The New Maine Cooking

D1472611

The New Maine Cooking

The Healthful New Country Cuisine

SECOND EDITION

Jean Ann Pollard

Down East Books

Front cover art © 1996
by Dawn Peterson

Illustrations
by Jean Ann Pollard.

Cover art and design
by Dawn Peterson.

Text design
by Phoebe McGuire.

ISBN 0-89272-388-2

Printed and bound at
Capital City Press, Montpelier, Vt.

5   4   3   2   1

Down East Books
P.O. Box 679
Camden, ME 04843
BOOK ORDERS: 1-800-766-1670

*To those wonderful cooks
who have shared recipes
with me in the past, and
who will share with me
in the future.*

Contents

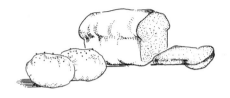

Introduction

Mainers, wise in the ways of making do and serving up in season, cherish traditions of heartiness and sensible, simple cookery. From the 1600s, when an explorer could reach into water a "yeard deep" to haul up a kicking lobster, people in Maine have relied on prodigious amounts and varieties of native ingredients from both land and sea.

Old traditions are still strong. Many a Maine cellar is stocked with "canned" foods for a long, white winter–shelves of green string beans, red tomatoes, pickled beets and eggs, golden corn, crocks of pickles, sauerkraut. There are bags of onions and braids of garlic in the kitchen; squash and pumpkins underneath the bed; dried beans in the closet.

But Maine cooking, true to its traditions, and reliant on its native abundance, has nevertheless changed profoundly through the years. In my own lifetime the days of codfish cakes, finnan haddie, and johnnycake have almost gone. So have overcooked vegetables and meat, a heritage from English country folk who first settled Maine. To their solid cooking traditions, and to those of French fur trapper and native Indian, waves of newcomers have added distinctive flavors over more than a century. These immigrants have included the Irish, Germans, Italians, Swedes, Finns, Russians, most numerously the French Canadians, and recently the Lebanese and Vietnamese.

Probably most important, in the past twenty years people from every other state have flocked to Maine to find "the Good Life." They have been young as well as older, often educated and sophisticated, open to the newest thinking but respectful of old ways and of the land. And some of Maine's native young people, eager to experience life to the fullest, have traveled far and wide, returning with new perspectives. In some ways, things have come full circle: many Maine people once again grow their own vegetables using composted "organic" methods–really, the old-fashioned way. Others seek out farmstands dedicated to the same principles. Many raise their own cattle and goats for both dairy products and clean meat. Rabbits and poultry have once

The New Downeast Nutrition

again become favorite backyard critters. Orchards advertise fruit produced with as few pesticides as possible; cheesemakers and wineries have appeared. In Maine there is a strong sense of the values of healthy eating, self-sufficiency, and quality living–*old-fashioned* values.

My life seems to have spanned "the good old days" in Maine and the natty new–with lots of world travel in-between. So this cookbook, though based on Maine's own culinary heritage and consciously relying on locally grown produce, is also rich with ideas gathered from the traditional, healthy, country cuisines of India, Japan, France, Mexico, North Africa, and the Near East. A combining of cuisines worldwide with the new life in

Maine and a building upon Maine's cooking heritage have produced the New Maine Cooking–both my book and the New Maine cuisine it represents.

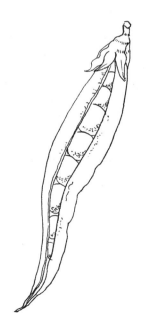

Good nutrition these days means using fresh vegetables–from your own garden, if at all possible–canning, if possible, in the fall; and relying on grains, legumes, and other whole foods to be the main part of the daily diet. As much as possible, too, I believe in choosing extra-virgin olive oil, cold-pressed sunflower oil, or clarified butter for fats; sautéing in water rather than oil wherever possible; omitting white sugar almost entirely (except when it's used in preserving); using sea salt for its trace elements, when you choose to use salt at all; and buying only aluminum-free baking powder.

Peasant diets the world over have a well-deserved reputation for being the healthiest. Unlike the average

American diet based on four food groups, with the emphasis on meat, many peasant diets draw from five food groups. They rely on whole grains combined with legumes for their chief protein source. This combination yields protein equivalent to meat, with the eight essential amino acids in proper proportion. Vegetables are served for added vitamins and trace minerals, and green leafy vegetables are most highly prized for their nutritional content. The fourth food group provides the essential vitamin B-12: dairy products, especially cultured ones such as yogurt; fermented bean foods borrowed from oriental cuisines such as **shoyu** and **miso** (see Glossary); and animal foods—meat, eggs, fish, or fowl—in small quantities. Since B-12 is necessary only in small amounts, food from this group can be served once every few days. The fifth group consists of raw foods— salad greens and fruits, sprigs of parsley or mint, grated daikon radish (another oriental staple), bean sprouts—which may be grown in one's own garden or purchased from farmstands, farmers' markets, health food stores, and supermarkets.

Menu Planning

The basic menu most of my Maine generation grew up with fits easily into the nutritional frame recommended above. Keep in mind that if you need grain plus legume for complete protein you can serve the two anywhere in the meal, perhaps in the dessert and hors d'oeuvre rather than in the entrée. A salad of raw and cooked vegetables and greens can account for the day's servings of raw foods and vegetables. And a yogurt dressing spiced with miso will easily provide the necessary vitamin B-12. Soups can be based on yogurt or miso and vegetables, with added protein in the form of **tofu** (see Glossary). Any way you choose to combine the essential foods will meet your nutritional needs.

When serving soup, keep it light if your entrée is heavy or sauced, and heartier if your entrée is light. Offer a dessert in keeping with what you've served: rich if your entrée has been light, light if your entrée has been heavy. A satisfying menu is balanced.

Typical Daily New Maine Menu

Breakfast:
Piece of fruit or fruit "jams" (unsugared and barely cooked);

Oatmeal or other whole-grain cereal, cooked or cold;

Eggs or scrambled tofu with toast;

Pancakes, muffins, or whole-grain bread;

Low-fat milk (soy or dairy) or an herbal tea.

Snack:
Walnuts, hazelnuts, sunflower seeds, pumpkin seeds, sesame seeds;

Raisins, dried apples or pears, prunes;

Raw carrot sticks, pickled eggs, etc.

Lunch:
Raw green or grated vegetable salad or leftover marinated cooked vegetables with either a yogurt dressing or a light olive oil and lemon juice dressing;

Or fruit salad with cottage cheese, sunflower seeds, and raisins;

Whole-grain sandwich (greens and salad might be inserted into pocket bread, a bun, or a tortilla), perhaps peanut butter, **tahini** (see Glossary), cottage cheese, or other low-fat cheese;

A cup of low-fat dairy or soy milk;

Hearty soups are always good for lunch.

Afternoon Snack:
Matchsticked vegetables such as carrots, kohlrabi, turnip;

Celery with peanut butter;

Roasted soybeans;

Any of the nuts and dried fruits listed above.

Dinner (in Maine it's still *supper*):
Hors d'oeuvres;

Soup (optional–it could be the entrée);

Salad (usually raw);

Entrée (main protein, especially grain plus legume);

Cooked vegetables (particularly greens): hot, cold, or marinated;

A healthy dessert (such as fruit and cheese, crêpes, or an omelet).

Bedtime Snack:
Low-fat cheese or nuts.

Glossary: Nutritional Notes

This is to help out when you come across nutritional suggestions or food items which may be unfamiliar.

Agar Agar is a tasteless seaweed derivative rich in trace minerals that can be used for gelling salads and desserts in place of animal gelatin or pectin. It is available in flake, granulated, or cake form in any health food store or food co-operative. The down-Maine method of creating blancmange from Irish moss is related.

Apples Apples have always been an important food in Maine. Today they're more appreciated than ever, especially if one can get the low-spray or even unsprayed kind. Apples contain pectin which reportedly reduces cholesterol.
Dentists suggest that an apple after a meal can remove food particles from between the teeth.

Baking Powder Baking powder is an ingredient in pancakes, muffins, and quickbreads. It contains alkaline baking soda and an acidic component such as tartaric acid. When wet, the single-acting variety releases carbon dioxide when the batter is cold; double-acting does it again in the oven. A rule of thumb is to use no more than one teaspoon per cup of flour because any more may increase the loss in the body of thiamine (because of the powder's alkalinity). Most commercial baking powders contain sodium, lime, and aluminum salts. Aluminum, recent research suggests, may rest in the brain to cause senility, and may damage other vital organs.

You can make your own baking powder by sifting together three times one part potassium bicarbonate (available at some pharmacies; or substitute baking soda), two parts cream of tartar, and two parts arrowroot (both available in the spice section of most supermarkets). Cornstarch may be used in place of arrowroot.

Beans Beans, Maine's wonder food, are half of the vegetarian "complete protein formula." They're rich in protein, thiamine, niacin, folacin, phosphorus, potassium, magnesium, and good for zinc–which is apt to be low in some diets. They contain almost no fat and no cholesterol. Soybeans and tofu (made from soybeans) contain moderate amounts of fat (thirty-five to forty percent of their calories), but it is mostly unsaturated. Fiber in beans helps to lower

cholesterol. And beans contain no more calories than other high-protein foods. For a high-protein, low-fat food, beans are best! Combined with grains, nuts, and seeds, you receive whole protein.

Black Pepper Black pepper is an irritant. I recommend that it be used sparingly. When indulged in, however, freshly ground is always tastiest.

Bulgur Wheat Bulgur wheat, which comes fine, medium, and coarsely ground, is essentially cracked wheat which has been precooked and dried. It dates from ancient times in the Middle East. Bulgur is easy to prepare because all it needs is rehydrating as follows: cover with twice as much boiling water and allow to stand for half an hour or marinate in a salad dressing for a couple of hours.

Butter Although some people suggest that populations which consume a lot of saturated fat tend to have high rates of heart disease, butter fans retort that butter has never been proved causative in heart disease when the diet is otherwise low in fat and high in essential nutrients. Although it contains cholesterol, some cholesterol is necessary for proper bodily functioning. If one consumes only a modest amount of cholesterol, and has sufficient vitamin C (which helps keep cholesterol and fat levels down), butter may be harmless enough.

I suggest using it in moderation. Butter is fine for greasing baking pans and casseroles, and in pastries–which I do not recommend consuming in quantity! *Clarified butter*, from which milk solids have been removed by melting and skimming, will not burn or produce carcinogens at high temperatures; stores easily without refrigeration for up to six weeks; and tastes good. I recommend it for occasional sautéing.

Butter, Clarified In a heavy saucepan over low heat, melt a pound (or more) of butter cut into small bits. Bring to a slow boil. Remove from heat and skim off the froth. Repeat several times until all the milk solids have been taken off. Return saucepan to burner and turn off the heat. Allow to rest a few seconds, then remove the thin filmlike skin which will form. Strain the butter through a cheesecloth-lined sieve

into a small bowl, leaving the milky solids in the bottom of the pan.

Carob Carob powder or flour comes from the bean-pod-like fruit (called St. John's bread) of the carob tree, which grows in warm climates such as Spain, Italy, and Morocco. The ripe pods are crushed, and the pulpy portion is separated from the hard seeds and ground into a powder. Though it can be substituted for cocoa in any recipe, it is more than just a chocolate substitute. It lacks the caffeinelike substance and oxalic acid found in chocolate, and is therefore considered far more healthful. Carob is so sweet that less sugar is called for, and it contains one-tenth the amount of fat found in chocolate. It is a valuable food in its own right, rich in vitamins and minerals.

Cilantro *Coriandrum sativum*, or cilantro, the Mexican word for **coriander**, is also called Chinese parsley. A member of the carrot family, native to southern Europe and western Asia, it can easily be grown in Maine as an annual in a sunny location. It will self-sow. The powdered, dried seeds (which are actually fruits) are used in breads, cookies, sauces, and to flavor meats. The pungent green leaves and stems are enjoyed fresh (especially in Mexican, Indian, Spanish, and Chinese dishes) in anything from salads or soups to stir-fries or curries. Traditionally, the combination for Indian flavoring is one part turmeric, two parts cumin, and three parts coriander seeds. Cilantro is a "learned taste" but indispensable once one gets to know it.

Couscous Couscous is made from hard white semolina, which is the starch obtained from durum wheat's endosperm, wonderful for pasta-making. It is also the basis of the famous North African dish. Being precooked, the grain is easy to prepare as you merely rehydrate it. Pour on twice as much tap or boiling water or stock, wait fifteen minutes, and fluff with a fork.

Daikon Radish These enormously long, white radishes (sometimes up to fourteen inches and weighing some five pounds!) are easily grown in Maine and easily wintered (as one would turnips) in sand-filled boxes in the cellar. The Japanese cook with them, use them as a raw garnish, and consider them highly nutritious. The flavor is tangy.

Fats Fats are important for the overall health of brain, nerves, and hormonal systems; are necessary as a source of fuel; delay a too-rapid emptying of the stomach; and carry the fat-soluble vitamins. But Americans for the most part consume too much fat (about forty percent of our total calories), and most of that is chemically "saturated." Saturated fats have long been linked with high rates of heart disease and recently with cancer.

Unsaturated oils have been recommended for quite some time. Heating, however, changes all vegetable oils in a way that may be harmful. Heating an unsaturated oil to 200°F for fifteen minutes, for instance, has been shown to increase atherosclerosis in some animals that are fed it. Most supermarket oils have already been heated to 330-380°F for twelve hours to deodorize them.

Fat intake should probably be way below twenty percent of our calories. The fish- and tofu-eating Japanese, with practically no heart disease, and lower cancer rates, keep their fat intake at ten to fifteen percent and use vegetable oils for deep-frying, especially rapeseed (colza). Margarines are often suggested as an alternative to butter, but they are absolutely useless for frying, of course, and all the dangers of heated oils apply to them. Moreover, to solidify liquid vegetable oil a process called hydrogenation is used, and the result is a chemically saturated fat. Margarines also contain dyes and other additives.

My recommendation is to use butter (especially clarified butter), extra-virgin olive oil, cold-pressed peanut oil for deep-frying, and sunflower seed oil. Please refer to these items in this glossary for more detail.

Garlic Garlic has long been used by Maine country people and elsewhere to ward off colds. It is, of course, an ancient remedy. When cooked for a long time its aroma disappears. Parsley is said to be a breath freshener, and in most dishes will balance garlic's strong taste wonderfully well.

Gomasio Gomasio, or sesame salt, offers a taste treat and can help reduce salt intake for people on a low-sodium diet. A combination of sesame

seeds and sea salt, it can be made easily: rinse one cup sesame seeds and drain well. Brown in a skillet, stirring constantly, until they begin to pop— or on a cookie sheet in a 300° F oven. When the seeds crumble easily, they're ready. Grind them with a mortar and pestle (a Japanese mortar and pestle known as a suribachi works best). Or use a blender. If blending, place only one-quarter cup of seeds in at a time and whiz at high speed. Combine with salt to taste, store in a tightly capped jar.

Hot Peppers A hundred grams of hot red pepper contain four times the vitamin C found in a hundred grams of orange. Peppers also contain vitamin A and iron. This may partly explain the pepper's popularity in ethnic cuisines around the equator, although hot pepper used in excess causes mucous membranes to complain.

Laban Every cook has a "trademark," and I suppose mine might be this Lebanese "gravy" founded on yogurt. Laban takes only two minutes to prepare and is delicious on everything from bean burgers to fish. Where many a recipe calls for heavy cream, substitute laban. Here's how to make it: in a small saucepan combine one cup yogurt, one egg white, one tablespoon cornstarch, and one-half teaspoon sea salt. Cook over high heat, whisking constantly *in one direction only* until it bubbles. Then lower heat and cook gently, still stirring, till smooth and creamy.

Miso Miso is a thick paste made from soy-beans, sometimes rice or barley, salt, water, and is fermented by *Aspergillus oryzae* mold starter. A staple in the orient, it's high in protein, B vitamins such as niacin and riboflavin (increased during fermentation), and B-12, which is especially important to vegetarians as there are only a few sources among vegetable foods. (The B-12 actually comes from the bacteria.) Being very salty, its presence in a recipe usually precludes the need for further salting. Miso makes an excellent broth, delicious on its own or as a base for soups and sauces. It is a highly versatile seasoning agent, and a zesty topping for grains, legumes, and vegetables.

Varieties of color, flavor, and texture are many, but there are several basic types of miso. The "red" variety (komé miso), which is actually dark

brown in color, is made from soybeans, rice, and salt. It's rich and pungent and I enjoy it most of all. Mugi miso is made from soybeans, barley, and salt; hatcho miso, from soybeans and salt; and genmai miso from soybeans, brown rice, and salt. Mellow white miso, a Hawaiian product, is aged for only a short time and has less to offer nutritionally.

Okara When making tofu one is always left with a residue called okara. It's the sediment collected in the cheesecloth during the first stages of making soy milk. It contains some of the protein and all the fiber from the soybeans and makes fine burgers and loaves.

Olive Oil Olive oil has been a traditional component of Mediterranean cuisine for thousands of years, often combined with massive doses of onions and garlic. Monounsaturated olive oil appears relatively safe and is fine for sautéing. But buy it in its "extra-virgin" state, the product of the first cold pressing. So-called "pure virgin olive oil" is of lesser quality.

Oxalic Acid If too much oxalic acid floods the bloodstream from such foods as rhubarb and spinach, it binds with calcium which is then excreted. It may also help the calcium to form little crystals which may lodge in the kidneys, causing stones. The vitamin D in butterfat helps the body absorb calcium. Traditional cuisine, which often cooks spinach with milk or milk products, may circumvent the oxalic acid problem. At least it tastes wonderful!

Peanut Oil Peanut oil is a traditional oil, this time from the orient, where it is used in small amounts to cook curries and stir-fries. If not stored at the proper temperature or if stored in too humid an environment, peanuts (and corn and some other grains and nuts) may produce a liver-damaging mold toxin. But produced from healthy peanuts, peanut oil doesn't get rancid fast, has a high smoking point, and is perfect for deep-frying. I recommend using it strictly for deep-fat frying, and doing so sparingly.

Polenta Usually called cornmeal mush in Maine, polenta can be simple or complex (as in **Fresh Corn Polenta**) and is fine as a meal's main dish. To make simple cornmeal mush, combine one cup coarsely ground cornmeal with one cup

water and half a teaspoon sea salt in the top of a double boiler. Then add two cups boiling water and cook about twenty minutes, or until thick and creamy, stirring often.

Potatoes Potatoes contain vitamin C and fiber, and also supply some vitamins B-1 and B-2, calcium, potassium (more in a potato than you'd get in a large banana), zinc, copper, magnesium, iron, and protein. They're not fattening, and are Maine's proud product!

Powdered Milk When using powdered milk, I recommend the non-instant, low-fat, spray-dried variety. Instant milk is more bitter to cook with.

Safflower Oil
Although safflower oil is highly unsaturated and

highly recommended today for both salads and cooking, I tend to shun it. Indian tradition considers it capable of inducing a wide variety of disorders, and I am not taking any chances!

Saké From their main staple, rice, the Japanese make an excellent wine which is mild and very good to cook with. Saké provides a slightly sweetish flavor without the tartness of many white wines made from grapes.

Sea Salt Refined salt is a combination of about forty percent sodium (an excess of which is sometimes the culprit in high blood pressure) and chloride. The average human requirement for salt is probably half a gram a day, but Americans consume anywhere from two to six grams! Much of it is

hidden in such foods as potato chips. Sodium appears in the processing of many foods as well: sodium phosphate (an emulsifier), mono-sodium glutamate (flavor enhancer), sodium benzoate (preservative), sodium caseinate (thickener), sodium citrate (acidity control), sodium bicarbonate and sodium nitrate (flavoring and preservative). It occurs in some medications, drinking water, milk, and meat. Your intake should be controlled. Fresh herbs flavor food and lessen the desire for salt.

I recommend sea salt because it contains calcium, magnesium, zinc, and other trace elements not available in refined varieties, although, ironically, it doesn't contain iodine. Also, sea salt just seems more Maine-y.

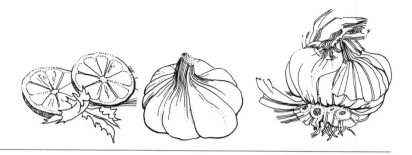

Seaweeds Maine's seacoast is decorated with many varieties of seaweeds, or sea vegetables as the Japanese call them, and health food stores or food co-ops are well-stocked. According to Larch and Jan Hanson of Steuben, Maine, who are professional harvesters, seaweeds are richer in organic iodine, potassium, and many other trace minerals than any other vegetable source. But note: you need only a hundred and fifty micrograms of iodine a day, according to the National Research Council, which is the amount in one-twentieth of a teaspoon of kelp. And too much iodine is as harmful as too little. Both can cause goiters. If you eat sea vegetables you can skip iodine-enriched salt. In fact, toasted, crumbled sea vegetables make good salt substitutes (see **Larch's**

Kelp or **Sea Lettuce**). Like their land cousins, seaweeds have prime maturity dates and suffer from pests: snails chew a sea garden just as slugs damage strawberries. For intrepid wild-food foragers they provide wonderful entertainment as well as good nutrition. In fact, family gathering is possible if you keep the following ideas in mind:

1) Seaweed vegetables grow in horizontal zones on rocky-bottomed, open-sea areas. You will find kelps in deep water, alaria a bit closer to shore; then, as you begin scrambling up the rocks, sea lettuce, the red zone of dulse and Irish moss, nori (which may be either olive or purplish), and finally the high-clinging rockweeds (fucus is the traditional variety used for clam-bakes).

2) The best time for

family harvesting is on the full moon or new moon tides in late May or early June. A clear, breezy day is best because harvesting can be done at low tide at dawn, the seaweed can be hung or spread to dry by ten o'clock in the morning, and you will have a dry product by evening.

3) Maine seawater is very cold. Harvesters should wear either a wet-suit or wool clothing which retains some warmth even when wet.

4) Harvesting is simple but often slippery. Larch advises carrying a stiff plastic laundry basket for lugging sea vegetables home–and also to fall on when you slip!

5) One sobering note: The only poisonous sea vegetable is a filamentous blue-green alga that definitely tastes sour. It

may also bleach other seaweeds it touches in your collection basket.

6) Collectible varieties are listed herewith, with drying instructions:

Kelp *Laminaria longicruris,* or kombu, is long-plumed and most crisp and vital in March, April, and May. By June it's softer, sweeter, and attracting snails. By July it's ragged. Another variety, *Laminaria digitata,* is many-plumed, with a prime season in April and May. Kelps grow in deeper waters, can be cut with a knife, and gathered from a boat at low tide. The long strips can be hung with clothespins on a clothesline to dry.

Alaria *Alaria esculenta,* similar to Japanese wakame, is kelplike, though it has a midrib and a little frill of "leaves" at its base. Peak growing season is during May and June. Alaria can be dried like kelp. Leave lots of space between plants.

Dulse Dulse is abundant by late June and toughens by September. Chewed raw it makes a healthy snack although its taste (like that for miso and yogurt) has to be "learned." Dulse is from four to twelve inches long and a deep red. Best quality is found in rock crevices away from the sun. Spread it on a nylon net attached to a frame off the ground for best drying, or even on a bedsheet on the grass, the leaves overlapping slightly. If it's not dry by evening, roll it up carpet-fashion and try again the next day. Unlike other seaweeds, dulse doesn't become brittle with drying but remains pliable.

Irish Moss *Chondrus crispus* is a mosslike little plant, about three to six inches high, which often carpets the sides and bottoms of tidal pools. It's usually raked commercially (and often bleached). Dry it as you would dulse. A little bit finely chopped and added to a stew makes it thicker and more nutritious, and it can be used for delicious, old-fashioned desserts.

Nori or **Laver** *Porphyra umbilicalis* and *miniata* is a narrow, leaflike, one- to two-inch-wide seaweed with wavy edges. It can grow from one to six inches long and is a rare find in Maine, although a regular food crop in the orient. To dry, simply spread it on a cloth on the ground. Chop it and put it out again on a sunny day, repeatedly turning till it's thoroughly black-ened and stiff.

Commercial Japanese nori is always chopped and rolled into neat sheets for such things as nori-maki (vinegared, rice-stuffed seaweed rolls).

Sea Lettuce *Ulva lactuca* is the largest of the bright green seaweeds, having very thin, translucent sheets. Drying is simple: lay it on clean wrapping paper in a warm attic room. It becomes black.

Sesame Oil Sesame oil is thick, rich, and used mainly for seasoning, but can also be used for stir-frying. Toasted sesame oil is an important seasoning agent in the orient.

Shoyu Shoyu is a dark, salty liquid seasoning which Americans call "soy sauce" or, erroneously, "tamari." What is usually

purchased in this country is an extremely salty, bitter, very dark-colored, poor substitute made without fermentation from hydrolyzed vegetable protein (de-fatted soy meal treated with acid), caramel coloring, corn syrup, salt, and water. Avoid it! The aromatic real thing is made from fermented soybeans, cracked roasted wheat, *Aspergillus sojae* mold spores (yeast), salt, and water. It is then aged in cedar vats for at least one year and no preservatives are added. Thanks to a historical twist of fate, natural shoyu is often labelled "tamari," although real tamari is quite a different oriental product.

The lovely salty taste of shoyu is good for seasoning soups, or using instead of worcestershire sauce on soy steaks, rice, vegetables, pilafs, salads,

anything at all. Because of the fermentation process it's high in B vitamins and protein. I refer to healthy, natural soy sauce as shoyu throughout the book. (Note: Soy sauce may also be made from soybeans alone. Check any health food store or food co-op for this variety.)

Sprouts When you sprout seeds their vitamin content is boosted. Vitamins C and A suddenly appear that seemed nonexistent. In fact, vitamin A in some sprouts is three hundred percent greater than in the original seed, and the vitamin C content may jump more than five hundred percent. One half-cup of alfalfa sprouts contains as much vitamin C as six servings of orange juice.

Sunflower Seed Oil Sunflower seed oil is

mild, basically unsaturated, and good for cooking when the taste of olive oil is not desired. I suggest using it for occasional stir-fries and curries, but most often for salad dressings. Sunflower seeds are twenty-two percent protein and thirty percent oil. The seed is rich in the B vitamins, calcium, phosphorus, and iron, and supplies vitamins A, C, D, E, and K. This is an oil which does not turn rancid quickly.

Sweeteners White cane sugar is a refined carbohydrate, the nutritional value of which is limited to the energy of calories it supplies. It can keep you going, but your body needs vitamins and minerals to be healthy. Most important, Americans now consume something like one hundred pounds of sugar a year per person! Research suggests that the combination of a high-fat, high-sugar diet may be extremely unhealthy. I recommend using sugar only occasionally or as a preservative. Sweetening should be mainly with the judicious use of maple syrup and honey, which contain some vitamins and minerals. When sugar is called for in recipes for pickles or preserved fruits, turbinado sugar, which is far less refined than other so-called "brown" sugars, is the best choice.

Some research states that heating honey makes it unhealthful, so I suggest that you do not cook with it. And never feed it to babies–it is reported to cause infantile botulism.

Although maple syrup is a powerful sweetener, it also contains B vitamins, calcium, phosphorus, and enzymes lacking in refined white sugar. It comes straight from the sturdy sugar maple tree. Use it sparingly but happily–it is a great Maine food tradition.

According to the American Foundation for Medical-Dental Science in Los Angeles, one tablespoon honey equals three teaspoons sugar; one tablespoon molasses equals three and a third teaspoons sugar; and one tablespoon maple syrup equals five teaspoons sugar.

Tahini Tahini is a "butter" akin to peanut butter but made from sesame seeds. Because the seeds are so high in calcium, tahini is a valuable food. It is used lavishly in the Middle East as the basis for marvellous sauces and dips.

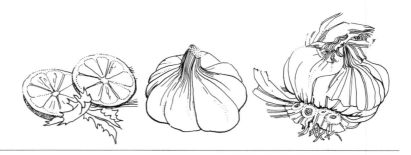

Tempeh Tempeh, Indonesia's most popular soy protein food, comes in neat burger-type cakes at most health food stores or co-ops. It consists of cracked soybeans, cooked tender, and bound together by a dense cottony mycelium of *Rhizopus oligosporus* mold. Tempeh contains more riboflavin, niacin, and B-6 than unfermented soybeans. Its protein is partially broken down from fermentation and is highly digestible. When sliced and sautéed till crisp and golden brown, it tastes rather like fried chicken. It can be cubed for croutons, sliced for stir-fries, hidden in casseroles, crumbled into tacos or pita pouches. Then there are tempeh burgers, TLT sandwiches, dressings, and spreads. Tempeh can also be produced from other legumes or legume products such as okara and grains such as barley.

Tofu Tofu can be made at home, or purchased from nearly any supermarket in one-pound blocks. It is actually soymilk cheese– a creamy, white substance, the density of which varies from fairly firm to very soft. Bland, it absorbs flavorings readily, can be crumbled and cooked, sliced, cubed, kneaded, frozen, fried, baked, boiled, or steamed. Tofu is high-quality soybean protein, often called "meat of the field" in Asia. Tofu is low-fat, contains no cholesterol, and is highly nutritious.

Vegetarian Strict vegetarians eat only vegetables and whole grains; others add milk and eggs to their diet; some add fish. If you are a strict vegetarian, be aware of the need to combine your foods carefully. In general, eat a whole grain plus half as much of a legume for complete protein. Add vegetables in an amount more than the legume but less than the grain, with emphasis on green leafy vegetables for vitamins and minerals. Getting enough vitamin B-12 is crucial, so indulge in yogurt and miso (also in tempeh produced with the addition of *Klebsiella*, a bacterium).

For people adapting to vegetarianism for the first time, a grain-based diet can be a problem, causing gas and a bloated feeling. But the body adjusts in time, producing the right enzymes.

Wheat Meat Wheat meat, or gluten steak (sometimes called seitan), can be made by rinsing the starch and bran out of whole-wheat flour until

The Wok

all that's left is a "steak" of gluten which can be fried, baked, or boiled. I prefer a variety which incorporates the whole grain. Best served in a spicy sauce, it offers meaty texture and contains all the protein and other nutritional qualities of whole grain.

Some readers may be unfamiliar with the wok, an oriental utensil ideal for stir-frying, which can also be used for other things. You can deep-fry and steam in it, for example. Because the wok allows extremely quick cooking, it is not only convenient, but a great saver of nutrients so easily lost during slower cooking methods. I recommend it highly.

Tips

1. Purchase a fourteen-inch wok. Small will be too small if you have guests, but you can use this medium-large one for very small amounts.

2. Choose the original kind of thin steel wok, an enameled wok (which needs no seasoning), or a heavy cast-iron type called a karhai in India.

Seasoning the Wok

1. Thin steel: Remove protective plastic coating, heat, and rub with peanut or other oil until no more brown color shows. If your wok ever becomes rusted, scour and reseason. But with proper use this shouldn't be necessary.

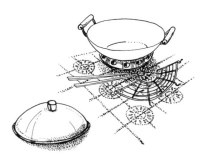

2. Cast-iron: Fill with water, bring to a boil, add two tablespoons baking soda, and simmer about twenty minutes. Then scrub off the nonrusting protective coating with a fine scouring pad. Repeat if necessary and you will never scour again. Heat wok and wipe inner surface with peanut oil using a paper towel. Cool. Rinse with warm water. Repeat heating and rubbing with oil until paper is no longer rusty or brown.

Cleaning a Seasoned Wok

Rinse wok in hot water. Fill with hot water and soak if necessary. Then scrub gently with a bristle brush. (Do not use steel wool.)
Dry over a heat source. Wipe lightly with peanut oil.

Don't store a wok in a closed cupboard. Hang it near the stove, or leave on the stove.

Accessories

Purchase an aluminum dome lid to go with your wok for steaming purposes. A wok chan, or frying spoon shaped to fit into the wok's curve, comes in handy for flipping ingredients, and for pressing them into the wok's sides for searing. A four-ounce ladle is also helpful. Twisted wire draining spoons of stainless steel are essential when deep-frying, and one shaped like a deep basket helps you dip food in and out of the oil. A metal ring for the wok to sit on completes your set, and will come in handy when improvising "double boilers" out of stainless-steel mixing bowls.

Cooking with a Wok

For good wok cookery, instantly controllable heat is wonderful. Perhaps the old woodstove is the heat source of choice as one can move the wok from front to back whenever more or less heat is required. Gas is easiest from the cook's point of view, but electricity is suitable if you remember a few hints:

1. If recipe calls for high heat and then medium heat, simply place wok on a burner heated to high, then switch to another heated to medium. Since stir-frying takes so little time, not much heat is wasted.
2. If you want really high heat, use your wok's ring with the large opening upwards.

3. If you want simmering heat, use the ring with the small opening uppermost.

4. In stir-frying, don't double quantities. Cook two batches instead. Quantity turns frying to stewing.

Some General Rules for Chinese Stir-fry Technique:

Your wok must be dry and clean or it will burn before coming to the right temperature.
Your wok must be preheated to a very high temperature. The rule is: **hot wok, cold oil.** Otherwise food will stick.

A quick outline of stir-frying goes like this:
a) Prepare all ingredients and have ready at hand.
b) Preheat wok to a very high temperature.
c) Pour in a tablespoon of oil. Add sliced and chopped vegetables immediately.
d) When three-quarters done (in two or three minutes), remove vegetables and keep warm.
e) Clean wok with a paper towel. Reheat to a very high temperature again and add about three tablespoons of oil.
f) Add the second set of ingredients: wheat meat, tempeh, tofu, poultry, or seafood.

g) When second set is three-quarters done, return first vegetables to wok with seasonings, mixing constantly–gently yet swiftly.
h) If recipe calls for a marinade, use just enough water to make a gravy. Never more.
i) Sprinkle on sesame oil immediately before food is served to give pleasant aroma.
j) Many dishes can be stir-fried in two or three minutes. Food is apt to be overdone if cooked more than five.

Bibliography

Below are a few of the books I have found most helpful in my nutritional research:

Rudolph Ballentine, M.D.: *Diet and Nutrition,* 1978 (The Himalayan International Institute, Honesdale, Pa.). Dr. Ballentine's book offers nutritional information on a grand scale, along with philosophical comment. For inspiration, this book is superb.

Adele Davis: *Let's Cook It Right,* 1947, and *Let's Eat Right to Keep Fit,* 1954 (Harcourt Brace Jovanovich, Inc., N.Y.). Adele's books are the great old classics of nutritious cookery and, although some of her conclusions now appear questionable (example: the intake of vast amounts of protein), she remains a valuable inspiration.

M. F. K. Fisher: *The Art of Eating,* 1976 (Vintage Books, N.Y.). Mrs. Fisher is surely this country's foremost food writer. With impeccable style and aplomb she writes about our basic necessity. Don't miss her description of the love-life of oysters!

Frances Moore Lappé: *Diet for a Small Planet,* 1971 (Ballantine Books, N.Y.). Ms. Lappé was the first person to explain protein complementarity. Every vegetarian is totally in her debt.

Irma Goodrich Mazza: *Herbs for the Kitchen,* 1975 (Little, Brown and Co., Boston). Mrs. Mazza's knowledge of herbs is unsurpassed, her cooking is superb, and her writing is delightful. Along with Mrs. Fisher she's my favorite cookbook writer.

Harold McGee: *On Food and Cooking: The Science and Lore of the Kitchen,* 1984 (Charles Scribner and Sons, N.Y.). This highly readable, inclusive book tells "all you ever wanted to know about everything to do with cooking"!

Joan Richardson: *Wild Edible Plants of New England,* 1981 (DeLorme Publishing Co., Yarmouth, Maine). Mrs. Richardson's style alone is worth reading, but her information is crucial to wild foraging.

William Shurtleff and Akiko Aoyagi: *The Book of Tofu,* 1975 (Autumn Press, Brook-line, Mass.) and *The Book of Tempeh,* 1979 (Harper and Row, N.Y.). With all their grand research, Bill Shurtleff and Akiko Aoyagi were the first to bring tofu and tempeh to the attention of

Americans. Their books constitute "the bible" of such cookery.

Lendon Smith, M.D.: *Feed Yourself Right,* 1983 (Dell Publishing Co., N.Y.). Dr. Smith tells about allergies along with nutritional do's and don'ts. With wit. Very helpful.

How This Book Is Organized:

1. Recipes, most of which serve a hearty six, are arranged seasonally. Vegetable follows vegetable as they emerge in Maine gardens, woods, or fields. Fish or fowl appear in their proper season, or at the time of year when Maine people most feel like cooking them.

2. If an item needs clarification, the **Index** can be referred to.

3. When other recipes in the book are referred to, they are set in bold type, or, if in the bold type of the ingredients, they are in initial capital letters.

4. Unfamiliar or foreign food items are fully described in the **Glossary** section.

5. I've tried to suggest serving notions and optional ingredients, so one can feel free and easy, not bound to exact directions. In other words, devoted to the true Maine maxim of "using what's to hand," experiment!

Spring

In the spring a Mainer's fancy often turns to fiddleheads and brookies.

"Greens are the spring tonic," Grandma used to say, handing over dandelions and handfuls of moist, wild mushrooms while she exclaimed over Junior's brook trout or rushed out to plant the peas, the radishes, the spinach.

Spring in Maine means the emptying of cellars and a lot of gardening before the blackflies hit.

It's an expansive time, exquisite with the sense of winter's ending, shedding of heavy clothing, putting away of boots.

But there are chilly days and frosty nights, and the garden won't produce till the end of June. So root cellar jewels are still appreciated along with the last jars of tomatoes, string beans, and pickles.

Grandma's Quick-Fried Smelts

(6 servings)

6 (6-8-inch) fresh smelts
    per person, or 36
    smelts
1 lemon, quartered
2 cups yellow cornmeal
1 heaping teaspoon sea
    salt
about 1/8 teaspoon
    freshly ground black
    pepper
1/4 teaspoon cayenne
3 (or more) tablespoons
    clarified butter
6 lemon quarters for
    garnish
6 teaspoons finely
    minced fresh parsley
    for garnish

1. Gut and quickly rinse the smelts. Pat dry and rub with a quarter of lemon.
2. In a large, shallow soupbowl combine the cornmeal and seasonings. Dip each smelt in the mixture. (If you run out of it, mix up more.)
3. Fry quickly, till flaking just begins near the backbone, in clarified butter. Use a cast-iron skillet and add more butter as needed. Don't crowd.

Grandma served smelts on a hot platter, sprinkled with finely minced fresh parsley and a quarter lemon, with potatoes, a tossed salad, and vegetables in season.

Smelts

I remember as a child waiting while my grandmother fried me up "a mess of smelts," and I remember holding them delicately in my fingers, crusted tenderly with cornmeal, and quickly cooked.

Parsnip Stew

(6 servings)

7 large parsnips, or 7
    cups sliced
3 cups cubed white
    potatoes
1 large chopped onion
    (or about 1 cup)
2 quarts whole milk
sea salt to taste
1/2 cup finely chopped
    parsley
cinnamon
pimento or Hungarian
    paprika for garnish

1. Wash parsnips and peel if necessary. Slice into quarter-inch disks. Peel potatoes and cut into cubes half an inch square. Peel and chop onion.
2. Simmer all together in a three-quart pot with a *little* water, over low to medium heat, till parsnips are barely tender—about twenty minutes. In a blender purée about two cups and return to the rest in the pot.
3. Add milk, and sea salt to taste, and bring to a simmer but *don't* overheat. Add parsley.

Parsnips

Parsnips are a wonderful early-spring root vegetable, wonderful in particular because they've wintered right in the garden. As the season progresses, their sweetness increases. By March or April they are moist and plump. They are perfect when washed well, peeled a little if very stained, sliced in quarter-inch discs, and simmered in just a little water or milk for about ten minutes. They can be topped with a sprinkling of cinnamon and served as a side dish to any meal, especially one rich in crisp greens.

That is the pristine way to serve parsnips. Leftovers can be mashed and added to soufflés (the taste is sweetness itself), or seasoned and baked with beaten eggs (for a fluffier version of the simple side dish). Or they can be made into patties. They also dignify a fine stew.

Sunchokes

Along with March's parsnips and the last of the well-mulched spring carrots, one can burrow in the garden for another blessing: the Jerusalem artichoke—which is neither from Jerusalem nor an artichoke. "Sunchokes" are the tubers of our native wild sunflower. They're knobby, tasty, and crisp enough to substitute for water chestnuts in any oriental stir-fry. They're also prolific growers, so once you've planted a bed of sunchokes you're set for life. Early Mainers (including our Indians) knew all about the sunchoke, although till recently they seemed

»

4. Just before serving, sprinkle with cinnamon. A garnish of pimento or Hungarian paprika is very pretty.

Serve with a tossed green salad or a winter salad tray (see **Winter Salads**), and fresh whole-grain rolls.

Storing Sunchokes
Scrub sunchokes carefully. Soil will cling to all the nooks and crannies. Store in bottom drawer of refrigerator, or in a plastic bag on a cool cellar shelf. They'll keep for weeks. (But do watch for mold.)

Sunchokes Stored in Lemon Juice

about 3 cups sunchokes
1/2 cup freshly squeezed
lemon juice

1. Wash chokes, cut off any knobs to facilitate cleaning. Peel and slice thin.
2. Pop into a glass quart container with lemon juice.
3. Add enough water to fill jar to brim.

These sunchokes, tightly covered and refrigerated, will keep about two weeks and come out tenderly tart and perfect for stir-fry or salad. (Keep your lemon water for adding to soups or bread.)

Stir-Fry Spring Goodies

(6 servings)

**2 cups sliced sunchokes
juice of 1 large lemon
2 tablespoons sunflower
 seed oil
1 cup asparagus cut in
 1/4-inch bits, lightly
 steamed fiddleheads,
 pea pods, or diced
 vegetable of your
 choice
1/2 cup sliced mushrooms
1 tablespoon shoyu
1 tablespoon water
1/4 teaspoon maple syrup**

1. Ahead of time, wash, peel, and slice sunchokes. Pop into a measuring cup (or bowl) with lemon juice. Top with water.
2. At dinnertime, heat a wok, then heat your oil in it. Add asparagus, fiddleheads, or other vegetables, and stir-fry.
3. Add mushrooms, shoyu, and one tablespoon water. Cover and simmer till the vegetables are tender, about two to three minutes.
4. Add drained sunchokes and toss again for about one minute.

Serve with mounds of short-grained brown rice and fresh whole-grain bread. A small raw salad topped with marinated beans and a yogurt dressing would round out the meal nicely.

forgotten. Now you often find the tan, knobby tubers in health-food stores. But don't ever hesitate to dig a basketful from abandoned gardens or wherever they've planted themselves. Come summer the flowers look like miniature sun-flowers—without the heavily seeded center.

They store well, and are delicious cooked simply, mashed, and seasoned with a dash of sea salt and black pepper.

(If you are unfamiliar with wok cookery, refer to my discussion of **The Wok***—see Index.)*

Steamed Fiddleheads

(6 servings with leftovers)

1. Collect three quarts of fiddleheads. Unlike most other greens, they don't shrink with cooking.

2. Wash quickly, lightly. This will rinse off most of the brownish "paper." If not to be cooked immediately, refrigerate.

3. When ready, steam till just tender, about five to seven minutes. Test with your teeth. *Overcooking makes them slimy, and you want them crunchy.*

Serve with freshly squeezed lemon juice, some olive oil (optional), sea salt (optional), and freshly ground black pepper. Also delicious served with a dribble of shoyu or **Arrowroot Lemon/Egg Sauce** or **Laban.**

Fiddleheads
Fiddleheads, or the first fiddle-shaped parts of the fern to show themselves come spring, were a favorite with both colonist and Indian, and remain popular today. The fern Mainers call the fiddlehead is the ostrich fern, **Mat-teuccia struth-iopteris,** *not the wooly-headed*

*bracken fern, **Pteridium aquilinum** (although that, too, is edible).*

*Thick, fat fern spirals of **Matteuccia** pop aboveground in May along the banks and bottomlands of streams and rivers. The heads are **not** fuzzy as sometimes described (like the bracken fern), but dark green with a brown papery skin which slips off easily. They don't need cleaning except to slip off the little skins.*

Wander along river banks with a good foraging guide. Once certain, pluck your tightly packed fiddlehead at three to six inches high. Late leaves are reputedly poisonous, so do not pick any heads that have begun to unfurl. And pick sparingly to ensure future harvests.

As for cooking: simple preparation is best. Do not overcook!

Leftovers can be used in innumerable ways, from salads (marinated or merely cooled) to lasagna (see **Lazy Time Lasagna**), from a soufflé such as **Maine Shrimp Rice Soufflé** (omitting shrimp and substituting fiddleheads), to a frittata such as **Suppertime Frittata**.

Fiddlehead Salad
(6 servings)

4 cups cooked fiddleheads
2 cups thinly sliced, large Bermuda and sweet white onions
2/3 cup extra-virgin olive oil
just under 1/3 cup freshly squeezed lemon juice
1 teaspoon sea salt (optional)
1/4 teaspoon grated lemon rind
1 tablespoon finely minced fresh parsley or other fresh herb
1 teaspoon shoyu

1. In a medium-sized bowl combine fiddleheads and onions.
2. Mix remaining ingredients in a small covered jar for a basic vinaigrette. Shake vigorously.
3. Pour over fiddleheads and marinate. Use immediately or chill, covered, in the refrigerator.

Serve as a refreshing side dish to any spring meal.

Freezing Fiddleheads

Blanch fresh, cleaned fiddleheads in a large pot of rapidly boiling water for two minutes. Remove and place in cold water. When cool, drain well, plop into freezer bags, remove as much air as possible, and freeze quickly.

Cooking Nettles

An old English cookbook suggests picking nettles in gloves, washing them, then pressing down well in a saucepan. Add a small piece of butter and a little pounded thyme. Little or no water is needed if cooked very slowly. Served on a layer of breadcrumbs, this dish "somewhat resembles spinach."

I suggest washing the leaves carefully and popping them, still wet, into a large kettle. (Wear rubber gloves.) Then steam them lightly till just tender. Serve with lemon or vinegar, or use in any way that you would spinach.

Wood Sorrel

(**Oxalis** species)

The ubiquitous three-petaled, heart-shaped wood sorrel, which seeds itself in everybody's garden and indoor plant pot, adds a piquant touch to bland winter and early spring salads. Its tartness is produced by oxalic acid (see **Glossary***), also found in spinach.*

Sorrel Soup

(6 servings)

2 tablespoons sunflower seed oil

3 cups wood sorrel leaves, packed

6 cups vegetable stock heavily seasoned with garlic if desired OR 2 tablespoons miso (see Glossary) plus 6 cups water

1 cup short-grained brown rice, rinsed briefly

3 large eggs

sea salt

freshly ground black pepper

1/2 teaspoon maple syrup

1. Heat oil in skillet or wok. Add sorrel and sauté for about one minute, tossing constantly.
2. Pour five cups stock or miso broth into a four-quart saucepan and bring to a boil. (If using miso, dissolve it in one cup boiling water, then combine with four cups water and bring to a boil.)
3. In blender combine sautéed sorrel and one cup stock or miso broth. Whiz for a few seconds.
4. Add rice to boiling stock or water. Cover and return to boil. Immediately lower heat and simmer gently about forty-five minutes, or until just tender.
5. In a medium-sized bowl

Wild Spring Greens

Fresh greens, free for the picking, adorn spring in Maine. Grandmother used to call them a tonic to "clean out the system."

Nettles

*The bane of hikers at midsummer because of the rash they produce, nettles (***Urtica dioica***) often grow six or seven feet high. They make a good potherb when young. You might call this revenge cooking. Found in May or June, they should be harvested before flowering. Once cooked or dried, the sharp-pointed leaves (with a heart-shaped base) lose their sting.*

Nettle leaves can also be dried (as you would mint, by tying together and hanging), then stripped from their stalks and stored in a tightly capped jar. Flake and sprinkle on soups, vegetables, or salads. Some folk infuse nettle leaves in boiling water and drink as tea.

For gardeners, nettles added to a compost heap are reported to activate the decomposition process.

Yellow Dock
(*Rumex crispus*)

or anyone who gardens, yellow or curly dock is always a problem. It seeds itself wherever it pleases, usually in the nice rich soil the gardener has so carefully composted and tilled. Dock knows what's good for it and puts down a long taproot.

But dock isn't just something to swear at. Down-Maine herbalists once gathered the roots for pharmaceutical purposes, and it was considered a potherb more nutritionally valuable than spinach during the 1930s' depression. Related to buckwheat, it tastes like spinach with a lemony tang because it, too, contains oxalic acid. Yellow dock is better-tasting than the broad-leafed variety, which is apt to be bitter. Identification is easy:

1. The leaves have a strong central vein which runs up the middle with branch veins curving off to join other veins, forming a scalloped pattern near the edge.

2. The leaf edge is somewhat wavy.

»

beat eggs till light and fluffy. Add sorrel mixture to it. Then skim off a cup of hot liquid from rice and add to eggs. (This heats eggs so they won't cook immediately.)
6. Combine the two mixtures and season to taste with salt, pepper, and maple syrup. Cook over moderately low heat, stirring constantly, about three to four minutes. Don't boil or the eggs will scramble.

Serve immediately, with fresh whole-grain bread.

Note: Substitute another suitable green. Add lemon juice to taste, and any herb of your choice.

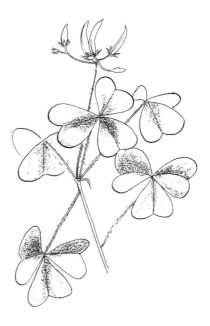

Steamed Dock

For early springtime dock, wash in cool water. Without shaking off the water, pop into a big pot. Cover and steam over high heat. After the first minute, use a long-handled fork to turn the mess over. (Maineiacs always speak of "a mess of greens.") Lower heat, cook another minute, and check for tenderness. Dock, with its piquancy, doesn't need much seasoning—just a little olive oil and freshly ground black pepper.

Use leftovers in omelets or soufflés; cut into cubes and serve with a vinaigrette dressing or with shoyu and a dash sesame oil; in **Green Custard**; or cubed and sprinkled on top of soups.

The Classic Fried New Maine Brook Trout

(6 servings)

6 fresh (9-inch) brook
　　trout (or whatever
　　size you've caught)
1 quarter-piece of lemon
1 cup yellow cornmeal
　　OR whole-wheat
　　flour
1 teaspoon sea salt
several grindings of
　　fresh black pepper
2 tablespoons clarified
　　butter (see Glossary)
freshly chopped parsley
6 lemon slices

1. Gut trout by slitting from belly vent to chin. Internal organs should come out easily through the slit belly. Cut off the head if you wish. Rinse and carefully pat dry. Then rub with a cut lemon.
2. Combine cornmeal or flour with seasonings. Dredge fish.
3. Melt butter in a heated, heavy, cast-iron skillet over moderate heat. Put in trout. Turn fish after two to three minutes, or as soon as golden, and fry the other side.
4. Garnish with parsley and lemon slices.

Serve on a hot platter, with fried or baked potatoes, and **Steamed Fiddlehead** greens.

3. At the base of the leaf a translucent sheet surrounds the plant stalk.

4. Areas of leaf injury (from insects or dryness) develop red pigmentation.

5. Leaves vary from a few inches to an entire foot or more in length and are usually tapering but sometimes heart-shaped.

Dock appears in late May, and in some areas produces new leaves in the fall. It freezes and cans well, and, unlike a lot of other greens, doesn't lose much bulk when cooked.

Trout in Batter

(4 servings)

4 medium-sized
　　brookies
1 cup beer (preferably
　　light)
1 cup unbleached white
　　flour
1 teaspoon sea salt
dash sugar
1 tablespoon Hungarian
　　paprika
1/2 cup freshly squeezed
　　lemon juice
sea salt
freshly ground black
　　pepper

about 2 cups unbleached
　　white flour in a soup
　　plate
about 2 cups peanut oil

1. Clean (see previous recipe), wash, and carefully pat fish dry. Set aside and keep cool.
2. Pour beer into a small bowl and sift in flour, one teaspoon salt, sugar, and paprika to make a beer batter. Whisk well and allow to stand, covered, at least one hour.

Springtime Fish

*In May, along with the blackflies and fiddleheads, the famous Maine brook trout begins filling creels and delighting freshwater fishermen. If you've been lucky enough to receive a gift of brookies or have caught some yourself, you'll find the traditional method of cooking still the best. But do observe three rules: **never** overcook, **try not** to let the internal temperature go over 150°F, and use **clarified** butter.*

3. Sprinkle trout with lemon juice, salt, and pepper. Dredge with white flour. Heat your wok (see **The Wok**) and pour three inches of oil into it. Heat to 360-370°F and maintain temperature.

4. Dip each trout into batter and slide carefully into the hot oil. Fry about four minutes each side or until golden. (Unless the wok is huge, do one at a time.)

5. Drain well. If you cannot serve immediately, place on a paper-towel-lined dish and keep warm in a 200°F oven.

Serve with lemon wedges, potatoes of any variety, whole-grain bread, and **Fiddlehead Salad**.

Sautéed Perch

(4-6 servings)

4-6 white perch
1 lemon, quartered
2/3 cup yellow cornmeal
1/3 cup unbleached
white flour
1/2 teaspoon cayenne
(optional)
4-5 tablespoons clarified
butter

White Perch

Preparing perch for cooking takes a little time! To scale, place your catch on a wooden board, hold fish by its tail, and scrape the blade of a knife from tail to head. Rinse, gut, and cut off head and tail. Wash carefully and pat dry with paper towels.

1. Rub perch with a lemon quarter (or squeeze the juice over for stronger flavor).

2. Combine cornmeal, flour, and cayenne in a soup plate.

3. In a cast-iron skillet heat butter until very hot, but not burning. Dredge perch in the cornmeal flour and cayenne mixture, and sauté over moderate heat. Brown slowly until golden and crisp, about ten minutes a side. Loosen fish almost immediately from bottom of pan using a thin metal spatula, and keep at it.

Serve with potatoes, spring greens (especially new beet greens if possible), and fresh whole-grain rolls with a tart preserve.

Marinated Tinkers

(4-6 servings)

2-3 tinkers
1/2 cup of sea salt per
    quart water
2 cups extra-virgin olive
    or sunflower seed
    oil
3/4 cup freshly squeezed
    lemon juice
    OR 1/2 cup dry
    white wine, or saké
    (see Glossary)
1 small onion, minced
4-5 garlic cloves, minced
1 teaspoon dried herbs
    of your choice (basil,
    oregano, thyme,
    rosemary)
1 teaspoon sea salt
freshly ground black
    pepper (optional)

1. Clean fish and soak for one hour, covered, in water and salt. (Mix enough liquid to cover all fish.)
2. In a medium-sized flat dish combine remaining ingredients.
3. Drain and dry fish. Split them to lie flat, if you prefer, and add to marinade. (Make additional marinade if necessary.) Allow to soak until fish have absorbed flavor, but not more than two hours.

Marinated mackerel are wonderful grilled out-of-doors and good broiled in your oven. If grilling over charcoal, use a hinged grill so fish won't fall apart when turned, and preheat to be sure grids are hot. The marinade's oil will have risen to the top and should be used often for basting. Let charcoal nearly burn down, and grill about five to six inches from heat for about ten minutes, or until done. Take care using charcoal: oil sputters and flares. It's important not to let flames scorch the fish. (If you broil in an oven, place the fish five inches from heat for about ten to fifteen minutes, turning once; then broil ten minutes on the other side or until done.)

Serve with fresh spring greens of any variety, and mashed or fried potatoes seasoned with sea salt, freshly ground black pepper, and grated lemon rind.

Tinkers

In the cold spring sea the tinker mackerel sport and play. These are immature darkly striped fish with flashing silver bellies.

Tinkers were one of Grandmother's favorites, always a staple in our house. Mother called them "oily fish," and she was right. But in the spring and again with fall they are less so, more tender and sweet. Mother baked them in milk in a slow oven until they flaked easily. We enjoyed them with mashed potatoes and dandelion greens served with vinegar.

Recent research suggests that eating "oily" fish once or twice a week may help prevent heart disease.

Tinkers also figure prominently in Japanese cuisine, where cooking is apt to be a prolonged marinade. Paul Peters, my local fish expert, offers this wonderful sample.

Classic New Maine Fish Chowder

(12 servings)

No coast in the world is more beautiful or more bountiful than Maine's. My people were coastal folk, fishermen and sea captains. I well remember their remarks about fresh-water fish: "They're soft!" "Wormy!" "Tasteless!" "No good at all!" Only firm and silvery salt-water varieties would do. Of course, chowder was the family mainstay.

1 pound fillet of hake
1 pound fillet of cusk or scrod
1 pound fillet of haddock or flounder (optional, but be sure you have 3 pounds fish in all)
1 cup shellfish, as available, such as freshly caught scallops or shrimps (optional)
at least 1 cup thinly sliced onion
2 tablespoons butter
2 quarts milk
3 cups barely cooked cubed potatoes
1 cup puréed cooked potatoes (optional)
1 teaspoon sea salt
1/4 teaspoon freshly ground black pepper (optional)
1 teaspoon grated lemon rind
1/4 teaspoon Hungarian paprika
3-4 drops hot pepper sauce and/or 1 table-spoon (or more) sherry
fresh parsley, finely chopped, for garnish

1. In a large kettle steam hake and cusk or scrod in a small amount (about an inch) of water until *barely tender*—only a few minutes. If using haddock, which falls apart easily, or delicate flounder, add them last. Be careful not to overcook. When cool enough to handle, remove any bones or skin, and flake. You should have six cups flaked fish.

2. *Lightly* sauté shucked shellfish and onion in butter.

3. In a large kettle scald milk. Add the barely cooked fish, barely sautéed shellfish, and onions (plus any leftover cooked lobster or crab meat), and potatoes.

4. If you like a thicker chowder and don't want to add cream because of fat and calories, add the optional cup of puréed potatoes to chowder. Add seasonings to taste. Allow to rest overnight if possible.

Serve *very hot (but not boiled)*, sprinkled with finely chopped fresh parsley; with a tossed salad and fresh whole-grain rolls.

The following recipe may be used for any white-fleshed fish from which you can slice good-sized fillets. It also calls for tiny, tender Maine shrimp, fresh or frozen.

Deep-Fried Fish with Shrimp

(6 servings)

1 pound large fillets of haddock, hake, cusk, pollock, or halibut
1 cup raw or frozen Maine shrimp (frozen is easiest to use)
1 teaspoon finely grated fresh ginger root
4 tablespoons diced onion (either a winter keeper or shallots)
3 tablespoons finely diced sunchokes or white potato
1 teaspoon sea salt
1 teaspoon cornstarch
1 teaspoon thick sesame oil
1-2 tablespoons finely chopped fresh parsley or other herb
3 cups peanut oil
garnishes of shoyu, lemon slices, and fresh chopped parsley

1. If necessary, remove skin and any bones from fish. Chop shrimp finely. Frozen shrimp are a bit easier to work with.
2. In a medium-sized bowl combine shrimp with ginger, onions, sunchokes or potatoes, salt, cornstarch, sesame oil, and parsley. Mash together thoroughly. Sesame oil is so thick and tasty it really can't be duplicated, although I suggest sunflower seed oil as an alternative.
3. Spread fillets out on waxed paper and spread shrimp mixture on top with a spatula. It will be cohesive but spread easily to a thickish depth. Use either a Japanese chopper or heavy French knife to slice fish and shrimp into pieces about one inch by one and a half inches.
4. Heat wok (see **The Wok**) and pour in peanut oil. Heat to deep-fry temperature of 370°F. When hot, add two or three pieces of fish, *shrimp side down*. Fry till golden, turning once. Remove with a wire spoon and drain on a rack.

Place on paper towels on a metal plate and keep warm in a 200°F oven till ready to serve.

Serve fish on a large platter, surrounded with steamed or stir-fried vegetables in season, with rice, another whole grain, or pasta, shoyu, and lemon slices. Garnish with a sprinkling of chopped fresh parsley.

After cooking, strain oil well. When cool, store it in refrigerator for future use.

Although the following recipe requires a lavish amount of olive oil, I assure you it's delicious!

Fish and Vegetable Casserole

(6-8 servings)

1/3 cup extra-virgin
    olive oil
1 small eggplant, peeled
    and diced
1 carrot, diced
2 green bell peppers,
    diced coarsely
3 onions, chopped fine
3 tomatoes, chopped
1 medium-sized potato,
    cut into small cubes
1 cup shredded red or
    white cabbage
1/4 teaspoon powdered,
    or 1/2 teaspoon
    fresh, thyme
1 bay leaf
1 teaspoon sea salt
1 teaspoon freshly
    ground black pepper

6 serving-sized fillets of
    white fish such as
    flounder, halibut,
    hake, or scrod (a
    large 1-pound fillet
    will do, cut into 6
    pieces)
1/2 teaspoon sea salt
1/2 teaspoon freshly
    ground black pepper
3 tablespoons fresh
    parsley, chopped

1. Place oil in a deep four-quart casserole, and heat.
2. In a large bowl gently mix vegetables with thyme, bay leaf, one teaspoon sea salt, and one teaspoon pepper. Add to hot oil in casserole and stir till just blended. Bake, covered, at 350°F for twenty minutes.
3. Place fish on top of vegetables and sprinkle with a half teaspoon sea salt, a half teaspoon pepper, and

»

parsley. Cover again and bake twenty minutes longer or until fish is done.

Serve immediately with fresh whole-grain rolls, rice or other whole grain, and possibly fruit for dessert.

Sorrel-Sauced Flounder

(6 servings)

12 small (2- by 4-inch size) flounder or scrod fillets, cut to size if larger
4 cups water
2/3 cup saké (see Glossary), dry sherry, or dry white wine
1 cup Laban
2 tablespoons finely chopped fresh wood sorrel
sea salt
white pepper

1. Place the flounder fillets in a lightly buttered lasagna pan.
2. Bring water and saké to boil. Pour over fish. Bake in a 325°F oven, covered, about five minutes (or until fish just begin to flake easily). Remove from pan and set aside on a serving platter in a warm place.
3. Measure one cup liquid from fish pan and place in a skillet. Reduce to a third of a cup. Add **Laban** and stir well. Then add wood sorrel and a sprinkling of pepper.

Spoon sauce over warm fillets and serve.

Flounder Fillets in Filo Flags

(6 servings)

Serve flounder fillets as hors d'oeuvres on a hot platter, or with a salad for lunch, or surrounded by cooked vegetables in season, with a crisp green salad.

**6 flounder or small
 scrod fillets**
**1 (8-ounce) box filo
 pastry (with sheets
 measuring 9 by 12
 inches)**
sea salt
**freshly squeezed juice of
 1 lemon**
**freshly ground black
 pepper**
**1/2 cup melted butter or
 extra-virgin olive
 oil**
**2 medium-sized
 tomatoes,
 quartered and sliced**
**freshly chopped
 parsley or cilantro**

1. Preheat oven to 350°F. Butter a large cookie sheet. Carefully rinse fish and pat dry. Cut each fillet into six one-by-two-inch rectangles and rinse again in freshly squeezed lemon juice and sprinkle with salt and pepper.
2. Unwrap filo dough and stack it. Cover with a slightly dampened towel to prevent drying. Remove one (nine- by twelve-inch) sheet and brush lightly with melted butter or olive oil. Fold it lengthwise in thirds making a long rectangle. Place a one- by two-inch bit of fish, folded in half, near the right-hand lower corner. Cover with a tomato slice and sprinkle with the parsley or other herb. Fold at an angle as you would a flag, keeping edges even, and continue folding to form a neat triangle. Set "flag" aside, under a slightly dampened towel. Repeat for all remaining fish and filo.
3. Place packets seam side down on cookie sheet and brush with melted butter or olive oil. Bake thirty to forty minutes, or till golden brown.

In Maine, fish is usually served with tartar sauce, which is unfortunately very high in fat. Tofu can be used to make a healthier version.

Lean Tartar Sauce

(makes about 1 cup)

8 ounces soft tofu
1 small onion, chopped
**1 teaspoon fresh,
 coarsely chopped
 tarragon or 1/2
 teaspoon dried
 tarragon (optional)**
**1 teaspoon fresh,
 coarsely chopped
 chervil or parsley**
1/8 teaspoon cayenne
**1 tablespoon Dijon
 mustard (optional)**
2 tablespoons yogurt
**3 tablespoons chopped
 sweet pickle or
 gherkin**

»

1 teaspoon Nasturtium
       Capers (optional)
1 teaspoon chopped
       chives, if available
1 tablespoon (or more)
       wine vinegar

1. Purée tofu, onion, herbs
(except chives), cayenne,
mustard, and yogurt in
blender until very smooth.

2. Once velvety, transfer to a
bowl and add pickle, capers,
and chives. Add wine
vinegar to taste.

Serve with almost any fish
dish, especially those deep-
fried or sautéed.

Variation: Substitute cottage
cheese or **Laban** for the tofu.
Or try **Chenna Tartar
Sauce**.

New Down-Maine Steamed Dandelion Greens

(6 servings)

about 3 pounds
       dandelion greens,
       carefully and freshly
       washed
vinegar
sea salt
freshly ground black
       pepper

1. In a large steamer kettle
place washed greens with
rinse water still clinging to
them. Add about half an
inch of water to the kettle.
2. Bring to a quick boil, then
lower heat and steam twenty
minutes (or a bit more),
depending on the age of the
greens. Fork over now and
again to ensure thorough
cooking and check water
level.
3. When tender, place on a
platter and cut into several
"blocks" with a sharp knife.
This makes them easier to
serve.

Serve with vinegar, sea salt,
and freshly ground black
pepper, or any salad
vinaigrette such as **Basic
Vinaigrette with Herbs**.
My children like shoyu,
lemon juice, and a little
sesame oil.

Dandelion Greens
(Taraxacum officinale)

In Maine, April, May, and June are dandelion months. If Grandma hadn't given you a spring tonic of sulphured molasses, then dandelions did it. They brought Maine folk out of winter in grand style and protected early settlers against scurvy.

To dig a mess of dandelions, use a long, sharp knife or a two-tined dandelion fork. I suggest you choose large single or double plants—budded perhaps, but not blooming. Maturity makes for bitterness. (Fall frosts, however, return the leaves to springlike satisfaction.) Shove knife or dandelion fork under plant so that root is severed just beneath the rosette of leaves. Then clean it, scraping off the brown, leaflike material at the plant's base with a sharp knife. Cut off root close to where leaves begin, but not so close as to make the plant fall apart. Shake off dirt. (One full brown grocery bag, weighing eight pounds, will cook down to about twenty-four cups of greens.) Be sure greens are scrupulously clean.

*The French serve
young, tender
dandelion leaves
raw, with a light
vinaigrette of olive
oil and lemon juice.
Garnish with a
sprinkling of finely
chopped chives,
garlic, parsley, or
borage, and some
chopped, hard-
boiled egg. It's
easiest to pluck
these young ones leaf-
by-leaf instead of
digging.*

*Dandelions also make good
pancakes. Here's a north
European recipe from Maine's
Finnish population, and you can
substitute spinach or any
leftover green when the
dandelion season is over.*

Finnish Green Pancakes

(20 pancakes)

**1 1/2 cups milk (soy or
    dairy)**
**1 teaspoon sea salt
    (optional)**
**scant 1/8 teaspoon freshly
    grated nutmeg**
**1 cup whole-wheat pastry
    flour**
**2 tablespoons sunflower
    seed oil**
2 eggs
**1/2 teaspoon maple syrup
    (optional)**
**1/2 pound greens, cooked
    (about 2/3 cup),
    squeezed dry (this is
    easily done by placing
    them inside a clean dish
    towel and pressing with
    both hands), and
    finely chopped**
**about 4 tablespoons
    clarified butter (see
    Glossary)**

1. In blender combine
first seven ingredients.
2. Add batter to greens
and mix well.
3. Brush moderately hot
skillet with a little butter.
Drop batter on, two
tablespoons per pancake.
Spread evenly, if neces-
sary, to form a three-inch
disk.
4. Cook about two
minutes on each side till
lightly browned. Keep
warm on a heated platter
until serving time.

Serve for breakfast, or
with a salad, vegetable
in season, and a bean
dish for lunch or dinner.

*Not only dandelion
leaves are
delectable—flowers
and buds make fine
eating as well.*

Sautéed Dandelion Buds

(4 servings)

2 cups dandelion buds
sea salt
**some freshly ground
    black pepper**
1/4 cup clarified butter

1. In the morning,
collect fresh buds. Ignore
really old ones. Choose
those which seem young
but ripe. Wash and
drain *well*. Sprinkle
with salt and pepper.
2. Warm a cast-iron

»

skillet over moderate heat, add butter, and bring to a foam. Sauté buds a few at a time until they burst into bloom, or nearly so. Remove and keep warm.

Serve hot as a side dish to almost any entrée. (Your children may dislike dandelion greens but they're bound to like these buds.)

Dandelion (or Day Lily) Fritters
(4 servings)

**about 2 cups dandelion
   blossoms**
2-3 cups peanut oil
**1/2 cup milk (either soy
   or dairy)**
**2 tablespoons
   nutritional yeast**
2 eggs
**1 cup whole-wheat
   pastry flour**
**2 teaspoons double-
   acting baking
   powder**
sea salt

1. Pick fresh dandelion blossoms just before cooking. Remove stems. Wash, drain well, and pat dry with paper towels. Work quickly or they'll close up.
2. Warm wok, then add about two inches of oil. Heat to 350° F.
3. Meanwhile, in a medium-sized bowl beat together milk, yeast, and eggs. Sift in flour, baking powder, and salt. Whisk until very smooth to make a batter.
4. Dip blossoms into batter and fry until golden. (You can also fry quickly in a skillet in a half inch of oil.) Drain on a rack. Keep warm on paper towels in a warm oven.

Note: This batter is enough for about two cups blossoms or day lily buds, or one very large sweet onion (for fried onion rings). It's very light.

The dandelion makes a fine wine which Maine folk have enjoyed for generations. This version is very sweet and makes a splendid, clear dessert wine—a lengthy process, but well worth the effort!

Dandelion Wine

(about 6 bottles)

2 quarts dandelion petals
1 gallon boiling water
2 lemons and 2 oranges
3 pounds white sugar
1 ounce wine-making yeast (available through mail-order or specialty shops)

1. Pick dandelion blossoms when fully open and bright yellow on a sunny day after the dew has dried. They close on rainy days and shortly after picking, so it's necessary to work quickly. Spread them out on a sheet of paper to get rid of insects, if necessary. Take care to discard every bit of bitter stems and green leaves, which spoil fermentation and taste. Hold stem part in one hand and pull out petals by digging into the middle with your other thumbnail.
2. Once prepared, place petals in a large, six-quart glass or stainless-steel mixing bowl. Add boiling water. Stir. Cover and leave for two or three days, stirring daily.
3. Squeeze lemons and oranges and reserve juice. Peel rinds thinly, omitting any white pith.
4. Pour petal mixture into a large pot and add thinly peeled rinds. Bring to a boil and simmer ten minutes.

5. Place sugar in a big crock. Strain boiled mixture onto it through several thicknesses of muslin or fine cheesecloth, or one thickness of cotton. When lukewarm, add fruit juice and yeast.
6. Allow to ferment in a warm room two to three weeks. By the end, petals will have utterly dissolved, leaving a sweet, brass-colored liquid.
7. Strain into a big pot or bowl, using a colander, through several thicknesses of muslin or fine cheesecloth.
8. Pour through a nonmetal funnel into a glass fermentation jar and seal lightly with an air lock. (Air locks are easily purchased from wine-making supply companies.) Store in a warm room two to three weeks, at an even temperature if possible.
9. Transfer to a cool place for two weeks or longer until little bubbles no longer rise to the surface when jar is moved. At this point you will notice a little sediment on bottom of jar. This is spent yeast and must be removed by a process called "racking." To do this, siphon wine into a clean jar using about four feet of half-inch rubber or plastic tubing. Stand wine jar on table and clean jar on floor and put

»

one end of tube into wine *above sediment.* Suck other end till wine comes down tube, then pop quickly into clean jar and let it flow. Be sure to leave the brown sediment behind! Insert air lock tightly closed (or simply cap) and leave jar in a cool place.

Rack again as more sediment forms; and again, if necessary, till wine remains clear for a week or so. (Clearing may take as long as four months.)

10. Wash wine or champagne bottles with detergent and hot water, rinse thoroughly, and dry in a warm oven. Cool with a plug of cotton wool in the top of each to keep them sterilized. Fill bottles by siphoning to within one inch of top. Soften new straight-sided corks in boiling water. (Note: A cork-flogger blows the corks home without a lot of fuss and is an inexpensive and useful gadget.)

11. Store bottles on their sides in a cool dark place (or wrap with paper). Age about one year.

Steamed Asparagus

(6 servings)

2 pounds asparagus, washed

1. Lay asparagus spears in a colander above an inch of water. Steam till *just* tender, perhaps five to ten minutes. OR
2. Tie asparagus in a bunch of nearly even height by popping a rubber band around the middle. Stand upright on a rack in a deep pot. (If you don't have a pot deep enough, or an asparagus steamer made especially for the job, invert another pot over it.) Add about an inch of water and steam until the asparagus is *barely tender*, about ten minutes.

Serve hot with **Arrowroot Lemon/Egg Sauce**, potatoes, rice, or another whole grain, a salad with marinated beans, and any cooked red or orange vegetables.

Asparagus
A once-wild native of southern Europe and Siberia, asparagus can be plucked on the roadside—it's gone wild again in many places. I keep a big bed of asparagus, which needs a fertile soil composted or manured yearly. As it ages, the spears grow ever larger and the season extends. We pick it now three and four times over. Best eating is when the spears approach seven to eight inches in height. A good test of tenderness is to see how far down stalk breakage occurs easily. Also, heads should be nicely closed.

Asparagus is traditionally served with Hollandaise sauce. Hollandaise, based on butter, is very rich. I've developed an alternative using arrowroot. Arrowroot sauce isn't supposed to "hold" very well, but this sauce, every time I've made it, has held from noon until supper.

Arrowroot Lemon/Egg Sauce
(6 servings)

3 egg yolks
1 tablespoon arrowroot
freshly squeezed juice of
**   1 lemon (5-6**
**   tablespoons)**
1 cup warm stock
**   OR 1 cup warm**
**   water, plus 1**
**   tablespoon shoyu**
sea salt
black pepper
1 tablespoon finely
**   minced fresh chives**
**   and/or 1 tablespoon**
**   finely minced fresh**
**   dill (half as much**
**   dried dill)**
**   OR 1 tablespoon**
**   finely minced fresh**
**   parsley or coriander**
**   (half as much dried**
**   herb) (substitute**
**   tarragon for fish**
**   dishes)**

1. In a small stainless-steel or enameled saucepan with a heavy bottom, combine yolks, arrowroot, and lemon juice. Whisk until smooth.
2. Add stock and place over medium heat. Cook, whisking vigorously, about four to five minutes, or until it comes to a boil.
3. After a minute of boiling, remove from heat and continue whisking for two to three minutes as it cools. Season with salt and several grindings of pepper. Add herbs and spoon over asparagus.

Serve immediately with mashed potatoes, rice, other grain, or pasta, cooked beans, fresh tossed salad, and any cooked root vegetable in season.

Note: This is also tasty cold.

*Asparagus is tasty in salads either raw or barely cooked, or cooked and marinated with any vinaigrette such as the simple one for **Fiddlehead Salad**. It goes well in tacos with cheese, tomato, onion, and dressings. And it enhances loaves, quiches, or soufflés.*

Gingered Asparagus
(6 servings)

2 pounds fresh
**   asparagus (about 5**
**   cups, prepared)**
2 tablespoons shoyu
1 tablespoon mild honey
**   (such as clover)**

about 2 teaspoons
**   toasted sesame oil**
1/4 teaspoon powdered
**   ginger**

1. Cut asparagus into bite-sized pieces (to use the oriental roll-cut method rotate each stalk a quarter turn while cutting on the diagonal). Peel the tough »

parts of the stalks and use–
they're edible.
2. Steam until *barely* tender
(ten to fifteen minutes) in a
colander over boiling water.
Drain well.

3. In a large bowl combine
shoyu, honey, oil, and
ginger. Adjust marinade as
you fancy. Add cooked
asparagus and toss. Chill for
about two hours before
serving, mixing gently now
and again.

Serve on a bed of green
leaves as individual salads.

*Omelets come in several
guises. The French, who
were among Maine's first
settlers, have given us a
lovely puffed one, by far the
fanciest. It can be filled with
asparagus, broccoli,
cauliflower, spinach, peas,
fiddleheads, thinly sliced
mushrooms, or finely
chopped, peeled, seeded
tomatoes.*

Puffed French Omelet

(for 1 hungry eater)

**1/4 cup diced asparagus
    or other vegetable**
2 eggs
sea salt to taste
**freshly ground black
    pepper**
**1/8 teaspoon freshly
    grated nutmeg**
**1/4 teaspoon grated
    lemon rind**
**1 tablespoon clarified
    butter (see Glossary)**

1. Steam asparagus or other
vegetable till *barely* tender.

2. Separate eggs and beat
whites till stiff peaks form.
3. Beat the yolks till light
and then add salt, a few
grindings pepper, nutmeg,
and lemon rind. Fold into
whites along with steamed
vegetable.
4. Set oven to broil. Warm
a well-seasoned, smooth-
sided, lightweight eight-inch
omelet pan over high heat
briefly and add butter.
When foam subsides and
butter begins to color, tilt
pan to coat the sides and
pour omelet in *gently*.

Do not stir. Lower heat to moderate and cook exactly one minute. Bottom should be browned and top *very* soft. Slip under your broiler for one to two minutes till top is set and slightly golden. Turn onto a hot plate, folding in half as you turn it out. The white will seem uncooked but there's enough heat inside to set it.

Serve at once! With whole-grain bread or rolls, fruit for breakfast, herb tea. For lunch and dinner add a tossed salad, lemon rice, barley, millet, or noodles.

Do not double the recipe. Make individual omelets.

The time-honored French soufflé treats asparagus with finesse and power. For the best in taste and texture, dairy butter is a must. Margarines cannot be substituted, nor can any fat such as lard.

Asparagus Soufflé

(6 servings)

4 cups (1-inch) pieces of asparagus (about 1 3/4 pounds)
3 tablespoons butter
3 tablespoons whole-wheat pastry flour
1 cup skim milk
3 egg yolks
1/2 teaspoon powdered mustard OR 1 teaspoon Dijon mustard
1 teaspoon dried thyme or 2 teaspoons fresh, minced thyme

sea salt to taste
freshly ground black pepper
freshly squeezed juice of 1 lemon
3 egg whites

1. Steam asparagus until *barely* tender. Drain and set aside.
2. In a small saucepan mix butter and flour. Allow to cook over moderate heat until flour browns slightly and gives off a nutty odor. Add milk, yolks, and seasonings, and cook till you have a thick sauce. Then add lemon juice and whisk till very smooth. Set aside.

»

3. Beat whites until very stiff. Combine sauce with cooked, drained asparagus. Gently fold in beaten whites.
4. Spoon into a buttered, two-quart soufflé dish (or two-quart casserole with high sides). Place dish in a large pan and add boiling water to come halfway up the sides. Bake in a preheated 375°F oven thirty to forty-five

minutes, or until a knife comes out clean.

Serve hot before it falls! (*Pull* soufflé apart by using two serving spoons back to back, tearing rather than cutting.) Complement with rice or other cooked grain and sliced tomatoes with basil, or a grated or marinated vegetable salad.

Steamed Lamb's Quarters

Lamb's quarters can be prepared like any other green. Pluck tender tops shortly before dinner. If very early in the season, use the entire plant. It cooks down a lot so gather twice what you imagine you'll need.

Wash gently and pop into a big pot with about a half-inch of water.

Cover and cook over medium heat, turning occasionally, for about ten minutes or until barely tender. Place on a hot dish and cut into large cubes for easy serving.

Serve as a side dish with cooked whole grain, a cooked legume (about half as much as grain), and colorful vegetables.

Wilted Lamb's Quarters Salad
(3-4 servings)

4 cups lamb's quarters (packed)
3 tablespoons extra-virgin olive oil
1 small onion, diced
2-3 cloves garlic, minced
1/4 cup vinegar or freshly squeezed lemon juice

1/4-1/2 teaspoon sea salt
freshly ground black pepper to taste
2 dried water chestnuts, soaked a half hour in boiling water, peeled and chopped fine (optional but very good for their smoky flavor)

1. Wash and chop greens coarsely.

Lamb's Quarters

Angrily thrown out as pigweed by most gardeners, this plant with the pointed, bluish-green leaves, which look powdered on their underside, and a stalk often ridged or grooved, also thrives under such names as wild spinach and goosefoot, and continues to produce edible greens till frost.

Originally introduced by settlers from Europe, lamb's quarters have run rampant over America, and no wonder. A single plant can produce seventy-five thousand seeds—which, ripe, taste good when ground and added with other flours to make pancakes and breads. They slightly resemble buckwheat.

I personally enjoy lamb's quarters' lack of "puckishness," and prefer its flavor to spinach. And one does not have to coddle it at all.

2. In a medium-sized skillet sauté onion and garlic over moderate heat in oil till limp. Add vinegar and seasonings. Bring to a simmer.

3. Add prepared chestnuts. Substitute finely chopped sunchokes if you prefer.

4. Pour sauce over raw greens and toss.

Serve warm, or chilled, with **Shoyu Sunnies** scattered on top (optional).

Far from being a nuisance, leftover cooked greens can be the basis for many delicious dishes, such as the following main-dish custard.

Green Custard

(6-8 servings)

1 tablespoon sunflower
   seed oil
   OR 2 tablespoons
   water
1 large onion, chopped
   fine
1 heaping cup sliced
   mushrooms
4 cups chopped, fresh
   lamb's quarters,
   spinach, Swiss
   chard, leftover
   cooked dandelion
   greens, comfrey,
   nettles, milkweed,
   fiddleheads, or any
   green of your choice
1 cup small-curd cottage
   cheese
   OR soft tofu,
   crumbled
1 cup thick yogurt
   OR Laban

1/2 teaspoon dried
   thyme
1 teaspoon dry mustard
6 eggs
1 teaspoon sea salt
   (optional)
freshly ground black
   pepper
1/8 teaspoon freshly
   grated nutmeg
1 1/2 cups shredded jack
   and/or cheddar
   cheese

1. Sauté onion and mushrooms in sunflower seed oil or water till limp. Spread over the bottom of a buttered nine- by twelve-inch lasagna pan (or pan of approximately this size).

2. Mix greens (well drained and patted dry) with cottage cheese or tofu, and yogurt or **Laban** seasoned with thyme and mustard.

»

3. Beat eggs till fluffy with salt, pepper, and nutmeg.
4. Combine the greens and egg mixtures. Spread over the onion/mushroom layer. Bake, uncovered, thirty minutes in a 325°F oven.
5. Then sprinkle with cheese and continue baking till cheese is melted and custard is set in center, a few minutes. Let stand ten minutes before cutting.

Serve for dinner with a yellow or orange vegetable salad, or sliced tomatoes, or serve for lunch with fruit and hot rolls.

Lamb's Quarters Flour

If you're a dedicated forager, go out on a dry fall day when all the leaves have fallen from tall pigweed plants, and the little pods are filled to bursting with ripe seeds. Knock them into a saucepan.

Spread the hard little black seeds on a cookie sheet and roast for one hour in a 300°F oven. Cool. Run through a coffee mill or blender till fine. Mix into regular flour for pancakes, muffins, breads, or biscuits in the same proportion as you would use buckwheat. Lamb's quarters flour can also be cooked as a breakfast cereal.

Fresh Cress Dressing

(about 1 pint)

1 cup well-packed fresh watercress
1 (16-ounce) cake of tofu
juice of 1 lemon (or less, to taste)
1-2 tablespoons shoyu
2 small onions, quartered
freshly ground white or black pepper (optional)

1. Pick cress, wash, drain, and pat dry with towel.
2. Purée all ingredients except tofu in blender. Then add tofu and continue blending till smooth.

Use on salads or as a dip.

Watercress

By June first our brook is green with new watercress standing four inches high, spicy, and just right for eating. If you gather your own, be certain it's from unpolluted water.

Miso soup is served daily in Japan. It's hearty and quick to prepare, but miso is salty, so be sure to use an unsalted stock. Topped with a few sprigs of fresh cress it's not only healthful but very appealing to the eye.

Miso Soup
(4 servings)

4 tablespoons mugi
    (barley) miso (see
    Glossary)
3 3/4 cups unsalted,
    clear chicken or
    vegetable stock
1 clove garlic, smashed
8 ounces soft tofu, cut
    into small cubes
    (optional)
8 sprigs fresh cress
    OR 4 tablespoons
    diced new onion tops
    or chives
    OR chopped parsley
    for garnish

1. Blend the miso with four tablespoons stock using a fork.
2. Whisk thoroughly into the rest of the stock. Add the smashed garlic, if desired. Bring to a simmer and stir gently to see that miso is well dissolved. (Do not boil.)
3. Add tofu if desired, and simmer just until it is hot (you are not cooking it). Remove garlic and pour into individual bowls. Top with cress or other garnish of choice.

Serve immediately, piping hot.

Rhubarb

Rhubarb is so much a part of Maine springtime nobody remembers it was originally brought over by Europeans. Every farm once had its backyard plot, heavily manured and bursting with huge green leaves (which are highly toxic). Many country homes still do—and it's wise to warn children that only stalks are edible. The best way to pick rhubarb is by pulling and twisting gently till stalk and root separate. Best when just mature, the stalks should be at least ten inches tall and about one inch thick—not old enough to be stringy. The outer skin doesn't need to be peeled until old age makes it tough.

Rhubarb is usually used for desserts—often with a lot of sugar. What follows is very different.

Sugarless Rhubarb Dessert
(4 servings)

1 cup raisins
2 cups water
1 tablespoon cornstarch
1/2 teaspoon powdered
    cinnamon
freshly grated nutmeg
5 cups rhubarb cut into
    1/2-inch pieces

1. Combine raisins and one cup water in a small bowl. Soak until raisins are very plump—about one to two hours. You can speed things up by using boiling water. Then purée in blender on high speed until most of the raisin fragments are very small.
2. Add cornstarch and spices.
3. Bring remaining cup of water to a boil and combine with rhubarb and raisin

»

puree in a saucepan. Cook over moderate heat until rhubarb is thoroughly soft, or pop into a buttered ten- by six-inch baking dish and bake in a 400°F oven about thirty minutes.

Serve hot, topped with **Tofu Whipped Cream** and sprinkled with chopped nuts; or **Cashew Cream**, yogurt, cinnamon, and chopped nuts; or **Whipped Cottage Cheese** and nuts; or use as a topping for **Almost Quiche**.

Oxalic acid (see Glossary)—also found in spinach, sorrel, beet greens, dock, and purslane plants—makes rhubarb tangy. One method of reducing oxalic acid is to pour boiling water over rhubarb, let it stand about ten minutes, then drain before cooking.

Stir-Fried Day Lily Buds

(2 cups–served as a condiment)

Pluck day lily buds just before mealtime when they're from one to one and a half inches long, tightly closed and yellow-green. (Don't forage from the roadside because of automotive exhausts.) Gather as many as you need to sprinkle rather thickly over a bowl of brown rice, about half a handful per person, and gather several stalks of scallions or shallots, which should be up by now, green and tall. When the rest of your meal is assembled and your diners are seated, stir-fry day lily buds briefly (see **The Wok**).

1 tablespoon extra-virgin olive oil
1/3 cup shallots or bunching onions, cut into 1/2-inch bits
about 2 cups day lily buds (no need to wash)
1/8 cup water
dried thyme to taste
sea salt to taste

1. Place wok over high heat and, when hot, pour in oil. In one minute add shallots and day lily buds and toss.
2. Quickly add water and seasonings. Cover, lower heat to moderate, and steam briefly, about two minutes.

Serve immediately, scattered over rice, with **Soylami**, **Soybean Sausages**, **Okara Bologna**, vegetables in season, and shoyu to taste, or yogurt seasoned with miso (see Glossary).

Day Lilies

When my husband and I first planned our solar house beside a roaring brook on the edge of a big field, I had a vision of planting my flower gardens only with edibles. I succeeded in part, but got carried away with delphinium, monkshood, narcissus, poppies, irises in all shapes and colors, and numerous other items rescued from my mother's gardens which I couldn't bear to part with. But there are also day lilies by the hundreds, and in June the garden borders look sunlit with both the big orange and the smaller lemon varieties. Day lilies are edible–not only flowers, but buds in all stages, as well as roots. Firm and smooth, the buds are exquisite stir-fried or steamed and used as a side dish.

*They're also lovely tempuraed. See **Japanese Tempura Batter**. If you do this, be sure to seat your guests and family before cooking; then serve immediately. Day lilies can also be cooked in individual soufflés, to be served immediately upon being done.*

The following recipe makes six rather large individual omelets with a blossom buried in the center. When ready to cook, collect day lily blossoms, including a bit of stem. Remove stamens and chop into the stuffing. Squash or pumpkin blossoms may also be used, but be sure to wash off any insect killer (such as rotenone) very carefully. Better yet, use only unsprayed blossoms.

Stuffed Day Lily Blossoms

(6 servings)

6 day lily blossoms
6 thin 2- by 1/2-inch bits
    of cheese
1/2 cup spinach filling,
    such as that from
    Spinach-Cottage
    Cheese Stuffed
    Crêpes
6 tiny bits of hot
    jalapeno pepper
    (optional)
6 large egg whites
1/8 teaspoon cream of
    tartar
6 large egg yolks
4 tablespoons whole-
    wheat pastry (or
    other) flour
1 1/2 tablespoons cold
    water
1/4 teaspoon sea salt, or
    to taste
clarified butter (see
    Glossary)

Dried Day Lily Buds

Pluck them in the morning after the dew has dried when they are about one and a half inches long. String on heavy thread and hang in a high, dry place about two weeks. Then store in a tightly covered container. A lovely addition to winter soups.

1. In each blossom place one bit of cheese, one tablespoon filling, and one bit hot pepper.
2. In a medium-sized bowl, beat egg whites until they make soft peaks, adding cream of tartar to help them hold.
3. In another bowl beat together the yolks, flour, water, and salt until light yellow and creamy. Fold yolk mixture into whites.
4. Over medium-low heat, melt a small amount of butter in a heavy-bottomed skillet. Place one-half cup of the egg mixture into skillet, making a mound. Into the mound place one stuffed blossom and enclose it completely by topping with a quarter-cup more egg mixture. Spoon it up from the sides to cover if necessary.
5. Cook for two to five minutes until golden brown on one side. Then gently turn and cook till just set. Butter pan between each one if they begin to stick.

Serve immediately! Good accompaniments would be a hot, clear miso soup or broth (see Glossary) to begin with, short-grained brown rice, and a huge tossed salad with a lot of greens and tomatoes. You could also serve it with heaping tablespoons of yogurt, tomato sauce, or salsa.

»

yogurt, tomato sauce, or
salsa.

Variation: Chili peppers
may be substituted for
blossoms. Choose either hot
or mild as your tongue
permits.

*Come spring, and all during
the summer when they are
unfolding, grape leaves can
be gathered for immediate
eating or future con-
sumption. Here is how to
preserve a gallon for
winter's feasting, according
to my friend Sadie Corey.*

Storing Grape Leaves

**a large basket of grape
    leaves**
canning salt as needed

1. Sterilize a one-gallon,
wide-mouthed glass jar.
Add a sprinkling of salt.
Cover with a layer of tender,
new grape leaves about four
inches in diameter, well-
rinsed.

2. Continue layering salt and
leaves. Cover. Store in a
cool place. Sadie says hers
have kept up to two years.
3. Before using, rinse
thoroughly under running
water or soak. And don't
add salt when you cook with
them.

For long-term storage, old-fashioned canning is the method of choice.

Canning Grape Leaves

(1 pint)

132 new grape leaves, 3-4
    inches across
10 cups water
1/2 cup canning salt
1 well-washed lemon
1 cup water
1 cup cider vinegar or
    white distilled
    vinegar

1. Collect one hundred thirty-two large, tender, new grape leaves–but not near the roadside because of lead from automotive exhaust. Trim stems to half an inch with scissors. Stack, shiny sides up, in groups of twelve.
2. Combine salt and water, and bring to a boil in a large canning kettle. Blanch grape leaves briefly–about thirty seconds. Drain thoroughly.

3. Bring water to high heat in a canning kettle (or improvise). Sterilize one wide-mouth pint canning jar by boiling for five minutes.
4. Once leaves are cool enough to handle, restack if necessary, and roll them up stem-first. Pack vertically into hot canning jar. Add one lemon slice (optional).
5. Bring one cup water and one cup vinegar to a boil and pour over leaves, tucking them down at the top, making certain they're covered, but leaving a half-inch headroom.
6. Process in a boiling-water bath for fifteen minutes. Store in a cool, dark place. Rinse before using.

Grape Leaves

Springtime grape vines provide splendid new leaves. Our Lebanese population has provided Maine with a delicacy everybody loves: stuffed grape leaves.

*Sadie places a long layer of towels on her windowsill, spreads her just-rinsed leaves (either fresh or refreshed) over it in a single layer, puts other towels on top, and forgets about them while she mixes up the stuffing. She uses chopped lamb, but I offer a vegetarian version. (See **Stuffed Swiss Chard** and **Soybean Sausages** for alternative stuffings.)*

Sadie's Stuffed Grape Leaves

(46 rolls, or enough for 6)

2 cups cooked long-grain
    brown rice
2 cups leftover Kasha
    OR any finely
    chopped vegetable
    you fancy
sea salt to taste (omit
    salt if using canned,
    salted leaves)
freshly ground black pepper

1/2 teaspoon cinnamon
about 46 grape leaves
about 3 cups stock
3 whole garlic cloves

1. Mix rice, kasha, salt, and spices together in a large bowl. If drier than hamburger consistency, moisten with yogurt.
2. Place grape leaf vein side up, pointed end facing you, and place a heaping tablespoon of stuffing in the

»

middle. Roll stem end toward you over mix, then roll in each side and roll up tightly to seal. Place in layers in a two-quart kettle or casserole.

3. Pour in enough stock to reach to top layer but not to cover. Smash garlic with broad edge of a knife blade and add to stock. Bring to a boil, then reduce heat and simmer about forty-five minutes.

Serve either hot or cold, as an appetizer or main dish, with lemon wedges and a runny sauce such as **Yogurt Tahini Dressing**. More cooked rice and a small raw salad would complete the meal.

Dandelion and Red Radish Salad

(6 servings)

4-6 cups fresh young dandelion (or other) greens
6-10 large, ripe olives, sliced
6 thinly sliced red radishes
1/3 cup freshly squeezed lemon juice
2/3 cup sunflower seed oil
1-2 teaspoons finely chopped green bunching onions (or scallions) or chopped chives
1 teaspoon sea salt

1. Pluck dandelion greens. Wash carefully, chill well, and tear into bits.
2. Toss with olives and radishes.
3. Combine remaining ingredients in a capped jar and shake. Pour just enough on salad to moisten it. Toss again gently.

Serve on a chilled platter (or individual plates) garnished with toasted sesame seeds.

Radishes
Everyone who gardens in Maine plants radishes. It is the first seed given to children to practice with, and experienced gardeners often scatter lettuce, radish, and carrot seeds together in a large bed. Mainers have always liked to eat radishes as a garnish, pulled fresh from the garden, and treated to a covering of sugar or even salt and butter. They make a fine salad with dandelion greens.

Summer

Long, warm days; brief, cool nights; garden fierce and bursting . . . History gives us pictures of men, stripped to the waist, scything hay by hand; women lugging buckets of switchel out to them at noontime, with hampers of hearty fare, such as freshly baked bread and chicken salad.

If today's workers, both men and women, tend to be office-bound, the need for good drink and satisfying eating is no less evident. Today's summer cooking in Maine tends to be lighter and, with a recent influx of ideas from the orient, simple and quick. (See **The Wok** for a detailed discussion of stir-frying technique if you are unfamiliar with it.)

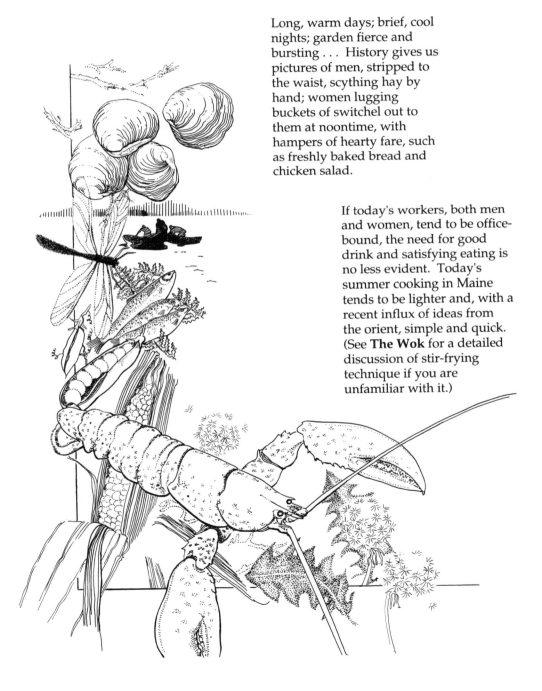

Milkweed

June-August is milkweed time in Maine. Beloved of monarch butterflies, it's also edible for humans. But note that raw milkweed can be dangerous to children if eaten in excess. And be certain to gather the edible variety, **Asclepias syriaca L.**, or common field milkweed! Common field milkweed produces large dusty-rose flowerheads, and its leaves, even when young, have a dense white nap on their lower surfaces. Its mature pods are warty. Don't mistake it for swamp milkweed, **Asclepias incarnata L.**, which enjoys wet areas as its name suggests, looks similar except that the flower clusters are smaller and the leaves narrower. And never confuse with dogbane!

As a vegetable, milkweed is versatile and can be eaten through all its phases as the season progresses. Gather the sprouts in June, about four to six inches high, to cook like asparagus. Later, for greens, pluck the four to six young top leaves that have just opened. In early summer, cook the large, tightly closed, flower bud clusters like broccoli. Until they begin to feel spongy, the inch-long pods too are edible.

Preparation
Wash the milkweed in salted water to flush out any odd denizens. Soak the greens about five minutes and drain well. Refrigerate till ready to cook.

Cooking Milkweed
I suggest cooking milkweed till al dente, as follows (but note that if the bitter taste is offensive to you, you should blanch it one or more times before the final cooking):

1. *Sprouts.* Blanch sprouts at least once, then steam about ten minutes, as you would asparagus. Serve with a lemon-juice/sunflower seed oil vinaigrette, or on toast with a light cheese sauce.

2. *Leaves.* Wash well and steam ten to fifteen minutes, without shaking off their wash water, as you would **Lamb's Quarters**. Serve with slices of lemon, sea salt, and freshly ground black pepper, with **Laban**, or with olive oil and shoyu.

3. *Steam buds* three to five minutes, like broccoli; or deep-fry in a batter such as the beer batter for **Trout in Batter** or the baking powder batter in **Dandelion Fritters**.

4. *Simmer pods* fifteen to twenty minutes, or sauté them with onions and mushrooms. They can also be dipped in batter and deep fried, or stir-fried with other vegetables. They can be cooked whole or sliced.

Cold, cooked milkweed greens make a fine salad topped by a vinaigrette or an olive oil/shoyu dressing. Simply heap your cooked greens on a serving plate, and cut through in several places (perhaps creating a diamond effect) for easy serving. You can also use a yogurt-based dressing with the recipe provided.

Milkweed Salad with Yogurt Dressing
(6 servings)

1 medium-sized bowl of cooked milkweed
1 cup yogurt
   OR 2/3 cup soft tofu
2-3 tablespoons thick tomato sauce
1 tablespoon finely chopped fresh parsley
1 teaspoon prepared horseradish, or as much fresh grated horseradish as you please
sea salt to taste (optional)

Combine all ingredients except milkweed and mix well. Whiz all ingredients in a blender if you use tofu.

Pour dressing over milkweed. Serve as a side dish to any seasonal meal.

Spinach

Maine folk have traditionally eaten spinach as a potherb, served simply as a side dish with butter, salt, and pepper. Often vinegar was added as a condiment. But lately spinach has come to the table fresh, dressed with vegetable oil, lemon juice, and toasted sesame seeds, or as the major ingredient in lasagna and **Spanakopita**, *tarts, quiches, soups, and salads.*

Almost any green in this cookbook, wild or tamed, can be substituted in spinach recipes. I personally prefer tetragonia, or New Zealand spinach, which is not a true spinach but can be treated like one in any recipe.

Cleaning
Wash three times in clean lukewarm water, allowing greens to soak no more than five minutes. A lukewarm temperature facilitates grit removal.

Green Feta Crêpes
(12 crêpes, or 6 servings)

1 recipe Tofu Crêpes
1 recipe Laban
1 1/2 pounds fresh spinach, blanched, well-drained, squeezed, and chopped fine (about 2 cups cooked)
1/2 cup diced mushrooms
1 medium-sized onion, diced
1 cup ricotta or cottage cheese
1/2 cup crumbled feta cheese OR crumbled firm tofu
1 beaten egg plus 2 yolks from Laban-making, above
1/2 teaspoon dried dill weed, crumbled fine or 1 teaspoon fresh dill weed, finely chopped
grated nutmeg
1/2 teaspoon sea salt
1/4 cup parmesan or gruyère cheese
chopped fresh chives or parsley for garnish
grated lemon rind for garnish

1. Mix batter for **Tofu Crêpes**. Use a bit more than a quarter-cup of batter for each crêpe, cook first side until freckled, then flip and cook second side about thirty seconds.

2. Make two cups of **Laban**. This will take only four minutes.

3. In a medium-sized bowl combine spinach, mushrooms, onion, ricotta, feta, eggs, herbs, seasonings, and half a cup **Laban**.

4. Preheat oven to 325°F. Place two heaping tablespoons of the spinach mixture on least-cooked side of each crêpe, slightly off-center. (Ends can be folded in.) Roll up the crêpes and place seam-side down in a buttered lasagna pan, side-by-side in one layer. Sprinkle with parmesan or gruyère. Cover and bake twenty to thirty minutes until bubbly. Pour remaining **Laban** over hot crêpes.

Serve garnished with chopped chives and/or parsley and grated lemon rind–as a one-dish meal or accompanied by a raw salad or with rice and salad.

Lebanese Spinach Salad

(6 servings)

1 pound spinach
1 teaspoon sea salt
1 large sweet onion,
    sliced thin
1/4 cup extra-virgin
    olive oil
juice of 1 large lemon
freshly ground black
    pepper
1 cup coarsely chopped
    walnuts (toasted if
    you prefer)

1. Cut spinach into small pieces, removing tough stems. Add salt and squeeze in a clean towel to drain. Combine spinach and onion in a large bowl.
2. Combine remaining ingredients except walnuts in a capped jar and shake well. Pour over salad and sprinkle walnuts on top.

Greek Spanakopita is truly a dish for a festive occasion–and easy to prepare even though the directions seem long.

Spanakopita

(8 servings)

2 pounds fresh spinach
about 2 tablespoons sea
    salt, to wilt the
    spinach
1 medium-sized onion,
    chopped
1/2 pound fresh
    mushrooms, diced
    (optional)
1 garlic clove, minced
    (optional)
1/2 tablespoon extra-
    virgin olive oil
1/4 teaspoon sea salt, for
    seasoning
freshly ground black
    pepper
6 medium-sized eggs

1/2 pound feta cheese,
    crumbled
juice of 1 lemon
1 teaspoon dried
    oregano, rubbed
    between the palms, or
    twice as much fresh
    oregano, finely
    chopped
1/4 pound butter
1 pound filo dough

1. Wash spinach and place in a large bowl. Rub salt into spinach bunch by bunch, tearing it up until it measures about a quarter of the original amount. Rinse thoroughly, drain, squeeze dry in a towel. Set aside.

Fava (or Broad) Beans

Fava beans are easy to grow in Maine, if you remember to plant them when you plant your peas. When we lived in North Africa they were a local delicacy–handfuls could be purchased straight from steaming bowls set over glowing coals and enjoyed salted, much as peanuts are in America.

My English mother-in-law serves shelled broad beans in a cream sauce. I think they're best this way, though you can also eat their leafy tops like greens, or serve them in their pods like snap peas when immature. Some folk, notably of Mediterranean descent, are allergic to them. If you do not have your own garden–or have not planted fava beans–limas make a good substitute.

2. In a heavy-bottomed skillet sauté onion, mushrooms, and garlic in olive oil till limp. Season with salt and pepper.

3. Beat eggs in a large bowl. Add feta cheese, spinach, sautéed vegetables, and lemon juice. Season with oregano and sea salt, and add black pepper to taste.

4. Preheat oven to 375°F. Melt butter. Oil a nine- by thirteen-inch lasagna pan. Spread out filo dough. Being careful not to tear, lay one sheet in pan, allowing edges to come out over sides. Lay a second sheet over the first, at an angle so that edges extend over pan in a different area. Use a pastry brush to cover with a little melted butter. Continue layering and brushing every other sheet so that corners fan out over

sides of pan until you have six sheets left.

5. Now pour spinach mixture into pan and smooth it out so corners are filled. Fold in all edges of the "filo fans" one by one. Layer remaining six sheets over top of spinach and turned-in dough, brushing each one with butter, and tucking edges down inside of pan. When finished, brush top with butter.

6. You can bake as is or cut half-inch-deep slashes on top, making diamonds or rectangles of serving size. Bake at 375°F for about an hour, or till the crust is puffed and golden brown.

Serve immediately with a whole grain or pasta, cooked, marinated vegetables, or a tossed salad.

Sauced Broad Beans

(4-6 servings)

**3-4 pounds unshelled
  beans**
sea salt
1 recipe Laban
white wine (optional)
**finely chopped parsley
  (optional)**

1. When bean pods are full to bursting, shell out enough beans to serve a hungry tableful.

2. Simmer over low heat, covered, in a heavy-bottomed saucepan in about an inch of salted water for approximately thirty minutes. Broad beans take about the same cooking time as lima beans. Check water level as the beans cook and add more boiling water as needed.

»

3. Make **Laban** (this will only take two minutes) and season with white wine and finely chopped parsley and/or summer savory. Add to the beans. (Note: A clear lemon glaze using arrowroot or corn starch is a tasty alternative.)

Serve with new potatoes or rice, a crisp salad, and fresh bread.

Summer Beanpot

(6 servings)

1/2 pound cleaned, dried
    fava beans
3 cups water
3 medium-sized onions,
    diced
1 clove garlic, minced
1 tablespoon extra-virgin
    olive oil
1 tablespoon komé or
    mugi miso (see
    Glossary)
1/2 cup tomato sauce
1 teaspoon minced fresh
    summer savory or
    half as much dried
    summer savory
1 teaspoon minced fresh
    marjoram or half as
    much dried
    marjoram
1 teaspoon sea salt
    (optional)
freshly ground black
    pepper
1 cup chopped Savoy
    cabbage
    (substitute red,
    regular, or Chinese
    cabbage if necessary)

1. Place beans in a large bowl and cover with water by more than three inches. Soak overnight.
2. The next morning, bring three cups water to a boil and add soaked beans slowly. Simmer on low heat about two hours or till tender. Drain, reserving cooking water.
3. In a heavy-bottomed, enameled skillet, sauté onions and garlic in olive oil until limp. Add two cups cooking water, miso, tomato sauce, and seasonings and simmer about ten minutes.
4. Add sauce to beans in a large heavy kettle, cover, and cook slowly one hour more. Stir occasionally.
5. Add cabbage and cook another hour. Adjust seasoning. Garnish with chopped fresh parsley if you please.

Serve with hot bread or a whole grain (for complete protein) and a fresh, piquant salad with a vinaigrette dressing.

I can fava beans (as you would shell beans) for easy winter eating, and store them dried for baking. This is really a late-summer recipe. Although it takes a long time to cook, little time is actually spent tending it.

Peas

Peas are one of Maine's earliest garden crops, and gardeners vie with one another to see whose green jewels appear first. Edible pod peas as well as the new snap peas prepared much like string beans are now enjoyed, along with yellow and green soup peas.

Peas are rich in vitamins and minerals. Matched with a whole grain, dried peas provide complete protein. (And pea plants fix nitrogen in the soil, as do beans.)

Simple quick cooking is best, although raw peas are wonderful in salads.

Fresh Green Spring Peas

**1 cup fresh-shelled peas
   per person
milk
a few mint leaves
   (optional)
salt to taste
a few grindings black
   pepper**

1. Shell peas.
2. Place in a heavy-bottomed saucepan with about an inch of milk. Add herbs. Bring almost to a boil, remove from heat, and let rest, covered, until peas are *just* tender, about fifteen minutes. Don't let milk burn.
3. Once done (*al dente*), remove mint leaves and serve as is with sea salt and black pepper. The milk makes a thin "sauce" to be eaten with the peas, wasting no nutrients.

Variation: If you prefer to use water instead of milk, limit it to just a small amount, bring to the boil, remove from heat, and allow to rest, covered, until *al dente*. Drain if necessary. Although Mainers in the past have served peas buttered, they have a delicate flavor all their own which doesn't need enhancing.

Leftovers: Cold cooked peas (which have been cooked in water) can be marinated in a little oil and vinegar or freshly squeezed lemon juice and used as a salad dish, or sprinkled over a leafy salad bowl.

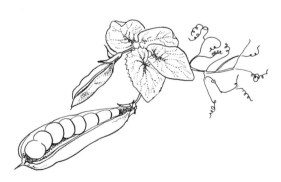

Pea Pod Stir-Fry

(4 servings)

2 cups pea pods
1 cup sliced sunchokes
1 small carrot
1 cup water
1 heaping cup Chinese
   cabbage, cut into
   1-inch pieces, OR
   chopped greens in
   season
2 tablespoons sunflower
   oil
1 clove garlic, crushed
1/2 teaspoon sea salt
1/2 teaspoon maple
   syrup
l tablespoon shoyu

1. Pluck two cups pea pods from your vines or purchase very fresh when they are *just* tender and barely ready. Rinse and set aside.
2. Drain sunchokes (see **Sunchokes Stored in Lemon Juice**). (These take the place of water chestnuts in traditional recipes.)
3. Bring one cup water to a boil and cook carrot slices three minutes. Drain and set aside.
4. Warm wok and then heat oil (see **The Wok** if unfamiliar with stir-fry technique). Add garlic and let it sizzle a few seconds. Discard. Add cabbage and stir-fry about one minute. Season with salt and maple syrup.
5. Stir in carrots and sunchokes. Turn a few times and add shoyu and pea pods. Mix quickly and allow to steam for one or two minutes.

Serve immediately with cooked brown rice, other grain, or pasta, and a small side dish of marinated beans to complete protein.

Pod Peas

Pod peas have a long history in oriental cookery, lending their tenderness and subtlety to many a stir-fry. With the arrival of Koreans, Vietnamese, and (to a lesser extent) Chinese and Japanese, stir-fry has become a familiar cooking method in Maine as in the rest of the country. As with many an oriental dish, vegetable preparation is half the game. Cooking is brief.

Simple Garam Masala

3 teaspoons powdered
   cardamom
3 teaspoons powdered
   cinnamon
1 teaspoon powdered
   cloves
1 teaspoon powdered
   cumin
1/2 teaspoon freshly
   ground black pepper

Combine and store in a tightly covered jar.

In India, "curry powder" is known only to foreigners–Indians pulverize and mix their own spices. They call the result "garam masala," and it differs from cook to cook. Beyond that, each cook adjusts her masala for the dish at hand.

India, too, has made its contribution to the New Maine Cooking. By July 4th Maine peas are popping, and nothing tastes better than a pea curry. Curries are simple. Spices are sautéed in hot oil, buttermilk, or stock, and vegetables are added, simmered till just tender, and served over hot rice with a whole array of condiments—a feast for the eyes and scrumptious to eat.

Snap Peas

Snap peas can be snapped and eaten like string beans, pod and all. Steam them lightly in a little milk or water, and season with sea salt and a few grindings of black pepper.

All three varieties of peas freeze nicely. Blanch for two minutes in rapidly boiling water, cool, drain well, and pack in plastic bags, squeezing out as much air as possible from the bag.

Pea, Panir, and Tomato Curry

(6 servings)

1 1/2 cups Panir (substitute tofu if necessary)
1 cup whey (from making Panir)
3 cups peanut oil
2 tablespoons sunflower seed or extra-virgin olive oil
2 tablespoons minced fresh ginger root
1 tablespoon minced garlic
1 cup finely chopped onions
1 teaspoon sea salt
1 teaspoon turmeric
1/4 teaspoon cayenne (optional)
1 teaspoon ground coriander
1 tablespoon Simple Garam Masala
2 cups finely chopped fresh tomatoes OR 2 cups canned tomatoes, drained
1 1/2 cups fresh green peas (about 1 1/2 pounds unshelled) OR pea pods or snap peas cut into 1/2-inch sections
1 teaspoon maple syrup
1 tablespoon finely chopped fresh cilantro OR 1 tablespoon parsley plus 1 teaspoon dried coriander powder

1. Make **Panir** the night before and save one cup of the whey. (If you haven't time, substitute purchased tofu and use water in place of whey.)
2. Cube **Panir** into half-inch squares. Heat three cups peanut oil in a wok to 370°F. Deep-fry the **Panir** cubes till golden. Drain and set aside. Remove oil and wipe the wok. Reheat and add vegetable oil. Then sauté ginger and garlic for thirty seconds. Add onions and salt and cook over moderate heat, stirring occasionally, till onions are limp.
3. Stir in a quarter cup of the reserved whey. Add spices and blend well. Stir in remaining whey and tomatoes and bring to boil over high heat. Reduce heat and simmer, partially covered, ten minutes, stirring occasionally.
4. Add peas, and sweetener if gravy tastes too acidic, and simmer three minutes uncovered.
5. Add **Panir** cubes and cilantro or substitute and heat through, perhaps two more minutes.

Serve in a large hot bowl, garnished with two more tablespoons chopped fresh cilantro or parsley, with heaps of steaming rice, other whole grain, or pasta.

»

Condiments might include **Yogurt Cucumber Raita,** carrot and orange salad, small dishes of raisins, yogurt, coconut, nuts, banana or apple slices (dipped in lemon juice), and chutneys such as **Green Tomato Chutney.**

Fourth of July Maine Poached Salmon

(6-8 servings)

1) Court Bouillon

3 1/2 quarts water
plus 1 cup cider
vinegar
OR 3 cups dry white
wine or saké (see
Glossary)
plus 2 quarts water
1 medium-sized onion,
minced
2 cloves garlic, smashed
(optional)
1/2 cup chopped celery
with leaves
1 bay leaf
1 teaspoon peppercorns
1/2 thinly sliced lemon
1 tablespoon sea salt
1 teaspoon dried dill
weed or thyme
1 clove (optional)

In a large pot combine water with vinegar or wine. Add onion, garlic, celery, lemon, salt, and seasonings.

Simmer about fifteen minutes or until flavor has permeated water.

2) Poaching the Salmon

1 (7- to l0-pound) fresh
salmon

Clean your salmon and gently wipe with a cloth. Wrap in cheesecloth, leaving ends free, and fold them over the top. Once the fish is done you can grasp the ends to lift the fish out easily. Place in a fish poacher or large bake pan on a rack. If you have no rack, some coarsely shredded lettuce leaves act as a buffer between fish and pan. (Lettuce also adds a subtle flavor.) Gently pour on hot **Court Bouillon** to cover, adding more hot water if necessary.

Bring to a boil, reduce heat immediately, and simmer ten minutes per inch of thickness (measured at thickest part).

Once flesh begins to flake easily along the backbone,

Salmon

*For generations of Mainers, the Fourth of July meant new peas with fresh-caught **Salmo salar**, the gorgeous Atlantic salmon. But, alas, industry dammed our rivers and neglected to build fishways. Salmon is now relegated to a few choice areas protected by ardent conservationists, but it is coming back. And it can be caught in a number of Maine lakes.*

*Poaching is perhaps the best cooking method for retaining natural moisture and keeping fish flesh tender. But how to bake, poach, or broil a truly large specimen, timing it correctly so that it emerges from the pan **barely** done, beautifully firm and juicy, has always been the challenge.*

*One prescription for odorless cooking and tender fish is to bake it **at a low temperature** in a preheated 300°F oven. Use a meat thermometer and remove your catch from the oven when its internal temperature reaches 145 to 150°F.*

lift out immediately. Drain well, place on a hot platter, and serve immediately. Or allow to cool on a rack before unwrapping to serve fish cold. Garnish with lemon slices and chopped fresh parsley or watercress.

Variation: If serving cold, boil down bouillon and use it to make a clear gel—see **Dilled Aspic**—and spoon gently over fish. Decorations such as paper-thin slices of carrot flowers, sliced pimento-stuffed olives, and flat sprigs of parsley can be added to the first layer of gel. Wash another thin layer over that to give luster.

Dilled Aspic

1 teaspoon agar powder or about 4 heaping tablespoons flaked agar (see Glossary)
1/4 cup cold bouillon or water
2 cups boiling Court Bouillon

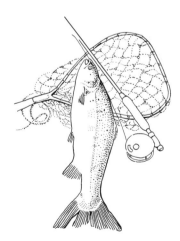

1. Simmer down **Court Bouillon** (above) until reduced by two-thirds. Check for taste and adjust seasonings as necessary. I often add more lemon juice and salt.
2. Mix agar into stock until dissolved.
3. Add **Court Bouillon** and stir well. Cool until beginning to set before using. Spoon gently over cooled fish, decorate, and spoon over another layer of aspic.

Serve with heaps of brown rice, mashed or baked potatoes; fresh green peas, shelled, podded, or snapped; and a tossed salad.

Larch's Kelp

Dry roast kelp in a 200°F oven until crunchy. This takes from fifteen to thirty minutes, depending on thickness and moisture content of the kelp.

Serve as a condiment crumbled over grains, vegetables, potatoes, in chowders, and sprinkled over popcorn along with brewer's yeast.

Digitata

Digitata kelp needs longer cooking than the single-plumed kombu so it's more suited for adding to stews. According to the Hansons it makes bean dishes more digestible and creamier. Jan makes a dish with water chestnuts, digitata, and buttercup squash which, she says, is very sweet.

Jan's Digitata-Buttercup Squash

(4 servings)

10-15 dried water chestnuts, soaked 30 minutes, or fresh chestnuts, steamed and peeled
1/3 cup dry digitata, cut into 1/2-inch pieces
1 small (6-inch diameter) unpeeled, buttercup squash, cut into small cubes
1 slice fresh ginger root

1. In a heavy-bottomed, two-quart saucepan cover chestnuts with water by two inches. Simmer till chestnuts break up when pressed, adding water as necessary to keep one inch in the pot.
2. Add digitata and ginger slice and simmer about eight minutes.
3. Add the squash cubes, more water to prevent burning if necessary, and continue cooking until the squash and chestnuts are soft.

Serve as a side dish for any festive occasion.

Alaria

Alaria, another kelp-like vegetable similar to Japanese wakame, is best soaked in fresh water, cut into small pieces, then simmered or steamed. Use the soak water for cooking. The Hansons suggest the following serving directions:

1. Add one part soaked and chopped alaria to three parts chopped carrots. Add one clove. Cook together.
2. Add one part alaria to three parts green string beans and a handful of walnuts. Simmer gently till tender. Serve with a dash of shoyu and some finely chopped fresh parsley.
3. Add one part alaria to one part onion and one part burdock. Cook together, with a dash of shoyu. Steamed scallions and dandelion greens are good additions to this dish.
4. Add alaria to aduki (or other) beans or lentils while cooking.

Dulse

Deep-red dulse has always been a down-Maine favorite. Chewed raw, it makes a healthy snack, although for some it's an acquired taste. Dulse is abundant by late June and toughens by September. Unlike other seaweeds it doesn't get brittle with drying, but remains soft and pliable.

How to Serve
1. Dulse makes a good condiment when dry roasted and powdered, especially for salads.
2. Larch Hanson suggests sautéing to get a crunchy chip.
3. Add to any bread or pastry dough that has a high corn/oat content; or is made from a combination of wheat and rye flours. (Note: Onions may also be added to bread dough to enhance flavor.)
4. Combine with potatoes, corn kernels, sautéed onions, chopped celery, fish if desired, and milk for a delicious chowder. Arrowroot can be used as a thickener.

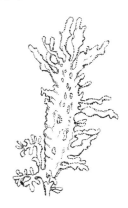

Irish Moss

Chondrus crispus *grows just below the slippery rockweed zone exposed at low tide. A mosslike plant, three to six inches high, it often carpets the sides and bottoms of tidal pools. Ranging from deep brownish red to olive green, it can sometimes be found flung up on shore, still useful although bleaching*

reduces nutritional content. Finely chopped Irish moss can be added to stews to make them thicker and more nutritious. One to two tablespoons suffices.

It is best known in the following delicious, old-fashioned dessert, some-times called Sea Moss Pudding.

Helen Marston's Blancmange

(4 servings)

4 cups milk
about 1/2 cup
well-packed Irish
moss
(a) 3 tablespoons honey
1 teaspoon vanilla
1/4 teaspoon
cinnamon
or nutmeg
(b) 3 tablespoons honey
1-2 tablespoons carob
powder
1/4 teaspoon
peppermint

1. Pour milk into a double boiler. Add moss washed *really* well to remove all sand, stones, and bits of shell. Put it into a little cheesecloth bag for safety's sake if desired.
2. Cook over boiling water half an hour, pressing moss occasionally to extract as much gel as possible. If not using a cheesecloth bag, strain. Flavor to taste with (a) or (b). Pour into molds. It sets while cooling.

Serve with a whipped topping and chopped nuts.

*Nori or Laver (**Porphyra umbilicalis** and **miniata**) ranges from olive to rosy pink-red. A narrow, leaflike, one to two inch wide seaweed with wavy edges, it can grow from one to six inches long. Although a regular food crop in the orient, and common in*

Ireland and Wales (known as sloke), it's a rare find in Maine. Commercial Japanese nori sheets are always chopped, rolled out, and cut into usable sizes for convenience. It's possible to make do with Maine's nori if you find some.

Maine Nori-Maki

2 cups cooked brown
    rice or bulgur
    wheat
1 cup finely ground nut
    meats OR crumbled
    tempeh (see
    Glossary)
1/4 pound mushrooms,
    finely chopped
a little shoyu
dried nori fronds

1. Combine rice, nuts, mushrooms, and shoyu.
2. Drop dried nori or laver fronds into boiling water and cook about one minute to soften. Spread out carefully.
3. On each frond (or group of fronds spread out so as to make a little square), place one tablespoon stuffing. Turn in the sides and roll up carefully–sushi mats made of bamboo help considerably. (These are available at many health food stores, kitchen supply stores, or specialty shops.)
4. Place in a colander over a pot of boiling water, and steam slowly about one hour.

Serve as you would stuffed grape or cabbage leaves.

Sea Lettuce

*Sea Lettuce **(Ulva lactuca)**
is the largest of the bright green
seaweeds, and has very thin,
translucent sheets. When dried
and crumbled or ground, it
makes a fine condiment and salt-
substitute. To dry, lay it on
clean wrapping paper in a warm
attic until black.*

I first enjoyed strawberries dipped in chocolate sauce on a porch overlooking Clarks Cove on the coast of Maine. And, like many another person smitten with chocolate, it was a rewarding experience. But, like many cooks today, I knew that chocolate wasn't healthful, thanks to its high fat content and an ingredient similar to caffeine. Could there be a substitute? There is. And it's delectable!

Strawberries in Carob Sauce

(2-4 servings)

1 quart fresh strawberries
1 cup dried raisins
1/2 cup dry sherry
2 tablespoons carob powder
1 teaspoon natural vanilla

1. Pick, wash gently, and hull berries. If prepared ahead of time, chill for freshness–but berries are really best at field temperature.
2. In a small bowl soak raisins in sherry for at least two hours. Drain.
3. When raisins are plump, purée in blender with carob and vanilla till velvety.

Serve absolutely pristine berries with hors d'oeuvre picks on a large platter and allow people to dip as they please.

Strawberries

Mid-July in Maine means strawberries: luscious red globes of juicy tartness. Best eaten straight out of the garden with dollops of honey-sweetened yogurt on top, strawberries can also grace innumerable dishes from soups to pie.

Strawberries are a fairly good source of vitamin C and other important nutrients. Besides making breakfast granola a real feast, strawberries make wonderful desserts–most Mainers would not want to endure a summer without a luscious strawberry shortcake. But the simplest way is to enjoy strawberries fresh from the field, pure and whole. And they are elegant served in champagne.

*When commercial berry varieties aren't available, there is always the wonderful wild strawberry **Fragaria virginiana**, the smallest but most flavorsome jewel of them all, available in almost any hayfield.*

Strawberries freeze easily for winter eating.

Frozen Strawberries for Winter

1. Dip fruit gently into cold water to wash off any dirt or pesticide residue.
2. Hull berries and allow to drain well.

3. Place on a cookie sheet and pop into freezer.
4. Once frozen, pour berries into freezer bags. This method permits you to remove as many separate berries as you please at a later date.

*One of my children's favorite ways to enjoy strawberries is in the making of a **Smoothie**–a thick fruitshake (full of vitamin C and other goodies) to start off their school days.*

Strawberry Smoothie
(for 2 children)

2 cups fresh dairy or soy milk
1 large banana
1 tablespoon nutritional yeast
1/2 teaspoon vitamin C powder (optional)
2 tablespoons yogurt
1 cup frozen strawberries or 10 fresh strawberries

1. Pour milk into your blender and add remaining ingredients.
2. Blend till the drink is stiff. Frozen fruit will make it icy cold.

Pour into tall glasses.

Jean Ann's Strawberry Shortcake

(4-6 servings)

2 cups whole-wheat
    pastry flour
1/2 teaspoon sea salt
4 teaspoons
    double-acting baking
    powder
1/2 teaspoon powdered
    cinnamon
1 teaspoon freshly grated
    lemon rind
6 tablespoons butter
3/4 cups milk
1 egg, beaten till light
    and creamy
1 quart berries
6 cups classic whipped
    cream, Crème
    Frâiche, Whipped
    Cottage Cheese,
    Cashew Cream, or
    Tofu Whipped
    Cream

1. Sift flour, salt, baking powder, and cinnamon at least twice and return bran to bowl. Add lemon rind.
2. Cut in butter, then add milk and egg, and mix together quickly but well.
3. Using a rubber spatula, smooth dough lightly into a greased eight-inch layer-cake tin. Bake at 500°F for twenty minutes. Remove from oven and split with a bread knife. It may crumble, but never mind! Put the bottom half onto a cake plate.
4. Cover with half the berries and half the preferred topping. Top with the second biscuit half. Crown with more whipped topping and remaining berries.

Serve hot, immediately, to (I guarantee) *very* appreciative people.

A Maine summer without strawberry shortcake is like a kiss without a squeeze.
The challenge for me was to create an old-fashioned biscuit without sugar, using whole wheat flour, and with only a modicum of butterfat. Butterfat, however, must remain high if the biscuit is to remain tender. The result is a large, light, round biscuit with a heavenly smell of lemon and cinnamon, just waiting to be topped with berries. Place in oven a half hour before serving time.

Strawberry Cream Puff Ring

(4-6 servings)

3 cups strawberries
    (freshly picked, if
    possible)
3/4 cup whole-wheat
    pastry flour
1/2 teaspoon sea salt
    (optional)
6 tablespoons butter
3/4 cups boiling water
3 unbeaten eggs

1 teaspoon freshly grated
    lemon rind
4 cups Crème Frâiche,
    Whipped Cottage
    Cheese, Cashew
    Cream, or Tofu
    Whipped Cream

1. Preheat oven to 400°F. Butter a large cookie sheet.
2. Rinse, drain, and hull strawberries. Set aside.
3. Sift flour and salt together. Set aside.

Another light shortcake can be made with French choux pastry or cream puff dough formed into a large ring. (My small son adores this.)

4. In a four- to six-cup saucepan heat butter in water just to boiling point. Add the sifted flour. Cook, stirring constantly, till mixture leaves sides of saucepan in a smooth, nearly compact ball. Remove from heat and cool one minute.
5. Blend in lemon rind and eggs, one at a time, beating with a wooden spoon till smooth after each addition. Spoon dough in a ring shape about eight inches in diameter on greased cookie sheet and bake at 400°F for thirty-five minutes. (Check after twenty-five minutes.)
6. Turn off oven and prick puff in several places with a sharp knife. Leave in oven ten minutes longer to dry out center. Slide it with a metal spatula onto a cake rack and cool. Then slice off top using a long, sharp knife.
7. Fill with two cups of berries and whipped topping of your choice. Top with remaining one cup strawberries as a garnish.

Toppings

Nothing can ever take the place of whipped cream from the big farm next door during my childhood, sweetened with a bit of white sugar and flavored with pure vanilla. But now delicious, natural substitutes—as opposed to the low-calorie, synthetic ones available commercially—can be used to make us all healthier and slimmer. Even children love them. I **am**, *however, including one cream-based topping.*

Crème Frâiche

(1 cup)

**1 cup heavy cream
1 tablespoon buttermilk**

1. Combine cream and buttermilk in a glass jar and cover tightly. Shake for at least one minute.
2. Allow to stand at room temperature about forty-eight hours, or till thick. Stir until uniformly creamy before serving. Stored in the refrigerator, it can keep for four to six weeks (but it won't!).

Tofu "Sour Cream"

(about 2/3 cup)

**8 ounces soft tofu
2 tablespoons freshly
    squeezed lemon juice
1/2 teaspoon sea salt
    (optional)**

**1 soft date, pitted and
    chopped, OR 1
    teaspoon maple
    syrup OR Raisin
    Butter**

Purée all ingredients in your blender till velvety. Chill before serving.

Tofu "Whipped Cream"

(1 cup)

8-12 ounces soft tofu, chilled
2 tablespoons maple syrup OR 2 tablespoons Raisin Butter OR Date Butter (see below)
1/2 teaspoon sea salt (optional)
1 teaspoon pure vanilla

1. Purée all ingredients in your blender till *very* smooth.

Serve as "whipped cream" topping on anything you like, or as a custard mixed with fruits such as orange sections, peach slices, strawberries, raspberries, blueberries, blackberries, plums, cooked prunes, or any other you fancy. Top with toasted walnuts or other nuts. If served as dessert after a course of vegetables and cooked whole grains, you have eaten complete protein.

Whipped Cottage Cheese

1 cup large-curd, low-fat cottage cheese
1/2-1 teaspoon mild honey or maple syrup (optional)
1/2 teaspoon pure vanilla (optional)
1 tablespoon freshly squeezed lemon juice (or to taste)

Whip all ingredients in blender until smooth and creamy.

Use sweetener and vanilla for a dessert topping. Omit for a savory salad topping, adding more lemon juice, salt, and herbs .

Cashew Cream

1 cup raw cashews
4 cups water
2 tablespoons Date Butter (see below)
1 teaspoon pure vanilla (optional)

Whip all ingredients in blender until smooth.

Julia's Tahini Dessert Topping (or Dip)

A simple topping which is fine for desserts, and especially fine for dipping fresh fruits, is made with tahini.

1 cup tahini (see
    Glossary)
juice of 1 lemon
1/2-2/3 cup water
1-2 tablespoons maple
    syrup
1/2 teaspoon pure
    vanilla
cinnamon, for garnish
    (optional)

1. Whip lemon juice into tahini with a fork.
2. Add water slowly, whipping constantly with a fork until light and fluffy but not runny.
3. Add maple syrup to taste, and vanilla. Sprinkle with cinnamon if desired. Chill.

Serve as a nutritious topping for fruit desserts, or as a dip with a platter of sliced apples, bananas, nectarines, and strawberries.

Raisin Butter

Raisin butter is a good sugar substitute, easy to use in all baked goods, as well as a replacement for molasses in old-fashioned recipes. It also makes a nice spread for toast.

1 cup raisins
1 cup water

1. Rinse raisins, combine with water in a small saucepan, and bring to a boil. Turn off heat, and allow to stand overnight. (If you're in a hurry, pour boiling water over your raisins and allow to stand a half hour, then proceed. It won't be as syrupy, but it will be as sweet.)
2. In the morning, purée in blender till smooth. For syrup, thin with water.

Date Butter

Another sugar substitute can be made from one of the few ingredients in this book which can't be grown in Maine. Date butter makes a good sandwich spread, especially with peanut butter.

1 cup chopped, pitted
    dates
1/2 cup water (increase
    for syrup)

Combine dates and water in a small saucepan and simmer till smooth (about five minutes). Stir a lot.

Yogurt

(makes nearly a gallon, but the recipe can be halved)

2 tablespoons yogurt
12 cups hot tap water
(between 90 and
120°F)
3 1/2 cups non-instant
low-fat powdered
milk

1. Combine yogurt with three cups hot water and two scant cups powdered milk in blender at medium speed. Always use plain yogurt for starter, or a dry culture of *Lactobacillus acidophilus* or *Lactobacillus bulgaricus*–two tablespoons per quart of liquid. Water should be *very warm*–between 90 and 120°F (115°F is optimal). Pour into a one-gallon thermos jug, the kind with a wide mouth.
2. On low speed, blend three more cups hot water with remaining powdered milk. Allow to mix a few moments but not to foam.

3. Rinse out the blender with six more cups hot water and add to the thermos. Cover thermos, shake a little to be sure it is all mixed up, and allow to stand overnight.
4. In the morning you should have the thickest, creamiest yogurt ever. Refrigerate in glass jars or in a large plastic "keeper." Covering keeps out extraneous bacteria which might make it sour further.

Serve over cereal or on pancakes; under fruit for breakfast, dinner, or dessert; in soups as a thickener or on soups as a garnish; in casseroles; mixed with lemon juice for salad dressings; blended with ice cubes for lassi, the traditional Indian dinner drink; alongside or in curries; with wheat germ for breakfast; or with mashed banana for baby food.

Yogurt

At our house we use a lot of yogurt, so I've developed a recipe for a week's supply (for a family of four to six), using a large thermos container, that really works. It's high in protein, minerals, and many vitamins including B-12 . I recommend that you use non-instant, low-fat, low-heat, spray-dried powdered milk (available at health food stores and food co-ops). Instant powdered milk makes yogurt bitter and runny.

Mainers have enjoyed clabbered milk for generations. I remember the story of my uncle who–to escape his seven sisters–would crouch in the cool cellar of their old farmhouse, over a pan of clabbering milk, relishing both freedom and food. Clabbered milk is soured by bacteria from the air, and yogurt by a special culture. The best-tasting culture comes from the Balkans, **Lactobacillus bulgaricus.**

The famously healthy people of Hunza in central Asia use a lot of milk products, usually from goats. Maine has a number of goat herds these days supplying both milk and cheese. The Hunza consume dairy products mainly in cultured form— yogurt, buttermilk, or cottage cheese— and combine them with a basic whole-grain/legume/vege-table/fruit diet. They cook with ghee (clarified butter) and drink the whey from cheese-making, which is nutritionally rich.

Yogurt can be transformed into your own low-fat "cream cheese." In India it's called chenna (and I thought I'd invented it).

Chenna
(1 quart yogurt = about 1 1/2 cups cheese)

4 cups yogurt

1. Set a colander over a pot and line with moistened, fine-weave cheesecloth. Add yogurt. Tie the four corners together, making a loop, and hang above the pot. (You can remove the colander.)

2. Allow to drip overnight, or until curds resemble cream cheese. Scrape cloth if necessary. Turn into a bowl and save whey for bread-making or soup.

Chenna can be stored up to one week in the refrigerator in a covered container, or it can be frozen.

Chenna Spreads
For each recipe below, simply mix all ingredients together well. Store, refrigerated, in a covered container.

Chenna Herb Garlic Spread or Dip (good with crackers, raw vegetables)

1/2 cup Chenna
1 teaspoon finely
    chopped parsley
1 teaspoon finely
    chopped green onion

1/2 teaspoon dried basil
    or 1 teaspoon fresh,
    minced basil
1/2 teaspoon dried
    thyme or 1 teaspoon
    fresh, minced thyme
1 clove garlic, minced
sea salt to taste

Hot Chenna Dip
(for raw vegetables, salad)

1/2 cup Chenna
1 teaspoon prepared
    horseradish
2 tablespoons tomato
    sauce

1/8 scant teaspoon
    cayenne or dash hot
    pepper sauce
about 1/2 teaspoon sea
    salt

Chenna Mustard Spread (good with cheese)

1/2 cup Chenna
1 tablespoon Dijon
    mustard OR 1/2
    teaspoon powdered
    mustard OR 1/2
    tablespoon each
    prepared mustard
    and prepared
    horseradish

1 clove garlic, minced
dash freshly squeezed
    lemon juice
sea salt to taste
freshly ground black
    pepper

Chenna Tartar Sauce

1/2 cup Chenna
1 1/2 tablespoons finely
    chopped green onion
1 1/2 tablespoons finely
    chopped dill pickle
1/2 teaspoon Dijon
    mustard

1 small clove garlic,
    minced
about 1/2 teaspoon sea
    salt
2-3 teaspoons freshly
    squeezed lemon juice
    (optional)

Dessert Chenna

1 cup Chenna
1 teaspoon cinnamon
1-2 tablespoons honey,
    Date Butter, Raisin
    Butter, or maple
    syrup
1/4 teaspoon powdered
    allspice

scant 1/8 teaspoon
    freshly grated
    nutmeg
1/2 teaspoon pure
    vanilla

Panir
(1 1/2 cups cubed)

Yogurt can be made firmer to become panir, another Indian food. Cubed and cooked with vegetables, panir adds delicious protein to the dish, is easy to make, and far less expensive than commercial cheeses. Use it often. Two large, nested, stainless-steel mixing bowls make a fine "double boiler" for this; but you can substitute whatever pots you have.

2 quarts milk
1/2 cup yogurt
2 tablespoons strained
    lemon juice, freshly
    squeezed

1. To make a simple double-boiler and ensure milk doesn't burn, place two quarts of milk in a four-quart stainless-steel mixing bowl (the kind used for bread-making). Set on a small circular rack in a larger stainless mixing bowl, and set both over moderate heat on a wok ring (see **The Wok**). Pour hot water into larger bowl to come two inches up sides of smaller bowl. Bring to a scald (about 130-150°F). Remove from heat.
2. Combine yogurt and lemon juice and gently and thoroughly stir into the milk. Curds will begin to solidify immediately and separate from the liquid whey.

3. Pour into a stainless-steel or enameled colander lined with a large square of double-thickness cheesecloth set over a bowl. Tie the ends of the cloth together, holding two ends in each hand (to form loop which can be hung over faucet or nail). Let drain till cloth is cool enough to handle. (Save whey for bread-making, soups, or curry.)
4. Twist cloth and wring to squeeze out all excess liquid. Place wrapped cheese on a slightly tilted cutting board and set another board or large skillet on top. Weight with about fifteen pounds for six to eight hours or till cheese is firm and compact. Unwrap and cut into half-inch cubes. Cover and refrigerate till ready to use.

Serve in curries, Italian dishes, on salads as croutons, and wherever you can use a fresh, firm cheese. It sautés well.

Summer Salads

Unlike California where *every* day is salad day, summer means salad days in Maine. What a relief it is to merely walk into the garden plucking whatever you please, and adding an herb or two. Town-dwellers can stop at Maine's many farmstands and choose freshly picked native produce. The long hot days produce greenery in abundance, and although Maine has had a tradition of overcooked vegetables, present-day cooks revere the salad (and believe in steaming vegetables until **just tender**).

Getting Ready

Gather your greens and vegetables just in time to chill before use. If you must purchase them, buy vegetables with roots and outside leaves left on if possible. Remember that deep green leaves contain greater concentrations of vitamins and minerals than lighter-colored leaves. Yellow spots usually mean anemic soil.

1. Wash greens quickly in cold water. Enzyme action is inhibited by cold and by boiling. Soaking or slow washing allows flavor and nutrients to pass into the water and be lost.
2. Drain and dry immediately. Swing in a wire basket or bag or dry on a towel by patting gently.
3. Chill immediately. Store, covered, in refrigerator. Leafy vegetables kept in light at room temperature can lose half their B and C vitamins in a day.

Preparing the Salad

If you like garlic, rub the inside of a large wooden bowl with a peeled garlic clove. Then add the greens, torn into bite-sized pieces, as well as vegetables cut into cubes or matchsticks, or shredded moments before serving. Cutting and shredding expose a large surface area to air which destroys more nutrients, so it must be done quickly at the last moment.

On top of the salad scatter : bits of raw potato, dipped in lemon juice and cut into strips or stars; julienned turnip, kohlrabi, fennel, or celeriac; any leftover cooked marinated vegetables; cooked, marinated dry beans (navy and garbanzo are especially good); raw or cooked peas; slightly steamed, chilled pea pods; onions sliced thin, and chopped chives; water chestnuts, sliced; toasted sunflower, pumpkin, or sesame seeds; tofu, cut into cubes (especially tasty when fried briefly in shoyu); croutons of whole-wheat bread, sautéed briefly in olive oil and seasonings; cheese (almost any kind) cubed or crumbled, especially panir or feta; and many other items.

Herbs, fresh and finely chopped, make wonderful salad ingredients and turn the "ordinary" into the "superior": chervil, chives, dill, sweet basil, mint, tarragon, burnet, marjoram, anise, lovage, oregano, thyme, and fennel. Use up to three different kinds. Collect fresh tips, bruise with your fingers, discard all large stems, and toss into salad. Nasturtium, violet, or day lily blossoms look lovely. And are edible.

Dressing the Salad

Dressing a salad is important to the salad's health as well as your own. Dress your greens at table just before serving.

I was once taught how to dress a salad by a Frenchman who first sprinkled each layer with olive oil, then salted every layer carefully before he tossed it. "Madam," he said, "the salt's the thing." But it isn't necessary to go heavy on the salt.

A Greek showed me how to make a **Basic Vinaigrette** by mixing oil and vinegar in a bottle, capping and shaking it vigorously, in the proportion of two-thirds of a cup extra-virgin olive oil to one-third of a cup freshly squeezed lemon juice, one teaspoon sea salt, and herbs.

I'd also recommend the following:
Wash your salad greens, shake very dry, then pat dry with a towel.
Chill.
Tear gently into bite-sized pieces.
Heap in a wooden bowl carefully rubbed with a naked clove of garlic.
Sprinkle with two to six tablespoons extra-virgin olive oil to seal in freshness.
Grind on a little black pepper and sprinkle daintily with sea salt.
Then sprinkle with a good wine vinegar (or any vinegar of your choice) or freshly squeezed lemon juice, add one tablespoon finely chopped fresh herbs, and toss again.
Taste and adjust seasoning if necessary. And never dress till your diners are waiting.

*In the same way
that a frame can
make or break a
painting, dressings
can enhance or ruin a
plate of good greens
and vegetables.
Most are high in fat.
For years this was
my favorite:*

My Favorite
Salad Dressing

(1 1/2 cups)

1 egg
1 teaspoon sea salt
**3 tablespoons freshly
    squeezed lemon
    juice**
**3 tablespoons vinegar of
    choice**
**1 cup chilled cold-
    pressed vegetable
    oil, such as sun-
    flower seed oil**
**1 tablespoon fresh
    parsley**
**1 teaspoon fresh
    chives or other
    onion, chopped**
**any number of herbs
    as desired**

1. Place first four
ingredients in blender
and whiz until fluffy.
2. Add oil in a very thin
stream until mixture is
velvety and thick.
3. Add herbs.

Note: This is a very
successful salad dressing,
and I learned to extend it
by adding an equal
measure of yogurt. But
other dressings can be
lower in oil or virtually
oil-free. And the
ubiquitous vinaigrette is
rather low in oil when
you consider how little
covers so much.

Vinaigrette with Herbs
(1 1/2 cups)

2 teaspoons minced,
    fresh (or 1 teaspoon
    dried) oregano
2 teaspoons minced,
    fresh (or 1 teaspoon
    dried) thyme
2 teaspoons minced,
    fresh celery tops
1 tablespoon honey
1 teaspoon dry mustard
1/3 cup red wine (or
    other) vinegar
2/3 cup extra-virgin
    olive oil

3 small cloves garlic,
    crushed
tops of 3 green onions,
    minced
1 teaspoon sea salt
    (optional)
freshly ground black
    pepper

1. Crumble dried herbs between your palms or mince fresh herbs.
2. Shake together in a pint-sized jar.
3. Refrigerate at least twenty-four hours. Then remove the garlic and enjoy. Shake each time before using.

The Vinaigrettes
Nothing much is new about vinaigrettes. They're basically mixtures of oil, vinegar (or lemon juice), herbs, and seasonings. It's seasoning that makes the difference, and the choice of oil is important. Polyunsaturated vegetable oils have been recommended for quite some time, but, even so, go light whichever oil you choose. For salads I recommend polyunsaturated cold-pressed sunflower seed oil or monounsaturated olive oil.

Nearly fatless vinaigrettes are also possible–and wonderful.

Lean Red Pepper Vinaigrette
(1/2 cup)

1 heaping teaspoon mild
    honey, such as clover
1 teaspoon Dijon
    mustard
2 tablespoons extra-
    virgin olive oil
2 teaspoons cider or red
    wine vinegar
2 cloves garlic, minced
1 red bell pepper, seeded
1 small onion, chopped,
    or one large green
    onion, top and all
3 tablespoons fresh
    parsley, minced
freshly ground black
    pepper

Whiz in your blender until absolutely velvety.

Serve on chilled, barely cooked Maine shrimp on greens already tossed with a simple oil and vinegar dressing, or on tomatoes. It's also good mixed with yogurt.

For a sweet-sour dressing–perfect with a juicy melon–this fatless one is fine. It's also good over cooked, cold string beans.

Lemon Juice Dressing
(about 1/2 cup)

**freshly squeezed juice of
2 lemons
1/2 teaspoon sea salt
2 tablespoons honey or
maple syrup
hot pepper sauce to taste**

Shake all ingredients together in a jar.

Nasturtiums are an indispensable part of Maine summer. Not only are leaves edible for salads, adding a spicy bit of flavoring, but blossoms offer an intriguingly hot, honey flavor. They can top any salad, or be chopped and added as an integral part. Blended with lemon juice they make a fatless dressing.

Nasturtium Dressing
(1/2 cup)

**1/2 cup freshly
squeezed lemon juice
15 nasturtium blossoms,
both yellow and
orange, rinsed
1-2 tablespoons honey**

Whiz all ingredients in blender till smooth and allow to chill overnight. This is particularly good over cold string beans.

Tahini, made of sesame seeds, makes a creamy dressing which is lovely for dipping raw vegetables into, or for drizzling over fruits.

Julia's Savory Tahini Dressing or Dip
(3/4 cup)

**1 cup tahini
juice of 2 freshly
squeezed lemons
2 cloves garlic, minced
1/2-2/3 cup water
1/2 teaspoon sea salt
dash of cayenne
freshly chopped parsley
for garnish**

1. Whip lemon juice into tahini with a fork.
2. Add water slowly, whipping constantly with a fork until light and fluffy but not runny.
3. Add garlic, salt, and cayenne to taste. Garnish with parsley.

Serve surrounded by black olives, tomato, cucumber, and **Pocket Bread** wedges, for lunch or as an appetizer. Or use as a low-fat dressing for coleslaw, or as a sauce for **Falafels.**

Yogurt Sunflower Seed Dressing

(1 1/2 cups)

1/3 cup sunflower seeds
1/2 teaspoon sea salt
freshly ground black
    pepper
1 tablespoon chopped
    fresh parsley, basil,
    tarragon, thyme, or
    dill

2 tablespoons freshly
    squeezed lemon juice
    or vinegar of your
    choice
1 cup thick yogurt

1. In blender, grind seeds
fine.
2. Combine with salt,
pepper, herb, lemon juice,
and yogurt in a small bowl.

Yogurt Dressings

Yogurt makes innumerable dressings–perfect for salads as well as baked potatoes, hot loaves, enchiladas, crêpes, and fruit.

Yogurt Tahini Dressing

(1 1/2 cups)

1 cup yogurt
1/4-1/2 cup tahini
sea salt to taste
1 garlic clove,
    minced

2 tablespoons freshly
    squeezed lemon
    juice, or to taste

In a small bowl combine all
ingredients thoroughly.

This is particularly fine
drizzled over **Falafel** in
Pocket Bread.

Low-Cholesterol Bean Dressing or Dip

(about 2 cups)

1 cup cooked small
    white or navy beans
juice of 1/2 freshly
    squeezed lemon
1/4-1/2 cup water
1 cup yogurt
1/2 teaspoon sea salt

1 clove garlic, minced
freshly ground black
    pepper
dash Hungarian paprika
1 tablespoon chopped
    fresh parsley

1. Blend or mash beans by
hand with lemon juice. Add
a little water if necessary for
a light, creamy consistency.
2. Combine with remaining
ingredients in a small bowl.

Cottage Cheese-Yogurt Dressing
(1 1/2 cups)

1/2 cup yogurt
1 cup cottage cheese
1 tablespoon chopped parsley (or more)
1 teaspoon chopped chives OR 1/4 teaspoon dried dill weed or 1 teaspoon fresh chopped dill weed
1 teaspoon sea salt (optional)
2 tablespoons freshly squeezed lemon juice (optional for salads)

Combine ingredients in small bowl. This is very good on baked potatoes as well as salads.

Tofu Dressings

Tofu–that wonderful, mild soybean "cheese"–can be used like yogurt to make tasty salad dressings. More important, serving with any whole grain forms a complete protein. And tofu contains no animal fat. (See Fresh Cress Dressing for a springtime tofu dip.) Here's a recipe based on one by a superb cook, Martha Rose Shulman .

Basic Tofu Dip
(1 1/2 cups)

8 ounces soft tofu
1/2 cup yogurt
1 tablespoon freshly squeezed lemon juice
1 clove garlic (optional)
1 tablespoon komé or mugi miso (see Glossary)
2 tablespoons tahini
2 tablespoons saké (see Glossary), dry sherry, or a light beer
1 small grating of nutmeg
a few drops hot pepper sauce

Whiz all ingredients in a blender till smooth. This firms up as it rests.

Shoyu Sunnies

**1 1/2 cups raw, hulled
sunflower seeds**
2-3 tablespoons shoyu

1. Toast seeds in a heavy-bottomed skillet over medium heat, stirring constantly, till tanning.

2. Then pour in shoyu and stir rapidly to coat all the seeds. Remove from heat immediately. When cool, store in a capped jar.

Serve as niblets, or as a garnish for casseroles, soups, salads, baked potatoes, or almost anything.

Sesame seeds are nutritious, being high in calcium, and good tasting. I use the brown variety instead of the milled white, but some folks feel the white is easier to digest. They're apt to be rather soiled when you buy them, so here is what to do.

Toasted Sesame Seeds

1. Pour as many seeds as can be comfortably stored in a small covered container into a sieve. Wash thoroughly under running cold water. Drain well.
2. Toast in a clean, ungreased skillet over moderate heat until brown, stirring constantly. They'll begin jumping around like popcorn in a bit. (If you have a mesh cover, use it.) When thoroughly dry and golden, but not dark brown, allow to cool. Store in a capped glass jar.

Serve sprinkled over nearly everything.

Use as a salt substitute as is, or grind in a mortar and mix with a bit of sea salt to make **Gomasio** (see Glossary).

Nuts and Seeds

Nuts and seeds–used in moderation because of their high fat content–are a nutritious, crunchy addition to any salad, excellent scattered over baked potatoes or other cooked root vegetables, or atop such succulents as broccoli and dandelion greens, or added to loaves and burgers. They provide a lot of protein, usually B vitamins depending on the nut variety, and trace minerals.

Although uniformly high in fat, most of it is unsaturated. Almonds, pecans, and walnuts contain the least amount of saturated fat, Brazil nuts the most. Walnuts, sesame and sunflower seeds top the list for polyunsaturates. Store in refrigerator or freezer.

Pumpkin, melon, and squash seeds are not only edible but good for you. So don't throw them out. Lady Godiva or "naked" pumpkin seeds are especially easy, although Burpee now suggests Triple Treat.

Toasted Pumpkin or Squash Seeds

seeds
boiling water to cover
sea salt

1. Wash seeds lightly and discard fibers. Place in a large saucepan with water and salt. Simmer gently two hours.

2. Remove from heat, drain well, and coat with sunflower seed oil. Spread on a cookie sheet in one layer. Sprinkle with sea salt. Bake in a 250°F oven until browned. Store in a capped jar.

Serve as a niblet.

Flat Breads

Heavy cooking doesn't sit well in summer. Flat, quick, whole-grain breads are appealing. Combined with legumes, they provide complete protein. Adding vegetables, as in tacos, ensures vitamins and trace minerals. Another way of combining proteins is to use tofu as an ingredient in the bread itself—unsurpassed for creating an elastic dough easy to handle and tasty to eat.

Flat breads come from southern cuisines. The classic favorites are tortillas, chupattis, and puris. But while tortillas are familiar to most Americans, Indian flat breads aren't. **Chupattis** *are like*

Basic Dough for Tofu-Wheat Tortillas, Chupattis, or Puris

[about 20 (6- to 7-inch) disks, or 40 (4- to 5-inch) disks]

6 ounces soft tofu,
**   drained and**
**   crumbled**
2 cups whole-wheat
**   pastry or bread flour**
1/8 teaspoon sea salt
5-10 tablespoons cold
**   water**

1. In a medium-sized bowl, mix tofu with flour, salt, and water, using your hands. Start out with one tablespoon water and add until your dough is very stiff but not quite at the stage where it cracks. Knead ten to fifteen times. Let rest at least thirty minutes to an hour at room temperature.
2. When ready to cook chupattis, tortillas, or puris, roll dough into a log about two inches in diameter and slice in half lengthwise. Then slice crosswise so you have twenty one-inch by two-inch pieces for tacos, or forty one-inch by one-inch pieces for chupattis or puris. Cover with a slightly dampened towel to prevent drying out.

»

»

95

To Cook Chupattis or Tortillas

1. Heat your griddle or heavy-bottomed skillet so that it's very hot. Take each piece of cut dough and roll it into a smooth little ball (one-and one-half-inch diameter for tacos, smaller for chupattis).
2. Flour a surface with white unbleached flour. Clap "marbles" between your palms to flatten. Place on floured board. Turn over to flour other side. Using a rolling pin, roll out very thin in all directions to a five-inch or a seven-inch diameter disk.
3. Place on very hot griddle and freckle each side quickly (only one to two minutes).

4. As chupattis or tortillas are cooked, stack them inside a slightly dampened towel to keep them moist and flexible.
Use your warm tortillas immediately.
(If not strictly fresh, rub each one with a little water, then reheat in a dry hot skillet until flexible. Keep warm, tightly covered, in a 200°F oven.)

Serve as **Tacos** or **Enchiladas**, chupattis with any Indian meal, scoops for spreads and dips, or as the bread for any lunch with a main-dish salad such as cottage cheese and greens, or fruit.

tortillas, though made with wheat flour instead of cornmeal, and are rolled flat.
***Parathas** are similar but rolled in layers with butter. Both are fried on a griddle.* ***Puris** are rolled small and deep-fried. A* ***papadam**, by the way, is a huge flat bread, difficult to make as it must be dried slowly in the sun.*

The basic dough recipe, which can serve to make everything from tortillas to chupattis, contains tofu. It's so elastic and strong you can easily roll it paper-thin.

Tacos #1

(2-3 per person)

Fill a fresh or refreshed tortilla with the following ingredients:
1. A heaping tablespoon of any cooked, seasoned beans, a heaping tablespoon grated sharp cheese (jack or cheddar), alfalfa sprouts, shredded lettuce or chopped fresh parsley, any raw vegetable of your choice such as chopped tomato, finely chopped onions, finely grated carrot.
OR 2. A heaping tablespoon crumbled tofu, chopped lettuce, tomatoes, pickles, hot peppers, hot tomato salsa, and some nutritional yeast flakes.
Fold over.

Serve with a hot pepper sauce (**Salsa Cruda**), or **Yogurt Tahini Dressing**.

Tacos #2

(2-3 per person)

fresh or refreshed
tortillas
cooked beans
grated sharp cheese
sunflower seed oil

1. Spread the middle of each tortilla with a heaping tablespoon of cooked beans and a heaping tablespoon of cheese. Fold over.

2. Heat two to three tablespoons sunflower seed oil in a heavy-bottomed skillet. Sauté tortillas on both sides till just crisp. Drain briefly on paper towels.

Serve immediately topped with **Salsa Cruda** or **Yogurt Tahini Dressing** or plain yogurt; alfalfa sprouts or shredded lettuce, radishes, grated carrots, and finely chopped tomatoes and onions.

*My puris don't swell up like little balloons, but they're delightful. Reheated in a slow (200°F) oven on paper towels and stacked in a large bowl on their sides, they make amusing party fare with **Chenna** dips and fresh vegetables. They even serve as an odd tortilla when stacked with taco ingredients–though of course they don't fold up. It's good to let folks load their own at the table.*

Jean Ann's Puris

(about 40)

1 recipe Basic Dough for
Tofu-Wheat Tortillas,
etc.
peanut oil

1. Roll out little one-inch diameter "marbles" into paper-thin disks. Place wok over high heat and pour in about three inches oil. Heat to 350°F.
2. Slip disks in, one by one, and allow to brown for one-half to one minute. Turn over with tongs and brown again. Drain on paper towels or rack (turning once).

Serve immediately, warm, or reheat in a slow oven. (If reheated on paper more oil will drain out.)

Whole-Grain Pocket Bread

(about 25 pockets)

**1 tablespoon dry baking
    yeast**
**2 1/2 cups lukewarm
    water**
2 tablespoons sugar
3 cups warm water
1 tablespoon sea salt
**about 9-10 cups
    whole-wheat bread
    flour**

1. In a large bowl soften yeast in two and a half cups lukewarm water. Stir in sugar. Let stand overnight (or at least four hours in a warm spot).
2. In the morning stir in three cups warm water, salt, and enough flour to make a stiff dough. Knead till smooth, using white flour on breadboard. Place in a well-oiled bowl, cover, and let rise till double in bulk.
3. Punch down and shape into a long, thick roll about three and a half inches in diameter. (If you like, set aside about a third of the roll. Refrigerate it, covered, and use the next day in place of yeast as the starter for another batch. See Note 2.) Preheat oven to 500°F. High heat is the secret to making the disk's "pocket." Cut remaining roll into chunks or slices about one and a half inches thick. Roll into smooth balls (my favorite size is a glob which would measure two-thirds of a cup). On floured board roll out into quarter-inch-thick disks (being careful not to crease) about five inches in diameter.
4. Place on oiled cookie sheets. The breads rise brilliantly when cookie sheets are hot, so place your disks on a cookie sheet hot from the oven. Bake at 500°F on the *lowest oven rack* for about eight minutes, or till browned.

Note 1: Pocket bread should puff up grandly. *Don't overcook.* Hard pockets won't make envelopes for stuffings. To keep pockets soft after baking, cover with a damp towel. You can also cover and pop them into a brown paper bag for fifteen minutes to ensure flexibility. Pockets can be frozen well. Warm before use.

Note 2: *If you kept some dough aside* for use the next day (about a third of the roll, see 3 above), dissolve this starter in three cups salted water and stir in enough flour to make a stiff dough– four to five cups. Add to reserved dough, then let rise and continue shaping and baking as above.

Mainers in the Waterville area are lucky–a large Lebanese community ensures a good supply of pocket bread in the stores year round. But you can make your own. Pocket breads are sometimes made with eggs, sometimes oil, and may be rolled out in large or small disks. My whole-grain version has an authentic feel.

How to serve

1) If you made smallish disks, serve hot as an appetizer with freshly cooked **Falafel** alongside (see below).

2) Cut into the "top" edge with a knife and gently open the pocket. Fill with shredded lettuce, chopped cucumbers, chopped bell peppers, grated cheese, hot **Falafel**, and drizzle with thinned yogurt or **Yogurt Tahini Dressing**. Serve for lunch.

3) Fill with anything you like, such as avocado and tomato. My children love peanut butter, banana slices, and alfalfa sprouts.

4) Cut into triangles and serve with **Hummus** and **Tabouli** as an appetizer or for lunch.

5) Cut into triangles and serve with any **Chenna** spread.

Falafel

*Falafel, grand little garbanzo balls, frequently accompany **Pocket Bread** in the Middle East, along with a tahini sauce and salad greens. Traditionally deep-fried, mine are sautéed lightly.*

Falafel

(38-40 balls)

1 cup dry garbanzo beans
3 cups cold water
1/2 cup cold water
2 cloves garlic
1 teaspoon sea salt
1 teaspoon powdered cumin
1/2 teaspoon powdered coriander
1/2 teaspoon chili powder
1/2 cup finely chopped parsley
clarified butter

1. *The night before*, pick over beans and wash well. Soak overnight in three cups cold water. One cup dry beans equals two cups cooked.

2. *On falafal day*, grind one and a third cups soaked garbanzos through a food chopper using medium blade (you'll have a few left over). Blend two-thirds of the ground garbanzos with a half cup cold water till very fine. Add garlic, salt, cumin, coriander, and chili powder and blend again.

3. Combine ground and blended garbanzos in a bowl with parsley.

4. Dip out with teaspoon, roll into small balls (less than one inch in diameter) and sauté lightly in a skillet in butter till golden brown on all sides. (Or deep-fry at a temperature of 350-370°F.)

Serve hot in **Pocket Bread**, with **Yogurt Tahini Dressing**, chopped cucumber, tomato, shredded lettuce, and finely chopped green onion.

Hommus Tahini

(about 3 cups, or 6 servings)

2 cups cooked garbanzo
    beans
1/2 cup rinsed and
    well-drained sesame
    seeds
1 clove garlic
1/2 teaspoon sea salt
3 tablespoons freshly
    squeezed lemon juice

1 tablespoon chopped
    parsley (optional)

Purée all ingredients in
blender, with barely enough
bean broth (from the cooked
garbanzos) to make the
blender turn.

Serve with pieces of **Pocket
Bread**, crackers, or rolls, as
an appetizer or for lunch
with salad.

*Pocket Bread cut
into wedges is often
served with
hommus, a garbanzo
bean spread. My
recipe adds sesame
seeds. In the old
days spreads like
this were produced
by mashing, usually
in a mortar.*

Tabouli

(6 servings)

2 cups fine-grained
    bulgur wheat
4 cups boiling water or
    stock
1 small clove garlic,
    minced
1 1/2 cups green
    scallions, chopped,
    or 1 medium-sized
    onion, finely
    chopped
2 tablespoons fresh
    mint, chopped
1 1/2 cups finely
    chopped, fresh
    Italian broad-leafed
    parsley
3/4 cup peeled
    tomatoes, chopped
    fine (optional)
1/2 cup freshly squeezed
    lemon juice
1/2-1 cup extra-virgin
    olive oil
1 teaspoon sea salt
freshly ground black
    pepper

1. In a medium-sized bowl
soak bulgur wheat in boiling
water for at least ten
minutes, or till the bulgur
has absorbed all the water
and is tender. If the bulgur
remains wet, squeeze it dry
in a towel.
2. When cool, add
remaining ingredients and
toss together.

Served as a piquant side
dish, tabouli is especially
good with anything rather
bland and heavy, such as a
nut loaf. Or serve stuffed
into cucumbers cut
lengthwise and hollowed
out. Or stuff tomatoes or
small zucchini.

Note: Substitute cooked and
cooled millet for bulgur.

*Tabouli, as I first
experienced it in
North Africa, is a
finely chopped
salad made chiefly
of Italian parsley
and bulgur wheat.
We often enjoyed it
with Pocket
Bread, Hommus,
and couscous (see
Glossary if
unfamiliar with
bulgur wheat or
couscous).*

Mustard Greens

Although it is not native, early Mainers considered the mustard green peculiarly "theirs." Mustard is one of the greens richest in vitamins and minerals, ranking nearly as high as kale. And it tastes good. My husband doesn't consider a salad "done" unless it contains some mustard–often our salads contain a copious amount. In fact, we entertained one evening and I served our usual salad only to discover several guests crying as a result!

Swiss and Rhubarb Chard

Centuries ago, Swiss chard pleased Greeks and Romans. Together with its more modern, red relative, rhubarb chard, it still pleases. Chard is a good mineral-gathering plant–its root system is deep and extensive. Planted early, it will produce early. Consistent cuttings keep it succulent throughout the summer and into fall.

Tender Early Mustard Greens

1. Gather greens, a large handful per person. Discard stems (allow leaf to fold, then cut out stem from the back side). Rinse quickly but well and don't dry.
2. Steam wet greens in a kettle over moderate heat till very tender. Add half a cup more water if necessary to prevent burning. Ten minutes cooking time is a good bet.

3. Remove from kettle and drain well in a colander. Form into a thick lump (which you can fashion into a sort of square) on a chopping board, and, using a long-bladed sharp knife, cut lengthwise and crosswise. Then transfer to a heated platter using a large metal spatula.

Serve as a hot side dish, drizzled with shoyu or any vinaigrette. A curried gravy (see **Simple Millet with Curried Gravy**) would be a good addition.

Chard stems, which don't shrink, can be cooked rather like asparagus, and leaves are good in any stir-fry, soup, loaf, or salad; or use chard to replace spinach in any recipe, although its taste is stronger.

Swiss Chard Stems in Garlic
(6 servings)

**2 pounds chard (equals
    1 1/4 pounds stems,
    or 5 cups, cut into
    1-inch bits)
3 tablespoons sesame oil
freshly squeezed juice of
    2 lemons
1/2 cup water
2 garlic cloves
1/2 teaspoon sea salt**

1. Gather chard and wash well. Drain. Remove leaves (save for **Stuffed Swiss Chard**) and cut stems into one-inch pieces. Place them in a colander over boiling water and steam until *just* tender, about ten minutes.
2. Whiz remaining ingredients in blender.

Serve chard bits on a hot platter, sprinkled with a salad dressing. Good accompaniments would be a whole grain (either plain or in burgers or loaves) or noodles, and other vegetables in season.

Stuffed Swiss Chard

(30 stuffed leaves or 6 servings)

1 cup well-washed dry
    garbanzo beans (also
    called chickpeas)
3 cups cold water
1 bay leaf
2 peppercorns
1 cup medium-ground
    bulgur wheat
2 cups boiling water
2 pounds Swiss chard
    (equals 1 pound
    leaves, or about 30
    leaves; big leaves
    about 9 inches long
    are best)
1 medium-sized onion,
    minced
1/4 cup finely chopped
    fresh parsley
1 garlic clove, minced
1/2 teaspoon powdered
    cinnamon (optional)
3 tablespoons extra-
    virgin olive oil
1/4 cup peeled, seeded,
    and finely chopped
    tomato (optional)
AND/OR 1 tablespoon
    diced zucchini or 1
    tablespoon diced
    green or red bell
    pepper (optional)
water or stock
1 tablespoon sea salt
freshly squeezed juice of
    1 lemon

1. *The night before*, soak
garbanzo beans in three cups
water.
2. *In the morning*, drop
them into lightly salted,
boiling water. Add bay leaf
and peppercorns and
immediately reduce heat.
Simmer until done, perhaps
two hours. Check by biting
into one–it should be soft.
3. *An hour and a half before
dinner*, combine bulgur
wheat and two cups boiling
water in a medium-sized
bowl. Soak for half an hour
or until bulgur is tender and
moist. Drain off excess
moisture if necessary.
4. While bulgur is soaking,
wash your chard and select
the widest leaves. Cut the
bottom part off so that most
of the thick stem has been
removed and you still have
a wide green banner to work
with. (Save stems for other
dishes.) Place chard in a
colander over a pot of
boiling water and steam ever
so slightly in order to wilt it.
An old Syrian recipe suggests
placing chard leaves in a
single layer in the sun for
half an hour to wilt.
5. Grind garbanzo beans
finely in a meat-grinder or
food processor. Then
combine two cups of the
soaked bulgur (drained if
necessary) with one cup of
the well-cooked, ground
garbanzos, onion, parsley,
seasonings, and two
tablespoons oil. Add
vegetables if desired.
6. Next spread out chard
leaves in turn, placing one
tablespoon stuffing at the
base. Roll up slightly, turn
in sides neatly, and finish
rolling much as you would
grape leaves (see **Sadie's**

*Grape and cabbage
leaves are not the
only items suitable
for stuffing–the wide
chard leaf is fine
once most of the
thick stem is
removed.*

*The stuffing in this
recipe can also be
used for cabbage and
grape leaves, and for
eggplants and koosas
(small, straight,
summer squash).*

String Beans

We always called them "string beans," referring willy-nilly to string beans, stringless beans, pole beans, or bush beans—although we did give credence to yellow wax and shell. Then there were all the dried beans, which we considered a separate species. At least that's the way it appeared to my ten-year-old gardener's mind.

Beans have been a down-Maine staple from the very first, ever since Native Americans were discovered growing them among squash and corn in tiny plots carved out of river bottomland. From string to dried, they provide a lot of protein, vitamins, and minerals.

We eat pecks during the summer, can quarts for winter, and find they please virtually everyone either pickled or hot. They are, in short, as valuable a vegetable now as they ever were.

Stuffed Grape Leaves).
7. Place one tablespoon olive oil in a three-quart heavy-bottomed kettle. Layer in the bundles. Cover with water and add salt. Weight with a small plate so all the bundles are immersed. Bring to a boil, then lower heat, and simmer over low heat thirty minutes.

Simple Steamed String Beans

The bane of my childhood was limp, soggy beans cooked by other children's mothers; my own knew better.

1. Beans do not shrink, so pick or purchase a large handful per person. Snap off bean "heads" where they join the stalk. Mother always said to remove the little tail as well, but I never do; I enjoy the look of it. Pull off the string if necessary, then snap bean pods into bite-sized lengths. When I was a child the pig would get these leftovers. Now our compost pile does.
2. Rinse snapped beans and drain. Place a layer in a cast-iron wok or heavy-bottomed kettle. Sprinkle with a little sea salt. Repeat till all beans are in. Then add about a half cup of water, cover tightly, bring to a boil, reduce heat to

8. Add the lemon juice.

Remove carefully with a spatula when cool, and serve with heaps of a whole-grain bread and/or fresh **Pocket Bread**, a small raw salad, and fruit for dessert.

very low, and simmer for about a half hour or until barely tender. (The salt-free way to cook string beans is to heap them in a covered colander and steam them over boiling water until *al dente*.)

Serve hot or cold with yogurt dressing or vinaigrette; or shoyu and freshly squeezed lemon juice; or simply sea salt (unless cooked with salt), freshly ground black pepper, and herbs of your choice.

Served with sliced nuts, they provide the beginning of the daily protein base. Almonds are *de rigueur*, of course, but I also suggest **Shoyu Sunnies**, toasted sesame seeds, or chopped, toasted walnuts.

Beans with Tomato and Pepper

(4 to 6 servings)

2 tablespoons extra-
    virgin olive oil
garlic cloves
1 medium-sized onion,
    chopped
1 large red or golden
    tomato, coarsely
    chopped
1 tablespoon saké (see
    Glossary)
1 tablespoon finely
    chopped bell pepper
1 teaspoon minced
    lovage OR 1
    tablespoon finely
    chopped celery
    including top
2 tablespoons minced
    fresh parsley
1 teaspoon finely
    chopped fresh
    marjoram, summer
    savory, sage, oregano,
    or basil
a pinch powdered
    cinnamon

a pinch powdered
    allspice
freshly ground black
    pepper
4-6 cups string or yellow
    wax beans per
    person, steamed until
    tender (see above)

1. Heat oil in a heavy cast-iron wok or skillet. Sauté as many garlic cloves as you fancy, smashed with the side of a broad knife blade, along with onion, over moderate heat until the onion is limp.
2. Add tomato, saké, pepper, celery, herbs, and spices. Simmer three minutes.
3. Add steamed beans and stir gently but well. Cover and steam till just hot, about two minutes.

Serve hot with cooked brown rice or another whole grain or pasta, a small raw salad with vinaigrette or yogurt dressing and sesame seeds.

String Bean Salad

(up to 6 servings)

1 cup string beans per
    person, steamed until
    tender (see above)
scant 2/3 cup extra-
    virgin olive oil
1/3 cup vinegar or
    freshly squeezed
    lemon juice
2 tablespoons cold water
    or saké (see Glossary)

1/4 teaspoon maple
    syrup
1/2 teaspoon Dijon
    mustard
2 teaspoons shoyu
1 teaspoon freshly
    minced sage, lovage,
    marjoram, or
    summer savory
1 tablespoon chopped
    fresh chives
1 teaspoon Hungarian
    paprika

freshly ground black
     pepper
1 large firm tomato, red
     or yellow

1. Place freshly cooked beans
in a bowl.
2. Make a marinade of the
oil and vinegar, water,
maple syrup, mustard,

shoyu, herbs, and spices.
Pour over the beans.
3. Peel tomato, chop finely,
and drain well. Add to salad
and chill.

Serve with a slotted spoon,
as a side dish to any meal.

String Beans and Feta Cheese Salad
(up to 6 servings)

1 cup freshly cooked
     string beans per
     person, chilled
1 cup curly endive per
     person (or other
     green of your
     choice), shredded
1 Bermuda onion, sliced
     thin, or 3 scallions,
     sliced
a few bits of summer
     savory, minced
7 nasturtium flowers,
     rinsed briefly and
     coarsely chopped (or
     left whole for
     garnish) OR 1-2
     tablespoons Nastur-
     tium Bud Capers,
     minced
scant 2/3 cup extra-
     virgin olive oil

1/3 cup freshly squeezed
     lemon juice OR
     vinegar of your
     choice, such as
     raspberry or Japanese
     umeboshi
about 1/2 teaspoon sea
     salt (optional)
freshly ground black
     pepper
1/4-1/2 cup cubed or
     crumbled feta cheese

1. Combine all vegetables
and herbs in a bowl and mix
lightly together.
2. Make a dressing of olive
oil, lemon juice or vinegar,
salt, and pepper. Pour over
as much as necessary to coat
the vegetables lightly.
3. Sprinkle feta cheese on
top.

String Bean and Wheat Meat Stir-Fry

(6 servings)

3 shallots or other
    bunching onions,
    chopped
1 teaspoon finely grated,
    fresh ginger root
1 1/2 cups sliced
    mushrooms
1/2 cup diced carrot
2 cups green beans,
    sliced into 1/2-inch
    pieces
1 cup thinly sliced
    Wheat Meat (cut 1-
    inch long by
    1/8-inch
    thick)
2 tablespoons komé
    miso (see Glossary)
1 tablespoon thick
    tomato paste
1/2 teaspoon chili
    powder OR 1/8-1/4
    teaspoon cayenne
    plus 1/4 teaspoon
    cumin
1 tablespoon shoyu
1/2 cup water
1 tablespoon vermouth,
    dry sherry, or saké
    (see Glossary)
1/2 teaspoon maple
    syrup
1 teaspoon minced garlic
3 tablespoons sunflower
    seed oil
1 tablespoon sesame oil
    (optional)
2 teaspoons cornstarch
1/4 cup cold water

1. At dinnertime slice **Wheat Meat** and prepare vegetables. Set them close to wok.
2. In a bowl, whisk together miso with chili, shoyu, one and a half cups water, vermouth (or substitute), maple syrup, and garlic.
3. Heat wok and add two tablespoons oil. Swirl to coat the sides. Add shallots and ginger and fry a few seconds. Increase heat. Add sliced vegetables and stir-fry a minute or two. Toss with a spatula or slotted spoon so that all surfaces are coated. Remove and set aside.
4. Heat wok and add the remaining tablespoon sunflower oil plus one tablespoon sesame oil. Stir-fry sliced **Wheat Meat** over high heat until golden, about two minutes.   Stir in miso/chili sauce. Cover, lower heat, and simmer fifteen minutes to let **Wheat Meat** absorb flavor.
5. Meanwhile, combine cornstarch and a quarter cup water. Return vegetables to wok and cook another two minutes or until beans are tender, adding a quarter cup more water if necessary. Add dissolved cornstarch and stir until sauce boils and thickens.

Serve at once with rice, other whole grain or pasta, a fresh summer salad, and rolls of your choice.

Wheat Meat (see Glossary), a tasty vegetarian food, is made by consolidating the gluten in wheat flour. It combines beautifully with beans to make a high-protein main dish.

Cucumbers

August at last! Cucumbers are in and vines run rampant. My favorite slicing cuke is a Japanese variety which grows very long and thin. It's called Suyo Long, reaches maturity in about sixty days, and is considered "burpless." Suyo also makes good "bread and butter" pickles.

Cukes can be used in odd ways besides being served fresh in a dagwood sandwich with tomato, lettuce, tofu, and mayonnaise. Middle Eastern folk and Indians use cucumber with yogurt and/or mint for delicious soups and yogurt-dressed salads.

Two Ways to Prepare Cucumbers

1. Peel and slice cucumbers thin. Arrange on a large plate and sprinkle with sea salt. Place another plate on top for perhaps one hour at room temperature to press out both water and possible bitterness. When you dress cukes after this, the dressing will not be diluted with water. Drain well.
2. If you know your cukes to be bitter, toss slices with a little sea salt, sugar, and vinegar. Allow to rest thirty minutes. Then drain.

Yogurt Cucumber Raita

(6 servings)

1 tablespoon sunflower seed oil
2 teaspoons powdered cumin
1 clove garlic, smashed with broad side of knife blade
3 cups thick yogurt
about 2 cups prepared cucumbers, diced
sea salt to taste
white pepper to taste (optional)

1. Heat oil in a skillet and brown cumin and garlic slightly. Remove from heat and discard garlic.
2. When slightly cooled, add yogurt, drained cucumbers, salt, and pepper. (If you want to discard seeds, cut cukes in half lengthwise and scoop out seeds before slicing.) Mix well. Chill.

Serve with curried dishes, rice or pasta, and a leafy salad, or cooked greens. Fruit is fine for dessert.

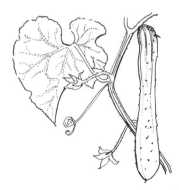

Cucumbers in Raspberry Vinegar

(6 servings)

3 large green cucumbers
1 tablespoon honey
2/3 cup raspberry
   vinegar
1 teaspoon sea salt
1/4 teaspoon freshly
   ground black pepper
   or white pepper

1. Score cucumbers lengthwise with a fork so that, when cut, the slices look rather like flowers. Test for bitterness (treat with salt, sugar, and vinegar as above if necessary). Cut in very thin slices.
2. In a small bowl, combine remaining ingredients. (Raspberry vinegar is wine vinegar flavored with natural raspberry extract–strong and lovely.)
3. Pour over sliced cukes. Water in cukes will help dilute the rather strong raspberry vinegar. Chill two or three hours. Drain before serving.

Serve as a side dish to any meal. These pinkish-green "flowers" are also good garnishes.

My father was wont to drown his sliced cucumbers in vinegar, salt, and pepper. Here is the New Maine version.

Chenna Cucumber Dip

(about 2 cups)

1 cup Chenna
2 large green cucumbers,
   peeled, seeded, and
   diced
1 tablespoon white
   distilled vinegar
1/2 teaspoon sea salt
1/8 teaspoon honey
1 small garlic clove,
   minced
2 tablespoons fresh
   chopped dill weed
1 tablespoon extra-virgin
   olive oil
three drops maple syrup
sea salt to taste
freshly ground black
   pepper
2 teaspoons tarragon
   vinegar

1. *The night before,* make **Chenna** using two cups yogurt.
2. *Next day,* combine cukes in the vinegar, salt, and honey in a small bowl. Allow to stand for an hour.
3. Drain well, pop into a square of cheesecloth, twist, and press out as much liquid as possible with your hands. Combine in a medium-sized bowl with **Chenna** and remaining ingredients.

Serve in a mound as an hors d'oeuvre, garnished with parsley and black olives (optional), with wedges of **Pocket Bread**, **Corn Crêpes**, **Puris**, or some freshly made crackers.

Chenna and cucumbers make a fine vegetable dip or spread for crackers or flat bread.

It is unusual to cook cucumbers in Maine. But with the typical hot summers producing in such abundance, cooking adds a needed dimension to the ubiquitous salad.

Potato-Stuffed Cukes

(6-8 servings)

3 cups water
1/2 teaspoon sea salt
2 teaspoons vinegar
2 very large, green
**   cucumbers**
1 1/2 heaping cups
**   cooked, mashed**
**   potatoes**
2/3 cup yogurt
1 teaspoon chopped
**   fresh dill or chives**
sea salt to taste
freshly ground black
**   pepper**
a little freshly grated
**   nutmeg**
a handful of Shoyu
**   Sunnies**

1. Preheat oven to 350°F. Bring water, salt, and vinegar to a boil in an enameled saucepan and add cucumbers, halved and seeded. Simmer three minutes. Remove and drain well. Then place, hollow side down, on paper towels until ready to stuff.
2. In a medium-sized bowl whip potatoes with yogurt and seasonings.
3. Turn cucumbers right-side-up and pile potato mixture into the hollows. Place in a buttered lasagna pan and sprinkle with **Shoyu Sunnies**. Bake about thirty-five minutes.

Serve with a tossed salad, steamed vegetables, and fresh rolls.

A Note about Desserts

Sweeteners are powerful chemicals. Refined sugar should be viewed as a condiment and preservative–not a staple–and honey should be used in moderation. Dessert can be a nutritious part of the meal if simple and complementary to the main dish. If your main course is grain-based or heavy, offer a light dessert; if your main course is on the slim side, have a grainy or creamy ending. If you're vegetarian, try serving rice with the savory course and tofu as a sweet topping for later on.

Red Raspberries in Red Wine

(6 servings)

2 quarts raspberries
a light red wine

1. Pick over berries, wash quickly, and drain well. Place in wine glasses.
2. Cover with light red wine. (I personally am fond of Bartlett's Maine Estate Coastal Red.)

Serve (but not to the little ones!) with fresh crackers.

Raspberries and Peaches in Port

(4-6 servings)

2 cups raspberries
2 cups sliced peaches
1 teaspoon freshly grated
   lemon rind
1 teaspoon grated fresh
   or candied ginger
   root
enough port to barely
   cover the fruit

1. Combine raspberries with peaches.
2. Stir in remaining ingredients and allow to rest, refrigerated, for two hours.

Serve chilled in small sherbert glasses.

Blackberry Cordial

(4-6 quarts)

8 quarts blackberries
2 quarts cold water
2 cups white sugar for
   every quart
   blackberry juice
1 tablespoon each whole
   cloves and allspice
1 cinnamon stick
1/2 teaspoon grated
   nutmeg
1 pint brandy or whiskey
   for every quart syrup

1. In a large enameled kettle simmer together blackberries and water until mushy. Strain through cheesecloth.
2. For every quart juice, stir in two cups sugar.
3. Tie spices into a little cotton bag and drop into the juice/sugar mixture.
4. Bring to a boil and boil fifteen minutes.
5. When cool, add two cups good brandy or whiskey to every quart syrup, pour into sterilized bottles, and cork securely. This will mellow. Store in a cool, dark place.

Raspberries and Blackberries
August 10–and the blackberries are ripe. The raspberries have been hanging like jewels to delight both birds and people. Berries turn any breakfast into a nutritious feast and also make superb desserts.

Raspberries and blackberries can be substituted for nearly all of the strawberry recipes. Try raspberry **Shortcake** *and raspberry or blackberry* **Cream Puff Ring** *in particular. Raspberries grow easily and well in Maine, produce in abundance, and for a long time.*

In the old days Grandmother always had blackberry cordial hidden on a back shelf. This was a combination of blackberry syrup and brandy or whiskey.

Broccoli

Broccoli is a **brassica** *of exquisite color, taste, texture, and nutritional characteristics. Lately,* **brassicas** *are being touted as some of the best anticarcinogens around (along with carrots). Broccoli is full of vitamins, minerals, and protein, yet very low in calories. Broccoli leaves, often thrown away, are especially high in vitamin A. The stems are nutritionally rich, too.*

The traditional method of preparing broccoli by lengthy soaking leaches out vital nutrients. Whether for stir-fry or any other dish, I prefer to **blanch** *broccoli. Simply bring a large pot of water to the boil, pop in broccoli (cut into florets or whole, stem trimmed short), boil one minute, and remove with a slotted spoon. (No worm will survive.) Drain and use in any recipe.*

In the past, Maine cooks sent broccoli stalks out to the hens along with the leaves. Now we know better–leaves are saved for stir-fries or added to other cooked green dishes, and stalks have many uses.

Broccoli Salad

(2-4 servings)

2 cups broccoli florets
1/2 cup extra-virgin olive oil
3 tablespoons wine vinegar of your choice
1 teaspoon Dijon mustard
1/2-1 clove garlic, minced
3/4 teaspoon sea salt (optional)
freshly ground black pepper
3 hard-cooked eggs, chopped

1. In a large pot boil enough water to cover two cups broccoli florets. Pop broccoli in, blanch one minute, and remove with a slotted spoon. (If you like your broccoli cooked a bit more, blanch four to five minutes longer.)
2. Plunge hot florets into icy cold water. Drain well and chill.
3. Combine olive oil, vinegar, mustard, and seasonings in a jar and shake vigorously. Pour over broccoli and marinate for about a half hour.
4. Immediately before serving, add eggs and toss lightly.

Serve on salad greens as a side dish to any meal.

Ways of Using Broccoli Stalks

Peel stalks by inserting a small, sharp knife under the skin and pulling.

1. Slice peeled stalks into disks or matchsticks. These are good for stir-fries.
2. Make thicker matchsticks and enjoy them with a dip.
3. Blanched matchsticks can be dipped into tempura batter and quickly deep-fried with other vegetables. Delicious!

Wheat Meat with Broccoli

(6 servings)

1 recipe Wheat Meat
3 cups combined
    vegetables (except
    onions or scallions)
    such as :
    broccoli stems
    (peeled and
    chopped), red or
    green peppers
    (chopped), string
    beans (cut into
    1/2-inch bits),
    sunchokes (diced),
    peas or pods,
    zucchini (diced),
    rhubarb chard (stems
    only, chopped)
3 shallots or scallions,
    sliced (or 1 medium-
    sized onion, sliced)
1 tablespoon miso (see
    Glossary)
1 tablespoon thick
    tomato paste
1/2 teaspoon chili
    powder OR 1/8
    teaspoon cayenne
    plus 1/4 teaspoon
    cumin
1 tablespoon shoyu
1/2 cup water
1 tablespoon of
    vermouth, dry sherry,
    or saké (see Glossary)
4 tablespoons sunflower
    seed oil
1/2 teaspoon grated
    fresh ginger root
1/2 teaspoon crushed,
    peeled garlic
2 teaspoons cornstarch
1/4 cup cold water

1/4 cup sautéed cashew
    nuts or walnuts, or
    Shoyu Sunnies

1. About two hours before dinnertime, prepare gluten for **Wheat Meat**.
2. At dinnertime, cut one cup prepared **Wheat Meat** into shreds about one inch long and an eighth-inch thick. Cut vegetables into pieces of similar size and set close to wok. (See **The Wok** if unfamiliar with its use.)
3. Combine miso with tomato paste, chili, shoyu, one-half cup water, and vermouth (or substitute).
4. Heat wok and add two tablespoons oil. Swirl to coat the inside. Pop in ginger and garlic and cook a few seconds. Add diced vegetables and stir-fry a minute or two. Toss with a spatula or slotted spoon so that all surfaces are coated. Remove from wok.
5. Add remaining two tablespoons oil and stir-fry **Wheat Meat** for two minutes or until browned. Stir in miso/chili sauce. Cover, lower heat, and simmer fifteen minutes to let **Wheat Meat** absorb flavor.
6. Meanwhile, combine cornstarch and a quarter cup water. Return vegetables to wok, turn heat to high, and cook another two minutes, adding a quarter cup more water if necessary. Add dissolved cornstarch and stir

until sauce boils and thickens. Add nuts.

Serve immediately with steaming brown rice, other whole grain, or pasta.

Lemon Broccoli Stir-fry
(4-6 servings)

1 medium-sized head of
   broccoli
2-3 thick celery stalks
2 tablespoons sunflower
   seed oil
2 medium-sized onions,
   sliced (about 1 1/2
   cups)
1/4 teaspoon celery
   seeds
1/2 teaspoon sea salt
   (optional)
2/3 cup vegetable stock
   OR water combined
   with 2 teaspoons
   komé or mugi miso
   (see Glossary)
1/3 cup freshly squeezed
   lemon juice
freshly ground black
   pepper
2 teaspoons cornstarch
   dissolved in 1/4 cup
   water
2 eggs
1/8 teaspoon freshly
   grated nutmeg

1. Cut off about four cupfuls of florets. Blanch in boiling water till *barely* tender. Drain and set aside. Peel (if necessary) about three inches of the tenderest stalks and cut them into thin discs.

2. Slice celery into quarter-inch half-moons. (You can substitute Swiss chard or pac choi stalks.)

3. Heat wok (see **The Wok**) and pour in oil. Add celery and onions and gently toss over high heat two minutes, or till vegetables just begin to brown.

4. Add celery seeds, salt, stock, lemon juice, and a generous amount of pepper. Bring to a boil, lower heat, and simmer, covered, about one minute or till vegetables are tender.

5. Then push vegetables to sides of wok and stir in dissolved cornstarch.

6. In a small bowl beat eggs till light and fluffy. Remove a quarter cup of the hot cornstarch liquid and combine slowly with the eggs. Then add the eggs to the vegetables and cook over low heat, stirring, till sauce is thick and smooth. Don't boil.

7. Add broccoli florets and mix gently but well until hot.

Serve hot, immediately, with brown rice, other whole grain, or pasta, garnished with **Shoyu Sunnies**.

The following main dish is perfect for leftovers.

Broccoli with Tempeh
(6 servings)

6 cups leftover cooked brown rice or other whole grain
8 ounces thinly sliced, crisply fried Tempeh Chips
8 cups broccoli florets and peeled tender stems cut into half-inch lengths (about 1 3/4 pounds broccoli)
2 cups Laban seasoned with 1 teaspoon dry mustard or 1 tablespoon Dijon mustard and 1/2 teaspoon thyme

milk (optional)
1/4 cup grated parmesan or other cheese

1. Butter a twelve- by nine-inch lasagna pan or shallow casserole. Spread with a layer of grain and a layer of **Tempeh Chips**.
2. Blanch broccoli in boiling salted water until barely tender. Layer it on top of tempeh. Thin **Laban** with milk, if necessary, to consistency of cream, and pour over broccoli.
3. Sprinkle with cheese and heat in a 400°F oven till sauce is bubbling and cheese is slightly browned.

Serve at once, sprinkled with **Shoyu Sunnies**, with fresh rolls, and sliced tomatoes.

Sweet 'n Sourish Broccoli with Deep-fried Tofu
(6 servings)

1 pound firm tofu, drained, OR 1 pound soft tofu, drained, and pressed under 3 pound weight for 30 minutes
2 cups water
2 tablespoons shoyu
1 tablespoon sea salt
1 teaspoon powdered ginger (optional)
1 teaspoon powdered coriander (optional)

6 tablespoons maple syrup, OR Date or Raisin Butter, thinned to a syrup
6 tablespoons red wine or cider vinegar, or freshly squeezed lemon juice
2 tablespoons shoyu
1/4 cup tomato purée
1 teaspoon cornstarch or arrowroot
1/2 teaspoon hot pepper sauce
1/4 cup stock or water
3 cups peanut oil
2 tablespoons sunflower seed oil
2 medium-sized carrots, diced

2 cups small broccoli
    florets, or peeled,
    diced stem
1 inch fresh ginger root,
    minced
1 large green tomato and 1
    large ripe tomato OR 2
    ripe tomatoes, cut in
    chunks (about 4 cups)
1 small zucchini, cubed
1 cup sliced mushrooms

1. Cut tofu into three-quarter-inch cubes. Combine water, two tablespoons shoyu, one tablespoon sea salt, powdered ginger, coriander, and add tofu. Allow to marinate at least one hour.

2. While the tofu is marinating, whisk together in a saucepan the maple syrup, vinegar, two tablespoons shoyu, tomato purée, cornstarch or arrowroot, hot pepper sauce, and a quarter cup of stock. Bring to a boil, cook for one minute, and set aside.

3. Mix up a batter such as **Cheechako Beer Batter**. Heat wok (see **The Wok**), add peanut oil, and heat to 350-370°F. Dip tofu into batter, and deep-fry till golden. Drain well and keep warm.

4. Empty wok and wipe after deep-frying. Add sunflower oil and heat to 350-370°F. Stir-fry carrots and broccoli for two minutes. Add ginger and stir-fry about three seconds. Then add remaining vegetables and sauce, cover, and simmer over medium heat till hot (about five minutes).

Serve immediately over brown rice, other whole grain or pasta, topped with fried tofu. Sprinkle lemon juice over the tofu if you like.

Note: Substituting whatever vegetables you have on hand–for example, thinly sliced turnip or small cubes of winter squash–works equally well. Keep in mind that slow-cooking vegetables should be stir-fried first, fast-cooking ones last. Winter squash or turnip, therefore, should be added with the carrots. The tomatoes in this recipe yield more liquid for the sauce, so if the vegetables you substitute are dry ones, mix up twice as much sauce (see 2).

Broccoli Pasta

(6 servings)

1 tablespoon salt
1 tablespoon extra-virgin
    olive oil
1 pound pasta (any
    variety)
1/4 cup diced red bell
    pepper
3 cups finely chopped
    broccoli
1 medium-sized onion,
    diced
6 tablespoons extra-
    virgin olive oil
1 clove garlic, smashed
1 heaping tablespoon
    finely chopped fresh
    basil
sea salt
freshly ground black
    pepper
grated lemon rind
    (optional)
chopped fresh parsley
    for garnish
toasted Shoyu Sunnies
    for garnish

1. Bring a large kettle of salted water to boil. Add one tablespoon olive oil, then pasta. Cook about eight minutes, or until *al dente*.
2. Steam peppers, blanched broccoli, and onion until barely tender (about ten minutes).
3. In a small saucepan heat six tablespoons olive oil and garlic.
4. When pasta is done, drain well and pour onto a heated ceramic platter. Toss with the hot oil, removing garlic. Add steamed vegetables, basil, and seasonings. Sprinkle with parsley and **Shoyu Sunnies**.

Serve with fresh bread, grated parmesan cheese, and a light wine.

Cooking Cauliflower

1 head cauliflower
about 3 quarts water
    plus 2 tablespoons
    white distilled
    vinegar

1. Wash cauliflower head. Remove most of core; then hollow out a bit, using small end of a melon scooper.

This allows cooking to proceed equally throughout.
2. Bring water and vinegar to a boil in a large pot. Pop in cauliflower, florets downward, and simmer about ten minutes. Cool by plunging immediately into a large bowl of very cold water. Remove and drain well. It's now ready to be sauced, chilled for salad, or used in any way you please.

Cauliflower

Cauliflower is a nutritious vegetable even though Mark Twain called it "just a cabbage with a college education." Although many people like to sauce cauliflower or purée it, it's best newly picked and served raw with a flavorful dip. But if you're dependent on the supermarket, here is how to prepare it.

*Like many Maine housewives, my mother was apt to overcook cauliflower, until she and I discovered its virtues semi-raw, if not absolutely raw. How to **cook** it and still retain that crispy texture became my goal.*

Fried Cauliflower

(4 servings)

3 tablespoons sunflower seed oil
1 teaspoon white mustard seeds
3 cups cauliflower, chopped very, very fine
1 teaspoon sea salt

1. Heat oil in wok. Add mustard seeds and stir for one minute.

2. Add cauliflower and salt and stir constantly over high heat for about three minutes.

Serve with vegetables such as baked zucchini with tomato sauce and hot peppers, new potatoes, corn on the cob, and a protein dish such as bean burgers or **Tempeh Chips**.

Broccoli-Cauliflower Casserole

(6-8 servings)

2 1/2 cups vegetable stock
OR 2 1/2 cups water seasoned with 1 tablespoon komé miso (see Glossary)
1 cup long-grain brown rice
2 cups broccoli florets
2 cups cauliflower florets
2 (6-inch) crookneck squash or zucchini, cut in slices 1/2-inch thick
1/2 cup diced celery stalk
1 cup sliced mushrooms
1/4 cup shredded carrot
1/4 cup chopped scallions or white onion, finely chopped
1/2 teaspoon shoyu
1 cup mild green chili sauce
20 cherry tomatoes OR 2 large tomatoes, cut in chunks
thin slices of jack and cheddar cheese (enough to cover)
3 tablespoons Shoyu Sunnies
OR Toasted Sesame Seeds

1. Bring stock to a boil and add rice. Cover, return to boil, reduce heat, and simmer forty-five minutes or till rice is tender. Remove from heat and uncover.
2. Blanch broccoli and cauliflower florets about four minutes, including about two inches of the tender stem. Drain and place in a colander set over boiling water with squash and celery. Steam five to ten

»

minutes or till *barely* tender. Add mushrooms and steam two more minutes. Remove from heat.

3. Add carrot, scallions or onion, and shoyu to the rice. Toss lightly with a fork. Spread rice evenly in a buttered, lasagna-type pan.

4. Spoon chili sauce over rice and top with steamed vegetables and tomatoes.

Cover with cheese, overlapping slightly. Bake, uncovered, at 350°F for fifteen to twenty minutes or till heated through.

5. Sprinkle with toasted sunflower or sesame seeds.

Serve as one-dish meal, with fresh fruit for dessert.

Stuffed Patty Pan Squash
(4-8 servings)

2 (5-inch) patty pan
    squashes
    OR 3 medium-sized
    yellow summer
    squashes
1 large onion, diced
freshly ground black
    pepper (optional)
1 teaspoon fresh dill
    weed, chopped
2 cloves garlic, minced
2 large beaten eggs
3/4 cup crumbled feta
    cheese
2-3 tablespoons finely
    chopped fresh
    parsley
2 tablespoons
    whole-wheat flour
1/2 cup diced, fresh
    whole grain
    breadcrumbs

1. Cut squashes in half across the widest part. Cut off the stem and a little piece of skin so the squash will lie flat. Remove seeds and some pulp (reserve this), leaving a half-inch rim. Blanch in a large kettle of boiling water until barely tender.

2. Combine squash innards, chopped fine, with remaining ingredients. Pile into squash "boats," mound up slightly, and place in a well-buttered lasagna pan with a half inch of hot water. Bake at 375°F about thirty minutes or till the filling is firm.

Serve with a tomato salad, fresh bread, and rice, another whole grain, or pasta.

Zucchini and Other Summer Squash

When I was a little girl zucchini was unheard of, although I remember yellow crookneck. To my mother and father squash meant Hubbard—the great green keeper which graced our winter board. We often grew them with the corn, which made corn-picking rather difficult for us as well as for the raccoons. But in due course zucchini arrived in Maine, much to the pleasure of many diners. Mother used to slice it thin, coat it with corn meal, salt, and pepper, and quickly fry it crisp. The Lebanese have brought us other notions. Now, zucchini is perhaps the most popular summer squash—but other varieties, such as patty pan, are delicious and versatile.

Suppertime Frittata

(6 servings)

2 tablespoons extra-
    virgin olive oil
1 medium-sized onion
    or 3 scallions,
    chopped
1 large clove garlic,
    minced
3 cups zucchini
    diced
1 large tomato, peeled,
    chopped fine, and
    drained
sea salt to taste
    (optional)
freshly ground black
    pepper
1 teaspoon fresh
    chopped herbs, such
    as basil, oregano, or
    thyme
7 large eggs
3 tablespoons thick
    yogurt
1 scant cup grated
    parmesan or other
    cheese
2 tablespoons butter
1 tablespoon finely
    chopped chives or
    parsley for garnish

1. Heat olive oil in skillet and sauté onion and garlic until tender. Add vegetables, seasonings, and herbs, and cook over moderate heat, covered, about ten minutes. Remove from heat, cool slightly, and drain well.
2. Beat eggs till fluffy; whisk in yogurt gently. Add cheese and vegetables.
3. Preheat broiler. Melt butter in a hot skillet. Pour in egg mixture. Cover tightly and cook over low heat about eight minutes till edges pull away slightly from sides. (If middle puffs up, prick with a knife or pull away from sides with a fork to allow uncooked egg to flow underneath.) When firm, brown lightly under broiler about one minute. This will set the top securely. Sprinkle with chives or parsley.

Serve at once, cut into wedges, with fresh bread.

Zucchini Lemon Soufflé

(4 servings)

4 cups diced zucchini
1 tablespoon freshly
    squeezed lemon juice
1/2 teaspoon sea salt
4 large eggs
1 cup Laban

1 tablespoon finely
    chopped fresh dill
    weed
    OR 2 teaspoons
    chopped fresh thyme
a dash of freshly grated
    nutmeg

1. Preheat oven to 350°F. Simmer zucchini in lemon

»

juice and salt till slightly tender–about four minutes. Drain well. Place inside a double-cheesecloth square and twist until pulp is quite dry. Zucchini is now reduced to one cup.

2. In a small saucepan, mix up **Laban**. This will take two minutes.

3. Separate four eggs. Beat whites till peaks form. Beat yolks in a small bowl till light. Add a little hot **Laban**, then pour yolks into **Laban** and mix well. Add zucchini and dill or thyme.

4. Fold yolk mixture into whites quickly. Pour into a buttered straight-sided, two-quart casserole or soufflé dish.

5. Place in a pan and add water to come one inch up casserole sides.

6. Bake from thirty to forty minutes at 350°F, or until golden and puffy.

Serve immediately with fresh rolls and a tomato salad.

Eggplant Casserole

(4-6 servings)

1 large unpeeled eggplant
1/2 cup fine, dry whole-grain bread crumbs
1/2 cup grated parmesan cheese
1/2 pound sliced raw mushrooms
1 tablespoon chopped fresh parsley
sea salt
freshly ground black pepper
1 1/2 cups tomato sauce, well seasoned with garlic and herbs

1. Place eggplant in a large pot of boiling water to cover. Reduce heat and simmer ten minutes. Drain and cool enough to handle. Cut into quarters lengthwise, peel, and cut crosswise into one-inch pieces.

2. Combine crumbs and cheese. In a two-quart, buttered casserole, place eggplant chunks, mushrooms, a sprinkling of salt and pepper, tomato sauce; top with the crumb/cheese mixture.

3. Bake, uncovered, thirty to forty minutes at 350°F.

Serve with a whole grain, potatoes, or pasta, and a leafy green salad.

Eggplant

An ancient cousin of mine (whose life history would make a wild-west movie look like a convention of cherubs) once showed me how to grow eggplant. It's not especially nutritious, but I love its color and slightly meaty quality. Originating in southern Asia, arriving in Europe during the Middle Ages, this member of the nightshade family makes wonderful dips, casseroles, and stuffed eggplant– always a favorite. Japanese eggplants are smaller than the variety to which most Westerners are accustomed.

Moussaka
(6-8 servings)

Although long in ingredients and time, moussaka is a wondrous casserole, especially for company.

1 cup garbanzo beans (also known as chickpeas)
6 cups water
1 bay leaf
2 garlic cloves, smashed
1 medium-sized eggplant, cut into half-inch cubes
1 medium-sized onion, chopped
2 tablespoons extra-virgin olive oil
3 cups sliced mushrooms
2 tomatoes, peeled, quartered, and sliced
1/4 cup chopped parsley
1/2 cup red wine or vermouth
1/4 teaspoon cinnamon
1/8 teaspoon nutmeg
2 tablespoons butter
2 tablespoons unbleached white flour
2 eggs
freshly squeezed juice of 2 lemons
about 1/2 cup grated parmesan or mandarini cheese
sea salt to taste
freshly ground black pepper to taste

1. *The night before,* pick over the garbanzos and wash thoroughly. Soak overnight in three cups water.
2. *About three hours before dinnertime,* simmer soaked beans in three cups of water for one hour till tender, with bay leaf and garlic. Once tender, drain well, and reserve liquid.
3. In a large, heat-proof casserole, sauté eggplant and onion in olive oil till slightly browned. Add garbanzos, mushrooms, tomatoes, parsley, wine, and spices. Cover and simmer slowly for twenty minutes. Drain resulting broth into bean liquid and set aside.
4. Meanwhile, in a small saucepan, melt butter, add flour, and brown the mixture slightly. Then add one cup of the reserved bean liquid and cook until smooth and thick.
5. In a small bowl, beat eggs till light and fluffy. Beat in lemon juice and two tablespoons reserved cooking liquid. Add sauce slowly to eggs while beating. Return to pan and cook slowly over very low heat or in double boiler, stirring often, till very thick.
6. Stir two tablespoons sauce into drained eggplant mixture. Butter a three-quart casserole. Layer with half the garbanzo/eggplant mixture, then half the sauce. Sprinkle with a quarter cup cheese, and season with salt and pepper. Repeat. Bake at 350°F, uncovered, for about one hour, till top is golden brown.

Serve with any whole grain, a lightly dressed leafy salad, and **Pocket Bread**.

Natalia's Eggplant Relish
(about 2 cups)

1 large or 2 medium-
     sized eggplants
3 large and meaty green
     bell peppers
2 garlic cloves
1 large onion
1 1/2 cups tomato paste
4 tablespoons extra-
     virgin olive oil
sea salt to taste
hot pepper sauce to taste
     OR 1/2 to 1 teaspoon
     cayenne powder

1. Preheat oven to 450°F. Pierce eggplant all over with a fork (to prevent explosions!). Lay it on a rack in a tightly covered pan and place in oven. Bake about forty-five minutes to one hour.

2. Roast peppers on oven rack, turning often, until skin separates and peppers are soft but not mushy. Remove from oven and place in a covered pan. When cool, remove skins— they should separate easily.
3.   Check eggplant. It should be soft but not mushy or charred. Place in a covered dish and allow to cool, then peel. Drain both eggplant and peppers by pressing lightly in a sieve.
4. Put peppers, eggplant, garlic, and onion through the fine cutter of a meat grinder. Add tomato paste, olive oil, salt, and pepper sauce.
5. Allow to rest two to four hours. Stored in a glass jar, refrigerated, it will keep two to three weeks.

Serve as a dip for **Pocket Bread**, **Puris,** or fresh crackers.

Russians started emigrating to Maine about thirty years ago, settling for the most part in and near Richmond. My friend Natalia makes a luscious eggplant dip, which she calls "poor man's caviar."

Eggplant Bryani
(6-8 servings)

2 cups brown rice
4 teaspoons turmeric
     powder
1 teaspoon sea salt
1 medium-sized
     eggplant
canning or sea salt
2 tablespoons sunflower
     seed oil
1 teaspoon poppy seeds
1 1/2 teaspoons white
     mustard seeds

1/4 teaspoon cayenne
     (optional)
1 teaspoon Simple
     Garam Masala
1/2 teaspoon powdered
     coriander
1/2 teaspoon turmeric
1 bell pepper, sliced
     lengthwise into thin
     bits
1 cup any variety cooked
     beans, such as pinto
     or navy
3 medium-sized
     tomatoes, peeled and
     chopped

Eggplant has long been a favorite of the Indian sub-continent. It makes an excellent bryani (a dish in which rice and vegetables are cooked together).

1/3 cup coarsely chopped
   walnuts
1/3 cup raisins or
   currants for garnish

1. Cook rice with four teaspoons turmeric and one teaspoon salt until tender (see **Jenny's Rice**).
2. Cut eggplant into slices three-quarters of an inch thick. Peel each slice, then cube into small bits. Sprinkle with salt, set in a colander, and allow to drain thirty minutes. Pat dry.
3. Preheat oven to 350°F. Heat wok and add oil (see **The Wok**). Add poppy and mustard seeds. Cover and cook one minute.
4. Then add cayenne, **Simple Garam Masala**, coriander, and half a

teaspoon turmeric. Stir a bit and add eggplant, peppers, beans, and tomatoes. Cook, stirring often, about seven minutes. Remove from heat.
5. In the bottom of a buttered, four-quart casserole spread a third of the rice. Cover with a layer of half the spiced vegetables. Repeat. Top with the last third of your rice. Cover and bake at 350°F about thirty minutes. Uncover, toss with nuts, and cook another five minutes.

Serve hot from the oven, sprinkled with a third of a cup raisins or currants. Pass **Chupattis**, yogurt, more raisins, and serve fruit for dessert.

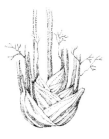

Fennel

A newcomer to many a Maine garden, fennel is ubiquitous in warmer climes. When I first met it in North Africa, its licorice-like taste dismayed then intrigued me. Now I grow it regularly and enjoy it immensely. The enlarged lower stalks are ready for eating when about two inches in diameter.

Plain Braised Fennel
(6 servings)

3 large fennel bulbs
1 tablespoon extra-virgin
   olive oil
freshly ground black
   pepper
1/4 cup water
freshly squeezed lemon
   juice

1. Rinse, then trim the stalks nearly down to bulb. Pare off any discolored outer ribs or soft spots.
2. Slice about half an inch thick, and simmer, covered, in a large skillet with olive oil, pepper, and water until easy to pierce with a fork.
3. Sprinkle with freshly squeezed lemon juice and sea salt to taste. **Laban** would sauce it nicely.

Marinated Fennel for Salads

(6 servings)

2 fennel bulbs
2 tablespoons red wine
    vinegar
6 tablespoons extra-
    virgin olive oil
1/4 teaspoon sea salt
freshly ground black
    pepper to taste
1 garlic clove, minced
a fresh herb of your
    choice, minced

2 large tomatoes, peeled
    and chopped
salad greens

1. Trim bulbs and slice thin
into a small bowl.
2. Add remaining
ingredients and toss lightly
with peeled, chopped
tomatoes. Heap on cos
lettuce, chicory, or some
other rugged crisp green.

Roasted Bell Pepper Salad

(6 servings)

6 fresh bell peppers
1 cup extra-virgin olive
    oil
sea salt to taste
1-2 cloves garlic, minced
freshly squeezed lemon
    juice (optional)
Hungarian paprika
    (optional)
black pepper (optional)

1. Select chunky, meaty
bells. Rinse, pat dry, then
broil about two inches under
your heat source, turning
frequently, for twenty
minutes or until skin is
blackened. (Or spear on a
long-handled fork and grill
over a gas flame two to three
minutes.) Place peppers
inside a brown bag to steam
until cool enough to handle.

2. To peel, start at the
blossom end and use a sharp
paring knife to pull off skin.
Then slice off the top and
discard seeds and ribs.
3.   Lay peppers on a platter,
sprinkle with sea salt, then
sprinkle with a quarter cup
olive oil into which you
have whisked two minced
garlic cloves. Allow to rest
for at least an hour,
preferably overnight, before
serving.
OR combine half a cup of
olive oil with two to three
tablespoons freshly squeezed
lemon juice and one
teaspoon Hungarian paprika,
a quarter teaspoon sea salt,
freshly ground black pepper,
and one clove garlic, minced.
Add peppers and toss lightly.

Serve with fresh whole-
grain bread or as part of a
salad platter garnished with
feta cheese and black olives.

Bell Peppers

*The bell pepper, a
tropical plant which
grows to eight feet in
native soil, is
extremely rich in
vitamins and
minerals, and can be
grown in Maine as an
annual if you plant
indoors in early
spring. When the
mature green bell
turns red, its vitamin
content multiplies
dramatically.*

*My favorites are the
big Ace Hybrid for
stuffing and general
salad use and Gypsy
for sautéing. I also
indulge in the semi-
hot Cubanelle and
some really hot
jalapenos. Like
other people of the
same latitude,
Mexicans sometimes
roast, marinate, and
serve peppers as a
nutritious salad.*

Stir-Fried Peppers and Tomatoes

(6 servings)

**1 tablespoon extra-
    virgin olive oil
1 medium-sized onion,
    chopped
1 clove garlic, minced
5-6 large bell peppers
3 large red or yellow
    tomatoes
1 teaspoon finely
    chopped fresh basil
1/2 teaspoon finely
    chopped fresh
    marjoram
sea salt to taste
freshly ground black
    pepper to taste**

1. Heat wok or skillet and add oil. Add onion and garlic and sauté until limp. Slice top off peppers, remove seeds, and cut into bite-sized bits. Add to wok or skillet, stir well, and simmer over moderate heat about five minutes.
2. Peel tomatoes and add to peppers with remaining ingredients. Stir gently, cover, and simmer briefly until the peppers are tender.

Serve on heaps of brown rice or other whole grain, with a leafy salad and cooked, marinated beans.

The bell pepper has long been known in Maine, and now hot chili varieties are beginning to burn their way north. Reputed to induce quicker digestion and promote good circulation, chili peppers are also very rich in health-giving vitamins. They have always been immensely popular with vegetarian cuisines worldwide—perhaps because a whole-grain/legume diet demands strong seasoning.

The California green chili (or Anaheim chili) grows well in Maine. Flavor ranges from mild and sweet to mildly hot.

Peeling Chili Peppers

1. Preheat broiler.
2. Wash, dry, and place peppers on broiler rack one inch below heat source.
3. Turn chilies frequently until blistered and lightly browned all over but not entirely limp. As each one is done, wrap it in a damp towel.
4. When all your peppers are blistered and wrapped, let stand till cool enough to handle.

5. Removing one chili at a time, peel by catching the skin with a knife and pulling it gently away. Try not to tear chilies if they're to be stuffed.
6. Cut a lengthwise slit in one side to about a quarter-inch of the stem end. Remove seeds, white core, and the pith with a spoon.

Chili Peppers in Rice

(6 large servings)

2 cups brown rice
    OR 3/4 cup barley
    and 1 1/4 cups rice
4 cups stock or water
    plus 1 teaspoon sea
    salt
6 California green chili
    (or jalapeno or
    Cubanelle) peppers
about 1 1/2 cups
    shredded jack or
    cheddar cheese
1 medium onion,
    coarsely chopped
2 large peeled tomatoes,
    quartered
1 teaspoon sea salt
freshly ground black
    pepper
1 teaspoon dried
    oregano or twice as
    much fresh finely
    chopped oregano
1 teaspoon dried basil or
    twice as much fresh
    finely chopped basil
2 cloves garlic, minced
1 cup corn kernels
    (optional)
2 cups yogurt
1/4 cup parmesan cheese

1. Cook rice in stock or water in a heavy-bottomed pot for forty-five minutes or until tender.
2. Peel chilies as described above. Remove seeds if you want a mild flavor; leave them in if you prefer it hotter.
3. Slit one side of each chili and stuff firmly with cheese.
4. Spoon half the rice into a three-quart, lightly buttered casserole. Then place the stuffed chilies on top like wheel spokes. Top with remaining rice.
5. In blender, purée onion, tomatoes, salt, pepper, herbs, and garlic. This should yield about two cups sauce. Add corn, if desired, and yogurt, and mix them in well with a spoon.
6. Pour sauce over rice. Sprinkle with parmesan cheese. Bake twenty-five minutes in a 350°F oven.

Serve with a hot pepper sauce, a tossed green salad with a light oil and lemon juice dressing, and fresh **Corn Crêpes**.

Handling Fresh Hot Chili Peppers

Handling fresh hot chili peppers is hot stuff!
1. Wear rubber gloves or oil hands generously.
2. Don't touch face or eyes!
3. Rinse pepper clean in cold water.
4. Pull out stem and break or cut the chili in half under cold running water.
5. Brush out seeds with a finger. They are the hottest part.
6. If ribs are fleshy, cut them out with small, sharp knife.
7. If you do burn your hands, pour salt generously onto them and gently rub together.
8. You can also soak fresh chilies in cold, salted water one hour to remove some of the hotness, but I suspect some vitamins disappear as well.

Using Dried Chilies

Dried chilies should be torn into small pieces, covered with boiling water, and soaked for at least thirty minutes before use.

Green and Red Tomatoes

Tomatoes, discovered in America, were immediately transplanted to southern Europe, where they ran rampant. Where would Italian cooking be without them? Orientals started growing them in the l700s.

A member of the nightshade family (related to potatoes, peppers, and eggplant) and at first thought to be poisonous, they've proved to be valuable nutritionally, and vitamin loss through cooking is minimal.

Because of our hot summers, Mainers can grow gorgeous tomatoes, but the season can be brief, depending on one's location. There are down-to-earth methods for prolonging the season—for example, save well-worn bedsheets and, when those clear, cold nights begin, cover the tomatoes. If they survive the first frosts, you can relax during Indian summer.

Fried Green Tomatoes with Herbs

(6 servings)

3-4 large green tomatoes
1 cup whole-wheat pastry flour
1 teaspoon sea salt
freshly ground black pepper
1/2 teaspoon well-crumbled dried oregano or 1 teaspoon minced fresh oregano
1/2 teaspoon well-crumbled dried basil or l teaspoon minced fresh basil
1 egg
1 teaspoon water

sesame seeds
1 tablespoon clarified butter
1 tablespoon extra-virgin olive oil

1. Slice tomatoes a half inch thick.
2. Combine flour, salt, pepper, and herbs, and dredge each slice. Beat egg slightly with one teaspoon water and dip tomato slices into it. Then dip into sesame seeds.
3. Heat butter and oil in a heavy-bottomed skillet. Sauté tomatoes over medium heat until golden brown, and barely tender clear through.

Serve as a side dish to any meal.

This soup freezes beautifully, and can be made in quantity for those cold winter nights ahead.

Bear Hill Green Tomato Soup

(6 servings)

6 tablespoons butter OR 3 tablespoons butter plus 3 tablespoons sunflower seed oil
10-12 coarsely chopped green tomatoes
3 large yellow onions, coarsely chopped

1 1/2 cups vegetable stock
1 heaping tablespoon arrowroot
1 1/2 cups milk (soy or dairy)
1/2-1 teaspoon sea salt
1/8 teaspoon freshly ground black pepper
1-2 tablespoons maple syrup
3 tablespoons chopped fresh chives for garnish

»

3 tablespoons chopped
   fresh parsley
   OR 1 tablespoon
   chopped fresh dill
   weed for garnish

1. Melt butter in a heavy
skillet or wok (see **The
Wok**). Sauté onions until
translucent, then add green
tomatoes, and simmer
briefly until soft.
2. Combine with stock and
purée in blender on low
speed.

3. Mix arrowroot with cold
milk and add to purée.
Bring just to a boil, stirring
constantly with a whisk.
4. Add salt, pepper, and
maple syrup carefully to
taste–you want the right
balance between savory and
sweet. Garnish generously
with chives and parsley or
dill weed.

Serve hot or cold, plain or
with a spoonful of fresh
yogurt on each serving.

Green Tomato Chutney

(7 half-pint jars)

4 1/2 cups finely
   chopped green
   tomatoes
4 1/2 cups peeled, finely
   chopped, tart green
   apples
2 lemons
2 cups onions
2 large cloves garlic
3 cup currants
1 1/2 inches fresh ginger
   root, grated,
   OR 3/4 cup
   crystallized ginger
2 cups dark-brown sugar,
   preferably turbinado
   (see Glossary)
1 cup cider vinegar
1 cup water
2 tablespoons white
   mustard seeds
1 1/2 teaspoons canning
   salt
1/2 teaspoon cayenne

1. Chop tomatoes. Peel and
chop apples. Wash, quarter,
chop, and seed lemons.
Finely chop onions, mince
garlic, and grate fresh ginger.
2. Combine all ingredients
in a large enameled kettle.
Cover. Bring to a boil,
reduce heat, and simmer
about sixty minutes or till
fruit is soft and syrup thick,
stirring often to prevent
sticking.
3. Pack into half-pint
sterilized jars leaving a
quarter inch headroom.
Then either process for five
minutes in a boiling water
bath or simply turn jars
upside down for a moment
after capping. (Heat will
create a vacuum seal.) Cool
right side up, and store in a
cool place.

*Though less
nutritious than when
red, green tomatoes
are good added to
any curry or stir-fry.
In a sense they can be
considered a
separate vegetable.
Their taste is tart,
their texture firm.
They can also be
cellar- or shelf-
ripened. Before
storing, rinse in a
very diluted bleach
solution, dry well
and lay between
layers of newspaper
in bushel baskets.
Pick over once a
week and watch
them ripen well into
November–but before
then, eat them
anyway! And don't
forget to make **Green
Tomato Chutney**.*

*Peeling
Tomatoes*

*Tomatoes are easy to
peel. Simply drop
them into a kettle of
boiling water for one
minute. Remove
with a slotted spoon,
then drop instantly
into cold water.
When cool enough to
handle, the skins
will slip off easily.*

A fresh tomato and pepper sauce is wonderful served in a bowl so that diners may spice their dishes to suit themselves. Hotness depends on the cook!

Salsa Cruda

(2 cups)

**4 medium-sized ripe
    tomatoes**
**1/3 cup finely chopped
    onion**
**1 tablespoon coarsely
    chopped fresh
    cilantro**
**1 teaspoon peeled, finely
    chopped, hot chili
    pepper (optional)**
**1/4 cup peeled, diced,
    sweet green chili
    pepper**
1/2 teaspoon sea salt

**1/8 teaspoon freshly
    ground black pepper**
1/8 teaspoon honey

1. Peel tomatoes (see
Peeling Tomatoes).
Remove stem area, slice in
half crosswise, and squeeze
gently to remove seeds and
juice. Chop fine.
2. Combine tomatoes with
remaining ingredients. Mix
well and refrigerate. This
salsa keeps about two days.

Tomatoes make a lovely soup, but they curdle milk. My Aunt Mae (a whiz with venison, plum preserves, and biscuits) solved the problem nicely with baking soda.

Aunt Mae's Tomato Soup

(6 servings)

1 quart milk
**rind of 1/2 well-washed
    lemon**
1 small whole onion
**1 heaping tablespoon (or
    more) arrowroot
    dissolved in 1/4 cup
    cold milk**
**1 quart stewed or
    home-canned
    tomatoes, simmering**
1 teaspoon maple syrup
1 teaspoon sea salt
**freshly ground black
    pepper**
1/4 teaspoon baking soda

1. Peel off lemon rind
thinly.
2. Scald milk with rind and
onion in a double boiler.
Add arrowroot mixed with
milk, and stir to thicken.
Remove from heat.
3. Combine remaining
ingredients quickly in a
bowl. Remove onion and
lemon peel from milk, and
quickly combine the two
mixtures.

Serve immediately with a
very crisp green salad and
fresh rolls.

Cream of Tomato Dill Soup

(4-6 servings)

1 tablespoon sunflower
    seed oil
1 finely chopped
    medium-sized onion
    OR 3 chopped
    scallions, including
    tops
1 large clove garlic,
    minced
1 teaspoon sea salt
freshly ground black
    pepper
4 large red tomatoes
1/2 cup diced celery
    stalk
1/4 cup diced carrot
    (optional)
1 heaping tablespoon
    tomato paste
2 cups milk
1/2 teaspoon maple
    syrup (if tomatoes are
    very tart)
2-2 1/2 tablespoons
    arrowroot OR cornstarch
    (as necessary)

1 heaping tablespoon
    minced fresh dill weed
    for garnish

1. Heat oil in a heavy, two-quart saucepan. Sauté onion and garlic until limp. Add salt and pepper.
2. Slice tomatoes in, and cook over moderate heat, covered, five to ten minutes, or until tomatoes and vegetables are soft. Blend, then push through a sieve or food mill to remove skins and seeds.
3. Whisk together tomato paste, milk, and arrowroot or cornstarch, combine with the tomatoes, and bring to high heat. Lower heat, cook until thick, then remove from stove. Adjust seasoning.
4. Sprinkle with dill.

Serve hot or chilled with a very crisp green salad, fresh rolls, and cheese.

Tomato Sauce

(4-6 pints)

10-15 large ripe
    tomatoes
    OR twice as many
    paste tomatoes
3-4 onions, chopped
several stalks celery,
    chopped
4-5 cloves garlic, minced
2-3 green bell peppers,
    chopped
1 tablespoon dried
    oregano

1 tablespoon dried basil
    OR fresh marjoram,
    thyme, and/or
    parsley
1 tablespoon sea salt
freshly ground black
    pepper
1-2 cups red wine
1 pound chopped
    mushrooms
1 tablespoon maple
    syrup, if sauce is
    really tart

Tomato sauce is absolutely necessary for getting through a Maine winter. It provides goodly amounts of vitamin C and lends cheerful color to any meal. Fresh, quick sauce is easy to make during hot summer weather and can be easily frozen or canned. It provides the base for hearty pasta dishes, nutritious soups such as minestrone and lentil, and favorites like chili beans or Spanish rice.

1. Drop tomatoes into a large pot of boiling water for one minute, then into cold water. Peel and quarter.
2. Combine in a large enameled pot with all remaining ingredients except mushrooms and maple syrup. Simmer over moderate heat until vegetables are tender and sauce slightly reduced. Add mushrooms and maple syrup and simmer slightly longer. (I often add finely shredded carrots, diced zucchini, and a lot of minced parsley.)

Tunisian Tomato and Pepper Salad
(4-6 servings)

The first time I tasted a salad of cooked tomatoes and peppers was in Tunisia, and we were served by the cook of an American Embassy official. I use less olive oil by sprinkling it over the salad rather than pouring it in as he did.

4 large, ripe but firm, tomatoes (red or yellow)
3 large bell peppers
about 3 tablespoons freshly squeezed lemon juice
sea salt to taste
freshly ground black pepper
1/2 cup finely chopped onions
about 2 tablespoons extra-virgin olive oil
black olives (optional)

1. Preheat oven to 400°F. Place tomatoes and peppers on a large cookie sheet. Roast on the middle shelf, turning often, about twenty minutes. (Tongs are a perfect help.)
2. Remove tomatoes and peel. Slice in half crosswise and squeeze gently to remove seeds and juice. Chop fine. Drain if necessary.
3. Remove peppers about twenty minutes later or when slightly blackened. Wrap in a damp towel and allow to steam five minutes. You can then peel them easily. Remove stem and white membranes and discard the seeds. Chop fine.
4. In a small, shallow serving bowl combine lemon juice, salt, and pepper. Add the tomatoes, peppers, and onions, and toss gently. Dribble on enough olive oil to coat. Scatter black olives, if desired, on top.

Serve as a side dish to any summer meal.

Pie Dough

(for two 9-inch pie shells or one 10-inch shell with leftover dough)

1 cup unbleached flour
1 cup whole-wheat
pastry flour
1/8 teaspoon sea salt
1/8-1/2 teaspoon grated
lemon rind
(optional)
2/3 cup butter, softened
to room temperature
6-8 tablespoons ice water
1 egg white OR milk OR
water (optional)

1. Sift together the flours and salt. Add rind.
2. Cut in butter with a pastry cutter or two knives.
3. Add ice water and toss with your hands as for salad. Add more water as necessary till dough clings together. Knead lightly. Shape dough into a firm ball but handle lightly. Refrigerate at least one hour before rolling out.
4. Roll out to one-eighth-inch thickness on a board lightly floured with unbleached white flour.

Fold in half and drape over your rolling pin. Place loosely over an upside-down pie pan. Cut dough one inch larger than edge of pan. Fold again and remove dough. Turn pan right-side up, fold dough again, and lay within pie pan. Tuck edge under and flute it.
5. Chill in freezer, well-wrapped, for at least an hour, or till ready to use.
6. Brush the entire piecrust with slightly beaten egg white to prevent sogginess.
7. Fill and bake as your recipe directs. Or bake at 400°F for ten minutes, cool, fill, and bake again.

Notes:
1. Freezing pie shells makes pastry even more crisp. Make ahead and store in plastic freezer bags, carefully removing as much air as possible. When using, fill and cook immediately before defrosting.
2. For golden-brown crusts, brush the top or rim with milk or egg white. For flaky top crusts, brush with water.

Wheat Germ Pastry

(for one 9-inch single-crust pie)

3/4 cup plus 2 table-
spoons unbleached
flour
2 tablespoons wheat
germ

1/8 teaspoon sea salt
6 tablespoons butter,
softened to room
temperature
2-3 tablespoons cold
water

1. Measure flour, wheat germ, and salt into a bowl.

This pastry is very short but very good-tasting. By adding wheat germ to white flour nutrition is improved.

2. With pastry cutter or knives, cut in three tablespoons butter until mixture resembles coarse meal. Cut in remaining butter until particles are the size of small peas. Add water, a little at a time, mixing slightly with a fork. Shape dough into a firm ball with your hands.

3. Roll out on a lightly floured board (or marble-topped counter) to one-eighth-inch thickness. Fold and place loosely over an upside-down nine-inch pie pan and cut it one inch larger. Fold and remove, and ease into pie pan. Fold edge under, moisten rim of pan, and flute edge.

While most quiches are rich with cream, mine is piquant and creamy with yogurt.

Tomato Onion Quiche

(4-6 servings, or one 9-inch quiche)

2/3 cup finely chopped onion
1 medium-sized tomato, chopped into small pieces
3 eggs, beaten till fluffy
1 cup yogurt
1 cup milk
3/4 teaspoon sea salt
freshly ground black pepper
1/2 teaspoon dried oregano, OR 1 teaspoon finely chopped fresh basil
2/3 cup grated sharp cheddar cheese
1 9-inch pastry shell (see above)

1. Spread onion and tomato in a nine-inch pastry shell.
2. Mix eggs, yogurt, milk, salt, pepper, and herbs (crumble dried oregano between the palms). Pour in. It looks best when custard comes just to the base of fluted edge.
3. Sprinkle cheese over top. Bake at 400°F for ten minutes. Then bake at 350°F thirty-five to forty-five minutes or till a knife inserted into the egg custard comes out clean. Allow to rest on a rack a few minutes before serving.

Serve hot or cold with a tossed salad and fresh bread.

Note: Substitute two-thirds cup steamed and chopped vegetables for the tomato, such as broccoli, asparagus, cooked greens, fiddleheads, or any other interesting leftovers.

Whole-Wheat Pizza

(4-6 servings or one 12-inch pizza)

2 tablespoons dry yeast
1 1/4 cups lukewarm
    water
2 tablespoons extra-
    virgin olive oil
2 1/2 cups whole-wheat
    pastry flour
1 teaspoon sea salt
    (optional)
1 cup cornmeal
olive oil for brushing
    (optional)
2/3 cup Tomato Sauce
your choice of toppings,
    such as 1 cup cooked
    fiddleheads, 1/2 cup
    thinly sliced bell
    pepper, 1/2 cup
    thinly sliced
    onion, 1/2 cup
    tomato chunks, 12
    sardines or
    anchovies, about 20
    pieces of sliced
    Soylami or Okara
    Bologna, 1/2 cup
    sliced black olives,
    sliced mushrooms, or
    sliced zucchini
1 cup (or more) grated
    mozzarella cheese
1 tablespoon extra-virgin
    olive oil (optional)

1. Dissolve yeast in a half
cup lukewarm water until
yeast bubbles.
2. In about fifteen minutes
stir in remaining water, oil,
flour, and salt. Knead about
five minutes. Dough should
be firm (but not hard) and
quite elastic–although

whole-wheat dough is never
as elastic as that made from
white flour.
3. Place in a large, oiled
bowl, turn to coat, and let
rise one hour or till doubled
in bulk. (You can hasten this
by placing it on a heating pad
turned to "low," or about
90°F.) Punch down. Divide
dough in half. Dust board
lightly with white flour. Roll
to about three-eighths of an
inch thick until you have a
twelve-inch pizza disk.
Sprinkle a cookie sheet or
pizza pan with cornmeal,
fold the dough in half, and
with a spatula carefully lift it
onto the pan. Gently brush
dough with a little olive oil
(optional).
4. Top with a thin layer of
tomato sauce and condi-
ments of your choice.
5. Sprinkle cheese over top.
Drizzle, if you like, with
olive oil. Bake on lowest
rack in oven at 500°F for
about ten minutes, or till
crust has browned and
cheese is bubbly.

Serve immediately with a
tossed green salad.

Pizza

*Pizza is every
child's (and most
adults') delight.
The two samples
presented here are
nutritious and very
tasty.*

Macaroni Pizza

(6 servings, or one 14-inch pizza)

**2 cups whole-grain
  elbow macaroni**
3 eggs, beaten
**1/3 cup finely chopped
  onion**
**1 cup shredded, sharp
  cheddar cheese**
2 cups Tomato Sauce
**1 cup sliced Soylami or
  Okara Bologna**
**3/4 cup sliced
  mushrooms**
**2 tablespoons sliced ripe
  olives**
**1 thinly sliced green
  pepper**
**1 cup shredded
  mozzarella or other
  cheese**

1. Cook macaroni until *al dente* (I recommend Jerusalem artichoke elbows).
2. Mix eggs, onion and cheese. Add cooked macaroni. Spread evenly on a well-greased eleven- by fourteen-inch cookie sheet (or fourteen-inch pizza pan). Bake on lowest oven rack at 375°F for twenty minutes.
3. Spoon tomato sauce over cooked "pizza crust." Top evenly with remaining ingredients, ending with cheese, and return to lowest oven rack. Bake for twelve to fifteen minutes or till cheese is bubbly.

Serve with tossed or spinach salad and warm bread.

Blueberry Sauce

**2 1/2 cups blueberries,
  fresh or frozen**
**juice of 1 lemon (about
  1/3 cup)**
1 tablespoon cornstarch
1/2 cup raisins
**1/4-1/2 lemon rind, well
  washed and chopped**
1/4 teaspoon cinnamon
**1/2 teaspoon pure
  vanilla**

1. Simmer berries in a small saucepan over low heat. Add a tiny bit of water if using fresh berries.

2. Pour lemon juice into a measuring cup and add enough water to make three-quarters of a cup. Place in blender with cornstarch, raisins, and lemon rind, and purée till smooth.
3. Stir into blueberries. Bring to a boil over high heat and boil one minute. Remove from heat.
4. Add cinnamon and vanilla. Store, covered, in the refrigerator.

Serve with muffins, waffles, pancakes, or the following "quiche."

Blueberries

*August 20–and we've had our first blueberries of the season. And so have the big black bears on the barrens and along the power lines. The misty blue berries are perfect for muffins, waffles, pancakes, breads, jams, sauces, or simply eaten by the handful. Pick your own if you can, remove all the little leaves and stems, rinse quickly if necessary, and serve plain or blanketed with toppings such as **Yogurt**, **Whipped Cottage Cheese**, **TofuWhipped Cream**, or **Cashew Cream**. They're also lovely substituted for strawberries in **Jean Ann's Strawberry Shortcake** and **Strawberry Cream Puff Ring**.*

Almost Quiche

(6 servings)

1 cup whole-wheat
    pastry flour
    OR 1/2 cup
    unbleached white
    flour plus 1/2 cup
    whole-wheat pastry
    flour
2 large eggs
2 scant cups milk (soy or
    dairy)
1 tablespoon maple
    syrup OR Raisin
    Butter
3 tablespoons butter

1. Sift flour into a small
bowl three times.

2. Beat eggs until fluffy.
Then beat in milk and syrup
(or substitute). Add flour
and beat until smooth, using
a rotary beater.
3. Melt butter in a ten-inch
glass or ceramic pie pan.
Pour in batter and bake for
thirty-five minutes in a
350°F oven. Cool slightly.
Edges may form a raised rim.
4. Before edges fall in, top
with **Blueberry Sauce**; or
jam; fresh, frozen, or canned
strawberries or other fruits;
or one-half to two-thirds of a
cup of **Sugarless Rhubarb
Dessert**.

Serve immediately.

*An odd style of
dessert "quiche,"
which isn't really a
quiche except that it
turns out to be custard-
on-almost-pastry,
comes from Finnish
immigrants who call
it a "pancake." You
can cut it up to serve
either hot or cold for
breakfast or lunch, or
topped with berries,
either cooked or
fresh, for dessert.
Blueberry sauce
makes it especially
delicious.*

Blueberry-Strawberry Ice

(6-12 servings)

4 cups thick yogurt
2 large egg yolks
1/2 cup maple syrup
    OR 2/3 cup honey
2 heaping cups
    strawberries
1 banana
4 tablespoons light rum
    (optional)
1 tablespoon freshly
    squeezed lemon juice
1/2 cup finely chopped
    walnuts (optional)
1 teaspoon grated lemon
    rind
2/3 cup blueberries

1. In a medium-sized heavy-
bottomed saucepan gently

whisk together one cup of
yogurt, egg yolks, and maple
syrup or honey. Heat over
moderate temperature till
just warmed through. *Don't*
boil. Pour into a large ice
cube tray or cake pan and
freeze till edges are just firm,
thirty minutes to an hour.
2. Transfer to a medium-
sized bowl and beat until
velvety. Gently whisk in
remaining three cups yogurt.
3. In blender, purée
strawberries, banana, rum,
and lemon juice until fluffy.
Fold into yogurt mixture.
Then fold in lemon rind.
Pour into a cake pan and
refreeze for thirty minutes.
4. Beat again with rotary
beater till smooth and
velvety. Repeat the freezing
and beating twice more. The

Blueberries make a fine wine. From the nutritional point of view, wine is considered a food, providing energy and nutrients. Primitive wines were apparently a rather good source of the water-soluble B vitamins–but today, thanks to modern filtration practices which remove yeasts from commercial wines, this is no longer the case. So if you drink wine, seriously consider making your own!

Before proceeding, read about **Dandelion Wine** *for explanations of utensils and procedures.*

last time fold in blueberries and walnuts. Freeze for about three hours before serving.

Serve plain or topped with any of the "cream" toppings (see Index), and **Blueberry Sauce** or plain blueberries.

Blueberry Wine

(about 10 quarts)

8 quarts blueberries
2 gallons boiling water
16 cups white cane sugar
1 tablespoon granulated
**   wine yeast dissolved in**
**   1/2 cup warm water**
freshly squeezed juice of
**   1 lemon**

1. Pick over blueberries; remove any stems, leaves, and blemished berries. Rinse quickly and drain well. Place in a large clean crock.
2. Pour boiling water over berries. Cover and allow to stand twenty-four hours, stirring often.
3. Place a large colander over a large bowl and cover with two thicknesses of finely woven cheesecloth. Strain juice. Rinse out crock and wipe clean. Return strained juice to crock.
4. Add sugar, dissolved wine yeast, and lemon juice. Cover well with a large lid (or cover with a polyethylene sheet and tie it

down tightly around rim). Allow to rest in a warm place (65-70°F) for three days.
5. Pour into an opaque fermentation jug or wrap a large, clear glass jug with brown paper to seal out light so as to protect color.
6. Fit with an air lock and allow to ferment until bubbling has stopped. Siphon out into sterilized bottles; cork, and store. You may wish to decant before serving at room temperature.

Corn on the Cob

(6 servings)

**12 ears of freshly picked
    corn**
2 cups water
**2 cups whole milk (or
    more if necessary)**
1 teaspoon sugar
**1 tablespoon sunflower
    seed oil**

1. Husk and remove silk.
Remove any corn borers
using the sharp point of a
knife; cut out and discard
areas where they have been
busy.

2. Place a shallow rack in a
very large pot. Bring water,
milk, sugar, and oil to a boil.
Add corn and simmer on the
rack about five minutes.
(Save cooking liquor for
bread-making or soup.)

Serve sprinkled with a bit of
sea salt, and perhaps some
freshly ground black pepper
and dried lemon rind; or
with **Larch's Kelp** or **Sea
Lettuce** or **Gomasio** (see
Glossary). Butter is
traditional—and
delicious—but not necessary.

Fresh Corn Fritters

**(an old New Maine
favorite)**
(about 20 fritters)

**4 ears fresh corn OR
    about 2 cups of
    kernels and milk**
**1/2 cup milk (soy or
    dairy)**
**2 lightly beaten egg
    yolks**
**1-2 tablespoons diced red
    or green bell pepper
    OR 1 teaspoon
    jalapeno pepper**
**freshly ground black
    pepper (optional)**
**1 1/4 cups whole-wheat
    pastry flour**
**1 1/2 teaspoons double-
    acting baking powder**
1 teaspoon sea salt

**1/8 teaspoon nutmeg
    (optional)**
2 egg whites
1/8 teaspoon sea salt
3 cups peanut oil

1. Scrape off kernels using
dull edge of a knife.
Combine in a bowl with
milk and egg yolks, bell or
jalapeno pepper, and a little
black pepper if desired.
2. In another bowl sift
together flour, baking
powder, and one teaspoon
salt. Stir the dry mixture
into the wet one.
3. Beat egg whites with a
pinch of salt until they hold
stiff peaks. Fold into corn
mixture. Preheat oven to
200°F.
4. In a deep-sided pan or
wok (see **The Wok**), heat
peanut oil to 350°F. Drop
batter in by tablespoons. (Dip

Corn

*With the corn
harvest, summer
begins to close and
August days bring
thoughts of school.
New hybrids have
lengthened the corn
season, and Mainers
enjoy corn on the cob
from July to fall.
Steamed till barely
tender, buttered and
salted, nothing
tastes better.*

*Corn has a long
history in the
Americas–Maine
Indians grew some,
the Aztecs
cultivated it as
early as the eighth
century, and
Columbus was the
first to introduce it to
Europe.*

*Yellow corn contains
more nutrients than
the white variety.
Combined with
beans, it produces a
complete protein–
the basis of the
native American
diet. Sweet corn was
introduced to New
England around 1779
and has remained a
favorite ever since.*

*Corn on the cob needs
careful handling–if
you're lucky enough
to have a garden,
pick the corn a half
hour before supper,
or early enough to
beat the raccoons. If
you live in town, find
a farm that invites
you to "pick your
own," and hurry
home.*

tablespoon into hot oil first and batter will slide off more easily.) Turn several times and fry till crisp and dark gold. Drain on a wire rack. Transfer to a hot plate and keep warm in a 200°F oven till ready to serve.

Serve with tossed salad, ripe tomatoes, fresh string beans, and new potatoes.

(Traditionally, corn fritters were served drizzled with maple syrup.)

Colache makes a quick, easy vegetable supper.

Colache
(6-8 servings)

2 tablespoons extra-virgin olive oil
3-5 tablespoons water
1 pound zucchini (or other summer squash), cut into 3/4-inch cubes
1 medium-sized onion, diced
1 green or red bell pepper, seeded and chopped
2 large peeled tomatoes, chopped
1 1/2 cups corn, freshly cut from the cob, with its milk
sea salt to taste
freshly ground black pepper
1 tablespoon fresh basil or oregano, finely chopped (half as much, dried)

a few drops freshly squeezed lemon juice
1 tablespoon finely chopped fresh parsley for garnish OR 3 tablespoons grated parmesan cheese

1. Brush a heavy-bottomed skillet lightly with olive oil. Add water, zucchini, onion, and chopped bell pepper. Cover, simmer, stirring gently but frequently, about five minutes.
2. Add tomatoes and corn and simmer about five minutes more. Add a little water if necessary.
3. Add salt, pepper, herb, and lemon juice to taste.

Serve sprinkled with finely chopped fresh parsley or grated parmesan cheese, and a whole-grain or pasta dish.

Fresh Corn Polenta

(4-6 servings)

2 ears fresh corn OR
    about 2 cups of
    kernels
2 cups milk
1 heaping teaspoon miso
    (see Glossary)
    dissolved in
    1 1/2 cups water
1 cup yellow cornmeal
1/4 cup diced red or
    green bell pepper
1/2 teaspoon sea salt
    (optional)
3-4 drops hot pepper
    sauce (optional)
a small amount of
    sunflower seed oil
2 tablespoons freshly
    grated parmesan or
    romano cheese

1. Scrape off kernels.
2. Combine milk and miso broth in a heavy-bottomed, medium-sized saucepan. Whisk in cornmeal. Cook over moderate heat, whisking often, until mush is thick and smooth, fifteen to thirty minutes. Remove from heat.
3. Stir in corn kernels and bell pepper, and season with salt and hot pepper sauce if desired.
4. Pour mush into a buttered seven-and-a-half- by eleven-inch cake or lasagna pan. Allow to rest, uncovered, for at least one hour.
5. Preheat oven to 375°F. Brush the top with oil and sprinkle with cheese. Bake fifteen minutes or until cheese is golden. Let stand fifteen minutes before serving.

Serve with a crisp salad, sliced tomatoes, and fish or beans.

Note: To serve as a leftover, slice cold polenta and sauté in butter or olive oil till golden.

*Cornmeal, an early staple of every colonial kitchen, was often served simply as cornmeal mush. (See **Polenta** in the Glossary.) It continues today as a timeless Maine favorite, influenced in this recipe by Italian cuisine.*

New (and Old) Maine Corn Chowder

(6 servings)

1-1 1/2 cups water
2 large onions, chopped
    fine
3 large potatoes, cubed
1 quart rich milk
2 cups whole-kernel
    corn (creamed-style is
    best)
sea salt to taste
freshly ground black
    pepper
3-4 drops angostura
    bitters

An old summer favorite of Mother's, especially on Thursday evenings before Friday's fish and Saturday's baked beans, was corn chowder, the corn fresh from the field. (But it can be made all year, thanks to canned or frozen corn.)

1. In a heavy-bottomed saucepan simmer onions and potatoes in water till barely tender.
2. In another heavy-bottomed saucepan scald milk. Add corn, and season with salt and pepper.

3. Heat. Then add cooked potatoes and onions, and bitters. *Do not boil.*

Serve hot with a sprinkling of finely chopped fresh parsley and fresh hot rolls.

Beets

Native to Europe and North Africa, the beet as we know it today didn't appear on tables until the mid-1500s, although its Swiss chard form was cultivated by Greeks and Romans, and spread to China in the Middle Ages. Both leaf and root are very nutritious.

Mother always served them with butter, salt, and pepper. Once in a while she added a thick vinegary sauce. And we never used fresh shredded beets in salad. The first baby beets were always eagerly awaited–pulled when still only three-quarters of an inch thick, and cooked, greens and all.

Baby Beets and Greens

baby beets and greens
water
shoyu, quartered,
**   lemons OR a simple**
**   Basic Vinaigrette**

Pull beets, wash carefully, and discard any dead leaves. Trim roots slightly, and steam till tender in a large colander over boiling water, about a half hour.

Serve on a large hot platter, chopped coarsely, with shoyu and lemon or vinaigrette.

Simple Cooked Beet Root

small beets to eat
**   whole, or large beets**
**   to slice**
freshly squeezed lemon
**   juice and mint**
**   (optional)**

1. Wash beets gently but do not break skins. Cut off leaves and stems to within one inch of top to prevent bleeding. Leave roots on unless terribly long, in which case trim to within three inches of bulb, also to prevent bleeding. Place

beets of uniform size into a large, heavy-bottomed kettle. Cover with cold water. Heat slowly to boiling, reduce heat, and simmer until tender–about forty-five minutes for medium-sized beets to over an hour for huge ones, such as the Lutz Greenleaf variety.
2. Place immediately in a large pot of cold water. Allow to cool, then slip off skins, root, and stems.

Serve whole or sliced, hot or cold, with freshly squeezed lemon juice and mint, **Horseradish Sauce for Beets**, or a **Basic Vinaigrette** seasoned with dill.

Horseradish Sauce for Beets

1 cup Laban or thick
    yogurt
1 tablespoon prepared
    horseradish

3 tablespoons finely
    chopped fresh dill
    weed
freshly ground black
    pepper

Mix together and pour over
hot, cooked beets.

Hot Beet Salad with Tarragon

(4-6 servings)

4 cups hot cooked beets
4 tablespoons sunflower
    seed oil
2 teaspoons finely
    chopped fresh
    tarragon
1/4 teaspoon maple
    syrup

1 tablespoon (or more)
    freshly squeezed
    lemon juice or cider
    vinegar

1. Slice cooked beets into a
hot bowl.
2. Add remaining
ingredients and toss gently.

Serve as a side dish to any
meal.

Cold Beet Soup

(4 servings)

enough cooked beets to
    make 1 cup purée
2 tablespoons vinegar
1 teaspoon salt
1 teaspoon mild honey
2 cups yogurt
2 medium-sized
    cucumbers, peeled,
    seeded, and diced
4 medium-sized
    scallions, sliced
3 red radishes, diced
2 tablespoons finely
    chopped fresh dill
    weed

4 tablespoons freshly
    squeezed lemon juice
sea salt to taste
freshly ground black
    pepper to taste
milk to thin

1. In blender purée beets
with vinegar, salt, and honey
until smooth.
2. Pour into a serving bowl
and add yogurt, vegetables,
dill, and lemon juice. Mix
well.

3. Season with salt and pepper to taste and, if necessary, thin with milk.

Serve immediately as is, or garnished with side bowls of diced cucumber; chopped cooked beets; croutons; chopped hard-cooked eggs; and thin slices of lemon. Leftovers may be used as a condiment to curry.

Potatoes

Potatoes, native to Chile where they were grown by the Incas, and probably brought to Maine by the Irish, are a staple in the diet of most Mainers. New potatoes have always been a late-summer treat.

Red Norlands

new potatoes
a simple lemon-juice vinaigrette (see Basic Vinaigrette)
fresh parsley, thyme, marjoram, or rosemary

Wash potatoes well, cook with skins on till tender, then toss with vinaigrette, and sprinkle with finely chopped fresh herbs.

Serve with anything!

New Potatoes in Lemon
(6 servings)

36 tiny potatoes
3 tablespoons butter
3 tablespoons sunflower seed oil
1 teaspoon grated lemon peel
1-2 tablespoons freshly squeezed lemon juice
a few drops maple syrup
1/8 teaspoon hot pepper sauce (optional) or cayenne

1 tablespoon finely minced fresh chives, coriander, lovage, thyme, marjoram, or tarragon OR 2 teaspoons rosemary

1. Dig (or purchase) tiny potatoes, wash thoroughly, and cook in boiling water about ten minutes till tender. Drain well and cool slightly.
2. Warm butter, oil, and seasonings in a heavy-bottomed skillet. Add potatoes, and roll around until well coated.

Serve on a hot platter sprinkled with sea salt and freshly ground black pepper.

Low-Fat Potato Salad

(6 servings)

4 cups cooked, cooled, peeled, and cubed white potatoes (3/4-inch cubes work well)
1 cup, or more, finely chopped onion, both white and green
1 cup chopped green or red bell pepper
1 cup yogurt
1 tablespoon freshly squeezed lemon juice
1 teaspoon (or more) sea salt
freshly ground black pepper
2 tablespoons fresh dill weed, chopped, or 1 teaspoon crumbled, dried dill weed

chopped black olives for garnish
sliced hard-cooked eggs for garnish
a sprinkling of Hungarian paprika
chopped dill weed for garnish

1. In a large bowl gently combine potatoes, onion, chopped pepper, yogurt, lemon juice, salt, pepper, and one tablespoon dill. Allow to sit from two to four hours to blend the flavors.
2. Garnish with olives, eggs, paprika, and dill.

Serve on a chilled platter on a bed of lettuce.

Spaghetti Squash

1 squash with pale yellow-buff skin, 1 to 5 pounds in weight

1. Pour water into a pot big enough to hold squash, and cover squash with water. Bring to a boil and cook about forty-five minutes or until the skin begins to give. (Flesh should be tender while skin remains shell-like.)

2. Drain, place on a large hot platter, and split squash down middle lengthwise.
3. Now fluff the spaghetti-like interior with a fork, removing as many seeds as possible.

Serve topped with tomato sauce and grated parmesan cheese. Return platter to the oven to reheat, if necessary.

Spaghetti Squash
A squash which has been more curiosity than serious fare has now come to Maine supper tables. It's simple to prepare.

Long-stemmed, male squash flowers fall off after producing necessary pollen, which gives the canny cook a grand chance to harvest them for eating.

Stuffed Squash Blossoms
(6 servings, 2 apiece)

1 tablespoon finely
    chopped onion, green
    or Spanish
1 cup cooked brown rice
1 egg yolk
    OR 1 tablespoon
    water and 1 teaspoon
    cornstarch
1/2 cup grated gruyère
    or other cheese
1/8 teaspoon sea salt
freshly ground black
    pepper
1/4 cup chopped fresh
    parsley
12 squash blossoms
3 cups peanut oil

1. Combine onion, rice, egg yolk, cheese, seasonings, and parsley.
2. Stuff blossoms with one tablespoon filling, allowing tops to close over stuffing.
3. Make batter (see **Stuffed Day Lily Blossoms**, **Cheechako Beer Batter**, or **Japanese Tempura Batter**).
4. Heat peanut oil in wok to 350°F (see **The Wok**). Dip blossoms in batter, and deep-fry till crisp.

Serve immediately with a crisp salad, additional rice, fresh rolls, and garden vegetables in season.

Bean Burgers
Children, especially, love "hamburgers" for summer feasts, but fat-filled commercial meat is an ever-decreasing part of Maine's new cuisine. Here are bean burgers, offering clean, complete protein when served on whole-grain buns.

Burger Buns
(12 lightweight buns)

1 tablespoon dry baking
    yeast
1 teaspoon barley malt
    OR maple syrup
1/4 cup warm water
4 tablespoons extra-
    virgin olive oil
1 egg, beaten
3/4 cup milk
1 tablespoon nutritional
    yeast
1 teaspoon vitamin C
    powder (optional)
3 cups whole-wheat
    bread flour
about 1 cup brown
    sesame seeds, rinsed

1. In a measuring cup soften yeast and sweetening in water.
2. When yeast bubbles, mix with oil, egg and milk in a large bowl.
3. Add nutritional yeast, vitamin C powder if desired, and flour. This will make a solid ball of rather sticky dough.
4. Turn out onto a *lightly* floured board, grease hands with butter, and knead until smooth and elastic about five minutes. To shape into round flat buns three inches in diameter, first roll dough into a fat, ten-inch sausage. Slice down the middle lengthwise. Then slice across each thinner sausage

»

five times to make twelve pieces. Form into balls by holding dough in fingertips and pulling dough down from sides to underside. This results in a smooth top and a bottom rather puckered and uneven. Flatten each ball with palm.

5. Place, seam-side down, on a large, greased cookie sheet, allowing space between each bun. Brush tops with cold water and sprinkle with sesame seeds. Cover with a damp cloth and set in a warm place to rise until doubled–thirty minutes to one hour, depending on temperature. Bake in a 375°F oven for fifteen to twenty minutes or until browned and crusty.

Sunflower/White Bean Burger

(about 14 3-inch burgers)

1 1/2 cups small white
    or navy beans
5 cups water
1-2 garlic cloves,
    smashed
1-2 sprigs fresh parsley
several grindings of
    black pepper
1 tablespoon fresh
    summer herbs of
    your choice (chervil,
    summer savory,
    lovage, thyme,
    oregano)
1 cup hulled sunflower
    seeds
1 teaspoon sea salt
freshly ground black
    pepper
1 cup diced onion
a few drops
    worcestershire
    sauce
1-2 cloves garlic, minced
2 tablespoons finely
    minced
    fresh parsley

1/4-1/2 cup bean
    cooking liquor
1 tablespoon cornstarch
    dissolved in 1
    tablespoon bean
    cooking liquor
white flour OR beaten egg
    and breadcrumbs
clarified butter or extra-
    virgin olive oil

1. About three to four hours before dinnertime, pick over beans for stones and dirt and wash well. Pop into a large saucepan with five cups of rapidly boiling water. Return to boil. Turn off heat and allow to rest two hours.

2. Turn on heat again and simmer gently until the beans are tender, one to one and a half hours, with smashed garlic cloves, parsley sprigs, pepper, and herbs as desired. Drain well and set aside. Reserve bean liquor.

3. In blender grind sunflower seeds fine. Once

beans are cool enough to handle, mash three cups of them coarsely and add to ground sunflower seeds. (Use the remainder for other recipes.) Mix well. Add salt, pepper, onions, worcestershire sauce, minced garlic, and chopped fresh herbs. Moisten as necessary with the reserved bean cooking liquor, plus cornstarch dissolved in one tablespoon of the liquor. (If you prefer your onions cooked, simmer them till limp with four tablespoons saké in a covered skillet.)

4. Form into patties and dredge gently in white flour OR dip in beaten egg and roll in breadcrumbs. Sauté in clarified butter or olive oil in a hot skillet until golden brown.

Serve on **Burger Buns** with fresh lettuce, sliced tomatoes, finely sliced peppers, and Bermuda onions, with Dijon mustard.

Note: This burger mix will keep about a week, refrigerated and covered. It also freezes well.

Red Lentil Burgers

(about 16 3-inch burgers)

1 cup red lentils, rinsed
1 1/2 cups water
4 medium-sized onions, chopped
1/4 cup saké (see Glossary)
1/2 lemon rind, grated
1 teaspoon sea salt (optional)
freshly ground black pepper (optional)
1/4 cup finely chopped fresh parsley OR 1 tablespoon mixed, minced fresh herbs
2 cups fine, fresh whole-wheat breadcrumbs
1 egg OR 1 teaspoon cornstarch dissolved in 2 tablespoons water

white flour OR beaten egg plus breadcrumbs
extra-virgin olive oil or clarified butter

1. Slowly cook lentils in water till soft and dry, about thirty minutes.
2. In a covered skillet steam onions in saké until limp.
3. Mix together the onions, cooked red lentils, lemon rind, herbs, and breadcrumbs. Moisten slightly with egg or cornstarch dissolved in water.
4. Shape into round, flattened patties and dredge gently in white flour or dip in a slightly beaten egg and roll in more breadcrumbs.

»

5. Sauté briefly in a hot skillet until golden brown.

Serve hot with tomato sauce or **Mushroom Gravy**, with new potatoes, and a tossed salad; or on buns with lettuce, sliced tomato, onion, and peppers.

Note: This burger mix will keep about a week, refrigerated and covered. It also freezes well.

There is only one way to cook a lobster properly from the vantage point of a good Maineiac.

Perfect Lobster

1-1 1/2-pound lobster per person
water
rockweed

1. Get your lobsters fresh out of the sea, if possible. Take them home in a hurry.
2. Heat an inch of water in a large pot and bring to a boil.
3. Add a six-inch layer of rockweed (the common deep-olive-green seaweed found growing on Maine coastal rocks like hair). Cover the pot.
4. As soon as a great steam arises, put lobsters in, head first. Cover with more rockweed, cover pot tightly, and steam for twenty minutes. No more. (If you lack rockweed, substitute two inches seawater, and if you lack that, substitute water plus two tablespoons sea salt.)

Serve hot with bibs and napkins, picks and nutcrackers, and hot melted butter, and vinegar or lemon juice, if you like. Potato salad is the accessory of choice.

Note: The rule of thumb is to steam one-and-a-quarter-pounders eighteen minutes, one-and-a-half pounders twenty minutes, two-pounders twenty-four minutes.

Lobsters

I grew up with lobsters. That is to say, a third cousin of mine, of ancient vintage when I was little, was an old-time lobster fisherman. Ralph's common conversation was so pickled with blasphemy as to represent an art; and his everyday appellation for young and old, male or female, was "deah." "Jesusgod, deah, wheah've you ben?" was his greeting. Where I "ben" was down in his fish house savoring all the equipment... the gaffs, the lobster pots, the brightly painted buoys with his initials on them, and his big lobster boat with The Edith Campbell *painted on her bow. Edith was my grandmother.*

"That little thing wants ta go fishin' with Ralph, don't she?"

She did. I perched in the bow completely unconcerned whenever we ran Hell's Gates at the mouth of the Kennebec, except for the one moment when my stuffed rooster fell overboard and had to be gaffed in. Otherwise I savored the rotten herring bait, the sound of the diesel engine, the feel of cold salt spray.

"That little thing ain't scared, are ya, deah?"

No. Enthralled. Remain so. And there's nothing like absolutely sea-fresh lobster for eating. In those days before over-fishing they were sizeable. Even I could put away a two-pounder.

If you purchase lobsters **make certain they're alive.** *Be wary of the swinging tail which can close painfully and dangerously on an unwary finger, particularly an immature one; and be certain those large claws are restrained with wooden wedges or rubber bands.*

Lobster Eating

For anyone who grows up with them it's basic. I suggest the following from years of carnivorous practice.

1. Break off the two front claws.
2. Break claws apart at each joint and, using pick, push meat out.
3. After removing wooden wedge or rubber band, break bottom pincer off each large claw. Pluck into this pincer's hole with pick, and meat will be pulled out. You may have to use a cracker to crush the large part of the claw until you can break it in half to remove meat. This is the most tender and succulent portion.
4. Turn next to the tail. Place lobster on its back, pick it up, and, holding body portion with left hand and tail with right, break tail from body by twisting.

5. Once tail is free, pull off the five little rudders at end. They contain a whisper of taste, so be sure to suck them out. Then poke your strongest finger into the end of tail and push meat forward until it spurts out the other end.
6. You will discover a log of red and white meat. Turn meat onto its "belly," and you will be able to lift off a thin, longish strip from the back, revealing a little grey or black vein. Carefully lift out the vein and discard.
7. Cut or break into bite-sized morsels, dip into butter, and savor.
8. After this, it's time to explore. There may be coral-colored spawn, and there will be gray-green "tomalley" in the body cavity. Enjoy.
9. Now separate body from back shell and crack it apart sideways, pressing down with your thumbs. There are bits and pieces of meat hiding here and there.
10. And last, milk the small claws with your teeth while sucking the meat out.

Serve your lobsters with enormous napkins or towels, and with a communal bucket handy to receive shells.

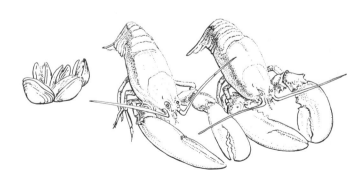

Lobster stew, a great Maine favorite, is simplicity itself—but it takes close attention to make it perfect. It's best if allowed to mellow a day or two before serving.

Grandmother's Lobster Stew

4 (1-pound)
  "chicken" lobsters
water
3 tablespoons butter
1 quart milk
1/2 cup cold milk
    plus 2 tablespoons
    arrowroot or potato
    flour (optional)
sea salt to taste
white pepper

1. Freeze lobsters for one hour, if you want a more humane method of killing them.
2. Bring water to a boil in a large pot and put in lobsters head first. Allow to blanch five minutes. Cool, shell, and cut the meat into bite-sized pieces. Carefully remove and set aside coral and tomalley.
3. Melt butter in a heavy-bottomed skillet. Add tomalley and coral, crumbled, and cook gently three or four minutes.

4. Add lobster meat and cook, stirring, three to four minutes. *Don't overcook.*
5. In a large, heavy-bottomed casserole, scald milk.
6. Add the sautéed lobster to the milk with all its butter and sauce. If you prefer a thicker stew, shake cold milk with arrowroot or potato flour in a capped jar and add. Season to taste with salt and white pepper. A lovely pink blush will appear on top. Allow to rest a full day (refrigerated in hot weather) before serving.

Serve hot but not boiling, sprinkled with finely chopped fresh parsley, with fresh whole-grain rolls, pickles, and tossed salad.

Variation: Adding a few drops of hot pepper sauce and a quarter cup of dry sherry just before serving may be considered a bit strange by some Mainers, but it is delicious.

Clams

A clambake nearly always involves lobsters—and any really adequate lobster dinner starts with steamed clams. A good trencherman or -woman will down two dozen clams within as many minutes, beg for more, demolish a two-pound lobster with nary a sigh, wallow in potato salad, and then ask for chocolate cake. So much for Maine **nouvelle cuisine!**

Maine's favorite clam is the soft-shell, also called long-neck or steamer. It's a two- to three-inch bivalve found abundantly in tidal flats from Labrador to North Carolina (though if there were fewer clam lovers, size would reach five inches). The shell is moderately thick and gapes at both ends.

Digging clams is fun if you don't do it for a business, and the easiest hoe to use is tined. It enables you to lift the clam out of the sand without creating a mound of mud or breaking the brittle shell. You can tell where clams are hiding because they spurt when you shake their world by walking near them.

Be certain you dig in a clean tidal zone.

Clams are available almost year-round except when the world is frozen. They're also apt to be in short supply come summer due to "red tides." My people used to say: "Never eat a shellfish during months that don't contain an 'e.' "

Clams tend to contain sand, which makes one's teeth suffer. My grandmother cleaned hers like this: She placed clams on a rack in a large kettle or tub and covered them with fresh water. Then she sprinkled in a small handful of cornmeal. The clams were soaked overnight, as I remember, then cooked, shucked, and eaten. Note: Clams must always be cooked live or they can make you very ill.

Clambakes are traditionally held on the beach, and there's nothing like them. But stovetop clambakes often produce better-cooked seafood, because fast-cooking items can be added last. You must have rockweed for the real flavor.

Simple Steamed Clams

20 cleaned clams per
person
water

1. Make certain shells are shut tight–throw out any that have opened. If you rap two clams together they must make a dull thud–a hollow sound means a dead clam.
2. Scrub shells and carefully wash in several waters. Place in a large kettle with about an inch of water. Cover, bring to a boil, and steam until shells open. Discard *any* that remain closed.
3. Pour clam broth into individual cups, and give each person a large soup bowl full of clams. (And a large napkin.)
4. Use fingers to tug clam out of its house. Then pull the thick black "skin" off the neck of the clam and discard. Dip clam first into broth to rinse; then into hot, melted butter flavored with lemon juice. (Shoyu and lemon quarters are also good, and fat-free.)
Clam broth is drunk once all the clams have disappeared.

Kitchen Clambake
(6 servings)

rockweed
water
6 (1-pound) lobsters
6 large potatoes, washed
and pricked with a
fork in several places
6 ears of corn
about 20 steamer clams
per person (120
clams)

1. In a very large kettle place about one inch water and a thick layer of rockweed. Place potatoes on top. Cover, bring to a boil, and steam about thirty minutes.

2. Add another layer of rockweed, lobsters, more rockweed, and corn (silk and corn borers removed) wrapped in a remaining bit of husk. End with a layer of rockweed and steam twenty more minutes.

Serve after removing rockweed with tongs. Heap each plate with twenty clams and one of everything else. It's *de rigueur* to serve with melted butter, but shoyu, freshly squeezed lemon juice, or an olive oil vinai-grette are fine. A tossed salad and fresh rolls would round out the meal.

Melon Salad

(4-6 servings)

1-2 fresh melons
Honey Lemon Dressing
    (see below)

1. With a melon scoop, fill a two-quart glass bowl with whatever melon or combination you please: cranshaw, honeydew, cantaloupe, watermelon.
2. Make dressing and pour it over the melon.

Melons

It's hard to grow melons in Maine, though some people do it easily. These people are invariably clever gardeners, rich in the lore of black plastic mulch, early starting, careful transplanting, and lots of watering.

Honey Lemon Dressing for Summer Fruit

(4 servings)

juice of 1 freshly
    squeezed lemon
2 tablespoons mild
    honey
1/8 teaspoon sea salt
1/8 teaspoon Hungarian
    paprika
    OR 1/2 teaspoon
    ground ginger

Combine all ingredients (increase for a larger bowl of fruit).

Variation: You may substitute any fruit juice for most of the lemon, and top the fruit with **Whipped Cottage Cheese** and a sprinkling of nuts, **Tofu Whipped Cream,** or yogurt sweetened with a bit of honey.

Flamed Cantaloupe

half a ripe melon per
    person
2 tablespoons madiera
    (or other wine) per
    person
1 teaspoon vodka per person

2. In a large serving spoon, heat madiera and vodka. Set it aflame and pour over melon. Repeat for each half.

1. Slice melons in half or quarters, and remove seeds.

Melons make good desserts, sliced into half-moons and served with cheese and wine, such as a young port, a liqueur such as Grand Marnier, or even vodka spooned into the cavity. The liquor can be flamed for a blazing dessert.

Fall

Now the garden is absolutely bursting with ripe tomatoes, drying beans, peppers bulging, last-minute zucchinis, lettuce bolting, brussel sprouts growing happily, cabbages expanding, cauliflowers looking seedy. It's time to spread sheets, tarps, and towels on summer's bounty against the expected frost.

Fall means sweeping out the cellar and lugging in bushels of potatoes; putting rutabagas, beets, and daikon into sand-filled boxes; admiring the rows of gorgeous canned goods on the shelves; and piling hay on top of the carrots and parsnips left in the garden. Life begins to fold in on itself, and it's time to feel cozy, to think of fireplaces, steaming loaves of bread, and soups.

Herbs and Spices

From colonial days, Maine people have been herb gardeners. Next to the rose- and lemon-scented geraniums outside my grandmother's kitchen door grew a sprawling catnip plant, mints for tea, and dill for pickling. From the nearby woods and fields she gathered witch hazel, sassafrass, pennyroyal, yarrow, and many other plants. My mother always grew wormwood in her garden, although she never used it medicinally.

Herb gardening is becoming popular once again. Through-out Maine, people are creating formal little gardens or planting herbs alongside vegetables to promote health, discourage insects, or simply for the joy of it. Commercial herb growers are successful–herbal vinegars, potpourri, and wreaths are sure sellers during holiday seasons. Awareness of the side effects of many potent prescription drugs is also drawing people back to the nearly forgotten lore of herbalism.

Only a few families of plants offer the pungent scent characteristic of culinary herbs, the two most important being the carrot family (**Umbelliferae**) and the mints (**Labiatae**). The carrot clan has three thousand species including anise, caraway, coriander, cumin, dill, fennel, and parsley. The mint family contains some thirty-two - hundred species such as basil, mint, marjoram, oregano, rosemary, sage, and thyme. The daisy family (**Compositae**), although the largest family of plants apart from orchids, gives us only tarragon and camomile!

In Maine, herbs must be garnered by fall unless one wishes to pot a few to bring indoors. I always rescue basil, chives, celery, parsley (which, because of deep roots, often wilts and dies), and a mint or two. Digging herbs from the garden means playing host to white flies and aphids. But after losing battles on several occasions, I became aware of a pyrethrum spray. Made from the blossoms of the Dalmatian Daisy, **Chrysanthemum cinearaefolium**, it is lethal to a wide variety of garden pests while being low in toxicity to people, pets, and bees. Soak your potted plant with it before bringing it inside. An alternative is to sow seeds indoors in sterile potting soil. Never having known the wild life, they'll be tame all winter.

Drying and Storing Herbs

Herbs should be gathered during their peak season in the morning of a clear day just after the dew has evaporated and just prior to blooming. Punch holes in some paper bags or cut out bottoms, tie the herbs together by their stems and hang upside down inside the bags, in a dry airy space, preferably shady. This allows oils to concentrate in the leaves and ensures freedom from dust. Good air circulation means faster drying, and shade protects herbs from sunlight which might blacken the leaves.

When the leaves are crumbly, stem-strip them and store in tightly stoppered glass jars. Dry organic material is less likely to spoil. Drying also breaks down cell structure and makes it possible to extract more oil–so dry herbs are a more potent source of flavoring than fresh. This explains why the cook uses half or a third as much dried herb as fresh. But oils are volatile and slowly evaporate–in time, even dried herbs lose their flavor. It's wise to store all herbs, when pefectly dry, in dark, air-tight containers.

Flowers should be harvested as soon as they bloom, and seeds when their color changes from green to brownish, but before the pods are so dry that they burst. Herbal roots are dug in the fall after leaves have dried or in spring before new growth begins.

Using Dried Herbs

The general rule of thumb in herb cookery is to use half as much of a dried herb as fresh. And crumble between the palms before adding to cooking to release flavor.

Herbal Condiments, Oils, Vinegars

One hundred years of French and Indian wars shaped Maine's early history, when we were truly a wild frontier. The French make up a large segment of today's population–and so it is especially fitting that many Maine culinary herbal customs are French. A fixed combination of three or four herbs, called **fines herbes**, is used to flavor *certain dishes. Examples would include: parsley, chervil, and chives; parsley, basil, and chives; or burnet, thyme, and parsley.*

*A **bouquet garni** is a little batch of herbs tied together with string or captured in a tiny cheesecloth sack, cooked with food to flavor broth or sauce. But I recommend simply adding herbs directly to the dish, allowing them to integrate. A simple **garni** would be a sprig or two of parsley and several spears of chives. The classic is three or four stems of parsley, a spray of thyme and half a bay leaf, tied together with string.*

Herbal Oils and Vinegars

Flavoring oils and vinegars with herbs is a custom of long standing in Maine. With the resurgence of interest in herbs in the 1970s several herb farms have appeared which sell herbal vinegar at high prices. It's easy to make your own.

Basic Directions for Herbal Vinegars

1. Fill a large glass or ceramic container (don't use anything metallic) with dried herbs crumbled in your hands. Choose tarragon, purple basil (which lends a burgundy color), dill seed, chive flowers, salad burnet, garlic, cloves, etc.
2. Cover with white or apple cider vinegar, or white, red, or rice-wine vinegar.

3. Steep several days, being sure herbs are covered with vinegar.
4. Cover with a nonmetallic lid. Acid corrodes metal, and you don't want the possible chemical contaminations.
5. When the vinegar is strong enough for your taste, strain and bottle. If it's too strong, dilute with more vinegar.
6. For looks, add a sprig of the fresh herb to the bottle.

Garlic Vinegar

1 cup vinegar
3-6 garlic cloves
1 teaspoon sea salt
cloves
freshly ground black
 pepper
1/2 teaspoon caraway
 seeds
3 cups red wine (or other)
 vinegar, simmering
 hot

1. Whiz one cup vinegar in your blender with garlic, salt, cloves, pepper, and caraway.
2. Pour into a glass jar and add three cups simmering vinegar.
3. Cover and allow to stand about one week, shaking occasionally. Strain through cheesecloth into sterilized jars or bottles and cover tightly with a nonmetallic cap.

Tarragon Vinegar

1 pint tarragon leaves
2 cups heated red wine or
 cider vinegar
2 garlic cloves, smashed
 with a broad knife blade

1. Crush tarragon leaves with your hands and place in a glass bowl.

2. Pour heated vinegar over them and add garlic.
3. Cover and allow to rest at room temperature for an entire day. Remove garlic and allow to rest two weeks more. Strain through cheesecloth, pour into a sterilized bottle, and cap tightly (preferably with a cork).

Salad Burnet Vinegar

fresh salad burnet leaves
cider vinegar

1. Fill a large glass jar with washed fresh leaves, patted dry.
2. Cover with cider vinegar.
3. Set in the sun to "cook" for ten days.
4. Strain and enjoy.

According to Madeleine Siegler of Monk's Hill Herbs in Readfield, Maine, salad burnet makes a magnificent vinegar and ought to be enjoyed more often. These are Madeleine's directions.

Red Wine Vinegar

1-2 tablespoons vinegar "mother," if available
1 gallon unpasteurized claret or sauterne

1. Pour "mother" into wine.
2. Cover top of bottle with a bit of cheesecloth held on by an elastic band. Set in a warm, dark place until the taste suits you. Then strain through clean cheesecloth, pour into bottles, cap, and store in a cool spot.

Wine produces a flavorful, robust vinegar. Wine vinegar is expensive to buy—but you can make it yourself for less. If you possess vinegar which has formed "mother," a thick jelly-like mass consisting of yeast and bacteria cells, you can produce vinegar rather quickly. If you haven't any "mother," uncapped wine will eventually become vinegar, but it will take a lot longer.

Herbal Oils

Flavored oils are as easy to make as flavored vinegars. I recommend an unsaturated variety such as sunflower seed, or a mono-unsaturate such as extra-virgin olive oil, although it already possesses a strong flavor of its own.

Garlic Oil

6 large smashed garlic cloves
4 cups extra-virgin olive oil OR sunflower seed oil OR peanut oil

1. Combine garlic with oil of choice.
2. Allow to rest five days.
3. Strain and store.

Herbal Teas or Tisanes

In recent years, along with the new interest in herbs, teas which do not contain caffeine have become popular. Some wild plants which can be gathered to make a dinner-type tea, or herbs you can grow and use either fresh or dried for the same purpose, are listed here. Unless otherwise noted, use one teaspoon of herb to one cup of boiling water and steep for five minutes.

Borage: A handful of fresh leaves steeped in a quart of water with a sprig or two of spearmint makes a cooling summer beverage, if chilled. The taste is reminiscent of cucumbers.

Catnip: Catnip leaves make a kindly tea, reportedly helpful for headache and indigestion. The flowering tops can also be used.

Chicory: The dried, grated root of *Cichorium* is often added to coffee, but it makes a good tea by itself. Dig the roots, wash, and slice into quarter-inch-diameter pieces an inch or two long. Roast in a 250°F oven one hour or till crisp. Grind in a coffee grinder or blender, and brew just as you would coffee, using a percolator or a filter drip system. Use about half as much chicory per cup as you would coffee--about one heaping teaspoon.

Clovers: Clover flowers and leaves make good teas. To dry *Trifolium* or red clover, pick the mature blossoms on a dry, sunny day and dry at room temperature. Rub into tiny bits, then seal in a capped jar.

Dandelion: Dandelion leaves make a good medicinal tea, which is mainly diuretic, and is considered to be a good blood purifier. The roots make a tasty coffee substitute. There are several ways to prepare it.

Dandelion Tea:
1) Pour one cup boiling water over a handful fresh leaves or a level teaspoon dry ones. Cover, brew for five minutes, and flavor with a dash of lemon and honey to taste.
2) Cooled, this tea may be taken in small glasses, flavored with a bit of honey and a dash of lemon as above.
3) Boil together one quart water and about two ounces of the roots, scraped and cleaned, or a handful of leaves. (Makes four servings.)

Dandelion Coffee:
Clean and dry dandelion roots thoroughly. Roast slightly to coffee color in a 200°F oven. Store in a tightly capped jar to be freshly ground when required to make "coffee." Brew as you would chicory. This drink is supposed to be good for delicate stomachs and even for children.

Mints: Mints make lovely, refreshing teas. Peppermint is probably the most popular herbal tea in America. Lemon balm and lemon » verbena are good either iced or hot. And you can add a sprig of fresh spearmint or lemon verbena to a cup of commercial dried green tea to add flavor.

Rose Geranium:

Adding rose geranium leaves and one clove to a pot of steeping tea lends a delightful flavor.

Rose Petals:
For rose petal tea pour four cups boiling water over five heaping teaspoons dried rose petals (or twice that amount fresh) in a porcelain teapot. Steep five minutes.

Rose Hips:
For rose hip tea gather hips when red but slightly underripe on a dry, sunny day. Pour one cup boiling water over one heaping teaspoon rose hips and allow to steep ten minutes. Reheat if necessary, but do not boil. Add lemon and serve with honey. The Irish add black currant leaves and several rose hips when brewing black tea.

Strawberry:
The leaves make a good tea, rich in vitamin C. Cover two handfuls of fresh green leaves with four cups boiling water and steep five minutes. For a cold drink, immerse newly picked, young, green strawberry leaves in boiling water, cover, and drink cold the next day.

Jams and Jellies

Elderberries are wonderful for both jam and wine. Grapes and rose hips also make preserves not to be missed. But I prefer to freeze blueberries and strawberries whole, only turning them into freshly made "jams" as needed, come winter. Raspberries usually get eaten by the bushel immediately!

These following traditional preserves are my favorites–simple, straightforward, but satisfying. All use honey or maple syrup instead of sugar. They have adorned the cellar shelves of Maine cooks in one guise or another for two hundred years.

Most jams contain as much white refined sugar as they do fruit. But there is a pectin which gels with the aid of a small amount of calcium rather than large quantities of sugar–low methoxyl pectin, made from the inner peels of citrus fruits instead of animal products. It is obtainable from Walnut Acres, Penns Creek, PA 17862, if not locally. You'll also need **dicalcium phosphate** *(also available from Walnut Acres).*

The first step in making sugarless jelly or jam is to prepare two separate water solutions.

1. Mix four tablespoons low methoxyl pectin with a quart of water in your blender. This can be stored, covered, in the refrigerator for use any time. If it gels, just mix again before using.
2. Combine two teaspoons dicalcium with a quart of water in your blender. This will settle and need more blending if stored for any length of time. To make jelly or jam, use a quarter cup pectin and a teaspoon calcium solution per cup fruit liquid. If a batch doesn't gel quite hard enough, reheat, and firm it up with a bit more calcium.

Storing Jellies and Jams

1. Fill small, hot, sterilized jam jars (resting on a folded towel) to within an eighth-inch of the top. Wipe rim carefully. Put a sterilized, hot metal lid in place and screw down the band. Turn jar upside down for a moment. As jelly cools a vacuum will form, and jars will seal nicely. Allow to cool. Then wash jars, wipe dry, and store in a cool, dark place. Label, with date.

OR 2. Heat canning paraffin in a small, heavy-duty bowl over boiling water. Pour hot jam into hot, sterilized jam jars to within a quarter-inch of top. Wipe the jar rim inside down to the jelly level. Ladle in an eighth-inch of hot paraffin. Once cool, wash off any spilled jam, top with metal covers and bands or any kind of covering available, and store in a cool, dry place.

OR 3. Pack into hot, sterilized canning jars leaving a half-inch headroom.

Process in a boiling water bath for ten minutes.

I recommend wiping cooled jars with a diluted bleach solution (one tablespoon bleach per quart water). This destroys lingering bacteria and discourages any that might try to colonize in storage.

The elderberry is a member of the honeysuckle family. It makes a lovely, deep purple jam.

Elderberry Jam

8 cups elderberries, washed gently and removed from stem clusters
8 cups apples, well washed and quartered (but not cored or peeled)
6 cups water (more if necessary)
maple syrup to taste
1/2 cup freshly squeezed lemon juice
1 part low methoxyl pectin solution to every 4 parts fruit
1 teaspoon calcium liquid per cup of fruit

1. In a large enameled pot combine elderberries and apples.
2. Add water and simmer till soft.
3. Mash with a potato masher. Place a layer of cheesecloth over a colander and pour in the elderberry-apple mixture. Gather ends and tie loosely to form a little bag. Then hang where it can drain into the enameled pot until the mush is quite dry. At the end, squeeze bag with hands to push through all you can.
4. Measure juice, add maple syrup, and lemon juice if desired. Stir and cook over low heat until mixture reaches a gentle boil.
5. Stir in pectin and bring to another bubble.
6. Mix in calcium liquid. Fill small, hot, sterilized jars to within one-eighth-inch of top and continue as directed in **Storing Jellies and Jams**.

Note: Substitute almost any fruit in the above recipe. I recommend tiny wild strawberries and small tart purple grapes. I also recommend chokecherries. They grew by the back fence of the schoolyard when I was a child–and one of our favorite "dares" was eating them. (What red-stained blouses and fingers, and faces with puckered mouths!) They make a lovely, deep-red jelly. Strain fruit first and use only the juice.

Rose Hip Jam

1 pound rose hips
1 cup water
small piece cinnamon
    bark
1-2 cloves
4 apples
1/2 cup freshly squeezed
    lemon juice
maple syrup to taste
low methoxyl
    pectin/dicalcium
    phosphate

1. Collect rose hips after the first frost. They'll be a deep red, have a mellower taste, and vitamin C content will have peaked. Avoid any which have been sprayed with pesticides or which grow at roadside and may be contaminated by roadside exhausts.

2. Wash well and drain. Remove any stray leaves and stems and cut out any rotten parts.
3. Place rose hips, water, cinnamon, and cloves in a large enameled pot.
Bring to a boil and simmer till hips are tender.
4. Remove cloves and cinnamon bark and rub through a sieve to remove seeds and skins. Cook apples in a little water until tender, then push through a sieve. Combine the rose hip and apple purées.
5. Add lemon juice and maple syrup. Return to boil slowly and add pectin and calcium solutions (see previous pages).
6. Pour into sterile jars and seal. Label, with date.

Rose hips, often called "haws," are another favorite of mine. The hip or fruit of the rose is enormously high in vitamin C. During the Second World War , when England was beseiged, children were given rose hip syrup because citrus fruits were scarce. In Maine, many a child of colonial days had the same. **Rosa rugosa,** *which sturdily decorates Maine's coastline, is a fine source of large red hips.* **Rosa magnifica** *produces hips the size of crabapples.* **Delicata** *and* **eglantaria** *are also fine. After enjoying a trip to the Maine coast, the new Maine cook often returns with pockets bulging to produce rose hip jelly.*

Helen Nearing's Roseberry Jam

1 quart large, cultivated
    blueberries
1 1/2 cups rose hips,
    halved and seeded
2 cups honey
1 small, well-washed raw
    potato, skin and all
1 small, well-washed
    green apple, skin and
    all

1. Place blueberries, rose hips, and honey in a large enameled saucepan over moderate heat. Stir.
2. While this is coming to a boil, shred potato and apple. Then add to the boiling mixture.
3. When you get three reluctant drops from a wooden spoon, put into jars and store (as previously described).

Helen Nearing, of **Living the Good Life** *fame, is a lovely lady with a down-to-earth attitude common to Maine. I once asked her how to make rose hip jam. Here is her response. You might prefer to substitute one cup maple syrup for the honey.*

Pickles

Fall is the time for jellying berries, bringing in the last of the garden produce, canning vegetables, and pickling the rest!

Capers are a condiment usually obtained commercially. They can easily be made at home, as Maine grandmothers used to.

Pickled Onions

(about 2 pints)

4 heaping cups small onions
2 quarts boiling water
5 cups water
1/2 cup canning salt
1 tablespoon mixed pickling spices
3 cups white distilled vinegar

1. Place onions in a wire basket and lower into two quarts boiling water. Simmer one to two minutes, or just long enough to let skins slip off easily when cool. Rinse in a bowl of cold water.
2. Cut off root and leaf ends and slip off skins. (This is a good method to remember come Thanksgiving with all those tiny, white, boiled onions to peel.) Rinse again. Place in a bowl with five cups water and salt. Stir till salt is dissolved and allow to rest forty-eight hours, covered.
3. Repeat, if you fancy really salty pickles;

otherwise, drain well. Dry by placing on a towel in a single layer and rolling them around with your hands under another towel (or a corner of the original).
4. Bring pickling spices and vinegar to a boil. Sterilize three twelve-ounce jelly jars or two pint canning jars. (To sterilize, bring jars to a boil in a large kettle and lift out with a wooden spoon or tongs.) Divide onions equally between jars, using a slotted spoon. Pour hot pickling juice over onions in each jar, dividing spices between them, to within a half-inch of top.
5. Wipe rims. Adjust lids and bands, and process in a boiling water bath for ten minutes (see **Processing by the Boiling Water Bath Method**). Remove with tongs and set on towel to cool. Wash jars and store in cellar or other cool, dark place.

Note: For variation, add one small, washed grape leaf, one small head dill, and six peppercorns per jar.

Nasturtium Bud Capers

(3 half-pint jars)

3 cups nasturtium seed pods
1/2 cup canning salt
2 quarts water
about 1 quart distilled white vinegar

1. Pick seed pods when green and fat (but not yellow).
2. In a glass jar combine salt with one quart water. Add rinsed seed pods. If they float, weight them down with anything handy, but don't use metal. Let rest twenty-four hours.
3. Remove seed pods from »

brine and place in remaining quart of cold water to soak for an hour. Drain.

4. Place capers in an enameled saucepan and add enough vinegar to cover. Bring to a boil. (Experiment with herbal vinegars.)

5. Place capers into hot, sterilized half-pint jars. Pour boiling vinegar to within a half-inch of the top. Seal and process in a boiling water bath (see **Processing by the Boiling Water Bath Method**) for ten minutes. Allow to stand at least six weeks before using.

Note: For variation, add one clove garlic to each jar.

Classic Pickled Beets

(2 quarts)

about 8 cups sliced 6-inch-long beets
4 cups 5% vinegar, such as cider or white distilled vinegar
4 cups white refined sugar
2 teaspoons canning salt

1. Cut off stems, leaving about one inch to prevent bleeding while cooking. Wash, being careful not to scratch. Pop into a huge kettle half-full of boiling water. Add boiling water to cover, as necessary. Boil over medium heat until skins slip off easily, maybe forty minutes, depending on size. (Test by placing a beet into cold water until you can handle it. Then push skin with fingers. It slides off if beet is done. Poke with a fork–beet should be firm but not hard.)

2. Place beets in a sink of cold water and, when cool, push off skins. Roots and stems can usually be pushed off with fingers as well. If not, trim with a knife. Remove *any* blemishes. Drain skinned beets in a colander. (They'll stain wooden shelves.)

3. Make a syrup of vinegar and sugar. Mix and heat to boiling. (Remember that white vinegar makes pickles more piquant.)

4. Slice beets into wide-mouth quart canning jars, sterilized by washing carefully in hot soapy water and rinsing with boiling water. (Since beets will be processed for thirty minutes, a more thorough sterilization isn't necessary.) Leave a bit more than half an inch headroom.

5. Add one teaspoon salt to each jar. Cover with boiling syrup, leaving a half-inch headroom. Adjust lids, and process in a boiling water bath (212°F) for thirty minutes. Start counting after water boils once jars are in it. Remove jars.

*Classically pickled is the only way my family really likes beets during the winter. They're absolutely necessary for anyone living where December, January, and February are totally white and very, very cold. My favorite variety for pickling is the long, cylindrical **Formanova**.*

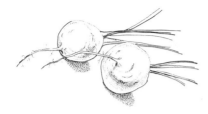

Complete seals if necessary. Label, with date.

Note: In case you discover, halfway through the winter, that you still have cellar-tubs of beets but your pickled beets are gone, pickle what remains, if still firm.

Pickled Pink Eggs
(one 2-quart jar)

When eating pickled beets, save the syrup and make pickled eggs with it. It's one very good way to keep extra eggs if you happen to have your own hens, as most every Mainer originally did. When egg production slows with winter, you can turn to your jars.

1 dozen small or
    medium-sized eggs
juice from 1 (or more)
    quart jars of pickled
    beets
1 medium-sized onion,
    sliced
1 teaspoon pickling spice
1 clove garlic (optional)
boiling vinegar, as
    necessary

1. Hard-boil eggs by placing in cool water, bringing to a boil, then allowing to sit for at least ten minutes. (Use eggs that are at least *three days old*. Young eggs are harder to peel, and their yolks tend to turn green.)
2. When cooked, crack shells under cold running water, allow to cool, and peel.
3. In an enameled saucepan bring pickling juice, onion, garlic, and spices to a boil.
4. Arrange eggs in a glass jar and pour pickling juice and onions over them. Cover eggs by adding boiling vinegar as necessary. Store, covered, in a cool place.

Red Cabbage Sauerkraut
(about 3 quarts)

Waldoboro is Maine's sauerkraut capital—come October the scent of kraut is heavy in the air. Red cabbage is my favorite because it's so pretty, tasty, and usually ready early.

about 7 pounds firm
    red cabbage heads
5 tablespoons canning
    salt
4-5 juniper berries
5-6 black peppercorns
buttermilk, as needed

1. Remove outer leaves, reserving some perfect ones. Wash each head, quarter, and cut out core. Pat quarters very dry, then shred or slice very thin into a large pottery or stainless-steel bowl. You should have six pounds shredded cabbage.
2. Sprinkle salt over cabbage and knead with hands until juices begin to show.

»

3. In a scrupulously clean two-gallon, ceramic crock, pack a firm layer of cabbage about two inches deep. Sprinkle with juniper berries and peppercorns. Press down firmly and sprinkle with one cup buttermilk. Repeat until cabbage is used up.

4. Cover with reserved leaves (washed and drained). Place a square of clean cheesecloth on top and tuck edges down against sides of crock. Place a plate or a clean, round wooden board (encased in a layer of paraffin) on top of cheesecloth. The plate or board will have to be chosen or made to fit just inside the crock.

5. Weight so that plate remains in exactly the right position to allow *juices to rise up and completely cover cabbage but not to rise over the plate*. This ensures that no air reaches the kraut. An alternative is to place a plastic bag atop the kraut and pour in two or more quarts of water. Use double bags to prevent leakage.

6. Cover entire crock with a fine-woven cloth to keep out dust and other unfriendlies. Set aside to ferment in a cool spot (65-72°F) for about two weeks. Check liquid level daily and adjust weight as necessary.

7. When fermenting has stopped and there is no more bubbling, you may freeze or can kraut. To can, heat to simmering, not boiling; fill clean, hot canning jars to within a half-inch of top; add juice to the same level; and process fifteen minutes for pints and twenty minutes for quarts, in a boiling water bath.

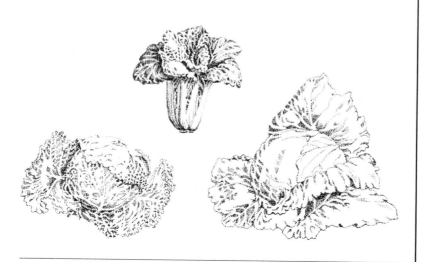

Pickled Mushrooms

(4 pints)

2 pounds (about 6 cups)
very small, tightly
closed, button
mushrooms
2 cups white distilled
vinegar
1/4 teaspoon dried
rosemary leaves,
finely ground
2 bay leaves
about 5 cups extra-virgin
olive oil
2 teaspoons sea salt
7-8 grindings of black
pepper
6 cloves minced garlic
1 teaspoon dried
oregano, thoroughly
crumbled between
your palms
1/8 teaspoon finely
ground rosemary
crumbled bay leaf

1. Wipe mushrooms with a
damp cloth or rinse quickly
to remove any trace of dirt.
2. In a large enameled
saucepan heat vinegar,
rosemary, and bay leaves.
Add mushrooms when the
vinegar comes to a boil and
simmer slowly, stirring
occasionally, three to five
minutes, or until heated
through but not limp. Drain
and discard liquid, bay leaf,
and rosemary leaves. Place
mushrooms in a clean towel
and press carefully to
remove excess moisture.
Spread out on another towel
to dry thoroughly. Cool to
room temperature.
3. Meanwhile, sterilize a
single half-gallon jar by
boiling fifteen minutes in
water to cover. Sterilize lid
as well. (You may also use
four pint jars.)
4. Place cooled mushrooms
in a large glass or ceramic
bowl and add about one-
quarter cup olive oil to coat
them; add salt, pepper, garlic,
oregano, and one-eighth
teaspoon rosemary. Toss
gently.
5. Using tongs, remove jar(s)
from kettle and place on a
towel. If using pint jars, pack
mushrooms to within one
and a half inches of top. Add
a bit of crumbled bay leaf to
each jar. Fill almost to top
with olive oil. Screw on
sterilized lid(s). Store in
refrigerator or a cool cellar.

Dilled Beans

(7 pints)

4 pounds young string
beans
21 peppercorns
14 tablespoons dill seed
OR 7 dill heads
1 3/4 teaspoons cayenne
pepper (optional)
7 cloves garlic, peeled
and rinsed (optional)
3 cups white distilled
vinegar
3 cups 5% cider vinegar
6 cups water
2/3 cup canning salt »

165

1. Pick and wash four pounds tender, young beans and remove stem end.
2. Pack, standing up, into seven pint jars, carefully washed. (Use a dishwasher or sterilize by boiling.)
3. To each jar, add three peppercorns, four tablespoons dill seed or one dill head, a quarter teaspoon of cayenne, and a clove of garlic.

4. In a large saucepan combine vinegars, water, and salt. Heat to boiling.
5. Pour over beans to within a half-inch of rim.
6. Dislodge and remove air bubbles by poking into each jar with a chopstick.
7. Place hot lids and bands on jars.
8. Process in a boiling water bath for ten minutes.

Processing by the Boiling Water Bath Method

Fill a large pot half-full of water and bring to a boil. Boil an extra pot of water to use as needed.

Wipe jar rims and adjust lids per directions from your jar company. Place hot, filled jars on rack and submerge in pot, making certain water covers jars by at least an inch. Add boiling water if necessary.

Start to count processing time from when water comes to a boil the second time after jars have been added. Remove jars, complete seals if necessary, and allow to cool. Wipe with a solution of two tablespoons bleach to one quart water and store in a cool, dark place.

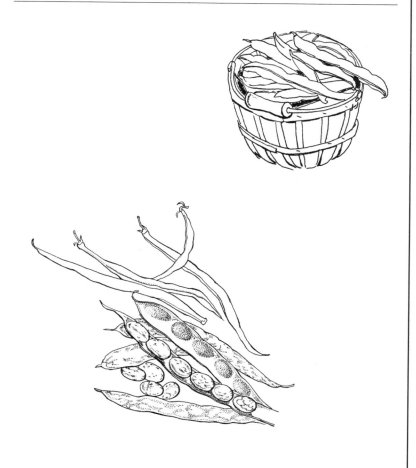

Apples

Maine is a storehouse of apple varieties old and new. Every fall my children relish going to an orchard and picking three bushels of "keepers," usually gorgeous Red Delicious, Northern Spy, and Ida Red (my favorite).

We also gather wild apples, driving country roads where old orchards once stood, finding lanes where wild apple trees bend loaded to the ground. Then we take them to the nearest cider shed to be pressed. Cider, frozen in leftover plastic milk bottles and stored in our big freezer, keeps the children happy for months. (You can add sugarless seltzer water for fizz.)

Apples pair well with cheese. Sliced apples, dipped quickly into lemon juice to prevent browning, are wonderful served with rocquefort, camembert, brie, any of the bleu cheeses, cheddar, or edam. Serving stilton cheese and walnuts with apples is a classic dessert.

Flamed Apples
(6 servings)

6 fresh apples
juice of 1 freshly
  squeezed lemon
cinnamon
12 tablespoons calvados
  or whiskey

1. Wash apples, peel, slice, and dip into freshly squeezed lemon juice a moment to prevent browning. Pile into individual ceramic serving dishes. Sprinkle lightly with cinnamon.
2. Warm two tablespoons calvados or whiskey gently in a ladle, set it aflame, and pour over one serving of fruit. Repeat for each serving.

Brandied Baked Apples
(6 servings)

6 huge Northern Spy
  apples
6 tablespoons raisins
6 tablespoons sunflower
  seeds
freshly grated nutmeg
cinnamon
1/2 cup brandy
2 cups apple juice or
  water

1. Wash apples well and core carefully with a melon ball scoop, leaving enough flesh at the bottom to prevent leakage during baking.
2. Place one tablespoon raisins and one tablespoon sunflower seeds in each hollow and add a dash of cinnamon and nutmeg plus one tablespoon of brandy per apple.
3. Place apples in a shallow lasagna or cake pan and add apple juice or water and remaining brandy.
4. Place in a 350°F oven and bake about thirty minutes, or until soft but not mushy.

Serve as is or topped with any of the whipped toppings such as **Crème Fraîche** or **Whipped Cottage Cheese**. (The extra sweet **Maple Sugar Topping** would also be delicious.)

Irish Colcannon

(4 servings)

1 pound kale
2 large potatoes
2 small leeks or 1
    medium-sized onion
1 cup milk
sea salt to taste
freshly ground black pepper
a dash of nutmeg
1 lemon quarter per
    person

1. Pick and wash kale. Strip leaves from stalks.
2. Simmer in one inch boiling, slightly salted water till tender but not overcooked (from twenty to thirty minutes). Drain thoroughly in a colander and chop fine.
3. In a separate saucepan cook potatoes till tender.
4. Slice leeks or onion and simmer in one cup milk till just tender.
5. When potatoes are done, drain, peel, and mash. Add salt, pepper, and nutmeg to taste. Stir in cooked leeks or onion, and milk, adding more milk (or yogurt) if necessary. Stir in cooked, finely chopped kale. Heat through.

Serve with lemon quarters, fish (especially smoked), carrots, and fresh whole-grain bread.

Kale

Kale is a cold-hardy, non-"heading" member of the cabbage family, particularly valuable for Maine gardens because frost heightens flavor, and in Maine frost comes early. Extremely valuable nutritionally, it can be wintered in cold frames to lengthen the "green season."

My Irish great-grandmother said that fairies ride kale stalks at the dark of the moon. Surely they do. The Irish also know how to cook it.

Curried Kale

(4 servings)

1/2 pound kale
3 tablespoons sunflower
    seed oil
1 or 2 cloves garlic,
    minced
1 tablespoon freshly
    grated ginger root
1 teaspoon cumin
2 teaspoons turmeric
3 teaspoons coriander
1/2 teaspoon sea salt
freshly ground black
    pepper
1 medium-sized onion,
    diced
1/2 cup water
1/2 teaspoon Simple
    Garam Masala

1. Pick and wash kale. Strip leaves off stalks, and chop fine.
2. Heat oil in wok, then sauté garlic, ginger, spices, and salt about one minute. Don't burn.
3. Add onion, and fry till limp. Then add chopped kale, toss well, add water, cover, and steam fifteen minutes.
4. Stir in **Simple Garam Masala**, and simmer five minutes longer or until tender.

Serve hot as a side dish to any curry dinner with plenty of a cooked whole grain and **Chupattis**.

Kohlrabi

Kohlrabi looks like an extraterrestrial with a big bulb growing above ground and leaves sprouting from it. When I first planted kohlrabi I expected something rather like a turnip—but, though related, it isn't. With a sleek outside (my favorite is purple), a smooth inside, and very edible leaves, it's best instantly peeled, then sliced or julienned for salad. Of course it may be cooked—but only briefly.

*Don't miss the fun of being the first to present it to some wide-eyed youngster who's sure to demand, "What's that **thing**?"*

Kohlrabi in Hot Pepper Sauce
(4 servings)

3 (2-inch) kohlrabi
1/2 cup Tarragon
    Vinegar
2 tablespoons maple
    syrup
1 teaspoon minced fresh
    ginger root
6-8 drops hot pepper
    sauce
1/2 heaping teaspoon sea
    salt
freshly ground black
    pepper
1/4 cup diced red bell
    pepper

1. Peel kohlrabi thinly, removing just the hard outer skin. Cut into thick matchsticks about a quarter-inch thick. Steam till tender in a colander set over a pot of boiling water, about five minutes.
2. In a small bowl combine vinegar, honey, ginger, hot pepper sauce, salt, and black pepper. Add cooked kohlrabi and toss well.
3. Chill, covered, for at least two hours in the refrigerator, turning occasionally.
4. Add bell pepper just before serving.

Serve scooped over lettuce leaves, sprinkled with toasted sesame seeds.

Red Cabbage Delicious
(6-8 servings)

1 green bell pepper,
    diced
1 small head red cabbage,
    shredded
1/2 cup water
sea salt to taste
freshly ground black
    pepper to taste
1/2 cup cider vinegar
1/2 cup Date Butter OR 1/4
    cup maple syrup
1 tablespoon celery seed
1 tablespoon white
    mustard seed

1. In a large enameled skillet simmer bell pepper and cabbage in water for a half hour.
2. Add salt and black pepper to taste, vinegar, sweetening, celery seed, and mustard seed. Cook three hours, adding more water as necessary to prevent sticking.

Serve with tossed green salad, potatoes or whole-grain fresh bread, fish, poultry, or baked beans.

Stuffed Cabbage Rolls: The Basics

1. Preparing leaves:
Cut about an inch of the core out of the cabbage, and stick a long-handled fork firmly into it. Hold head under boiling water about two or three minutes to loosen three or four leaves at a time. Use a sharp knife to further loosen leaf bases as necessary, and place leaves in a large bowl as you remove them. When cool enough to handle, remove part of the ribs, to make them supple. Cut large leaves in half lengthwise.

2. Filling and rolling:
Place about one tablespoon stuffing near core end of leaf. Roll it up a little, turn in sides, and finish rolling so as to make filled envelopes. Place envelopes in a buttered, heavy casserole side by side and then layer.

My Lebanese friend, Sadie, makes a gorgeous cabbage roll tasting of mint and cinnamon.

Sadie's Cabbage Rolls

(about 50 rolls)

cabbage leaves from one large head
stuffing of choice (see below)
3-6 cups seasoned stock
sea salt
freshly ground black pepper
1/4 teaspoon cinnamon
3-4 garlic cloves
1-2 tablespoons minced fresh mint leaves

1. Prepare cabbage leaves as described above.
2. Fill with a stuffing such as that for **Stuffed Swiss Chard, Sadie's Stuffed Grape Leaves,** or **Soybean Sausages.** Roll up and place in a casserole (as above). Weight with a plate.
3. Pour on stock seasoned with sea salt, freshly ground black pepper, a dash of cinnamon, and smashed garlic cloves. See that it just covers the rolls and doesn't come over the edges of the plate.
4. Bring to a boil, reduce heat to low, and simmer forty minutes. Then add a heaping tablespoon of dried mint leaves. Tilt kettle so broth goes all around leaves. Add some extra mint on top. Simmer five more minutes. Remove rolls with a spatula, and serve with yogurt, lemon quarters, rice, other whole grain or pasta, tossed salad, and **Pocket Bread**.

Note: Use tomato sauce in place of stock, seasoned with minced garlic, sea salt, black pepper, and a little cinnamon.

Cabbage
Cabbage has been a mainstay of Mainers for generations. From early to late varieties, this common vegetable provides us with a good abundance of vital nutrients. Of the many varieties, I most enjoy Primax for early eating, Ruby Perfection for glorious purple color, and big Danish Ballheads for keeping. The best method of wintering is to bed cabbages underneath high piles of hay directly in the garden. But they also store beautifully in a cool root cellar, well-wrapped in newspaper. Besides providing wonderful mid-winter salad munching (often simply dressed with a flavorful vinegar such as Japanese umeboshi) cooked cabbage is delicious.

Cole Slaw

Cole slaw is an all-time favorite. It was always served with baked beans and brown bread on Saturday nights during my childhood, and usually dressed with mayonnaise. The dry crispness of cabbage seems to need that oily taste. I now extend the dressing with yogurt for leaner results.

Brussels Sprouts

Like cabbage, brussels sprouts come along with fall, tolerating frosts and cold better than most other vegetables except kale. And like cabbage they are high in vitamins. My English husband couldn't endure Christmas without a dishful!

Simple Brussels Sprouts

Sprouts mature fastest at the bottom of stalks so pick there first. When picked, trim stems and pull off any loose outer leaves. To cook, simply pop into lightly salted boiling water and simmer, covered, about fifteen minutes or until fork tender. When done, plunge sprouts into cold water to stop cooking.

New Downeast Cole Slaw

(6-8 servings)

1 recipe My Favorite
    Salad Dressing
1 cup yogurt
1 small head of green
    cabbage, shredded fine
2 large carrots, shredded
1 small onion, diced
1 cup rinsed raisins
    (plumped, if you like, in
    sherry for a half hour)
1 teaspoon caraway seeds

1 tablespoon finely
    chopped parsley

1. Prepare **My Favorite Salad Dressing** and mix with thick, fresh yogurt.
2. In a large bowl combine remaining ingredients.
3. Add enough of the salad dressing/yogurt mixture to allow all ingredients to cling together nicely. Sprinkle with more parsley, and serve with **Baked Beans** and **Brown Bread** on Saturday night.

Hot Brussels Sprouts

(4-6 servings)

4 cups brussels sprouts,
    rinsed and trimmed
2 tablespoons extra-
    virgin olive oil
2 whole cloves garlic,
    smashed
2 tablespoons freshly
    squeezed lemon juice
sea salt
freshly ground black
    pepper
1 tablespoon fresh
    chervil, parsley, or
    tarragon, minced

1. Pop sprouts in lightly salted boiling water, then simmer, covered, until fork tender and drain. *Don't rinse with cold water.* Place in a heat-proof serving dish.
2. Heat oil in an enameled skillet. Brown garlic slightly and add lemon juice. Stir well and pour over tender sprouts.
3. Sprinkle with salt, pepper, and herb of choice.

Remove garlic and serve at once as a side dish to any meal.

Seasoned Sprouts

Cook, then halve or quarter each sprout and toss with sunflower seeds. Pour on any vinaigrette or a dressing of **Laban** seasoned with lemon juice, a dash of hot pepper sauce, and nutmeg. Serve warm or cool.

Whole-Grain Flours

As that cozy season of fall arrives, bread making, **real** bread making, comes to mind. No more chupattis or baking powder quickbreads. Fall is definitely the time for high-rising, yeasted beauties.

In the following dictionary of grains I have emphasized those easily obtainable as flour. For cooking these grains in their whole form, please refer to the Index.

Amaranth: *Amaranth grows in Maine. According to the Rodale company of Emmaus, Pennsylvania, which is bringing amaranth to public attention, it was a significant crop in parts of both the old world and the new for centuries. Johnny's Selected Seeds of Albion, Maine, has been researching it in association with Rodale.*

Although amaranth flour lacks gluten and some folks don't enjoy its earthy flavor, it's fine for flat breads like chupattis or tortillas. It mixes well with other flours for yeast breads, and is also good for pancakes, muffins, and quickbreads using baking powder. Combining amaranth with cornmeal yields a complete protein. Even its leaves can be cooked like spinach!

Barley: *Barley is easily grown in Maine. It can be purchased whole or as flour. The pearled type is similar to white rice–lower in nutrients. Brown whole barley has only the outer layer removed. It can be cooked like rice and, like brown rice, takes longer.*

It's great in soups, pilafs, and stuffings and can be added whole to breads.

Lightly toasted, its flour is nutty, but being low in gluten it's not good for making raised breads. Cakelike loaves are possible, and barley adds sweetness to wheat breads.

Buckwheat: *Buckwheat is an old Maine favorite. Surprisingly a member of the rhubarb family, it's actually not a grain at all. The three-cornered seeds, called groats, can be removed from their hulls only with a special buckwheat huller. Sometimes called kasha when toasted, it's wonderful in pilafs, stuffings, and loaves. Groats can be purchased light (untoasted) or dark (toasted). Unhulled groats are good for sprouting.*

Buckwheat flour can be made into noodles (often called soba noodles) and pancakes. Dark flour contains the hull; light flour has lost it.

Buckwheat is high in vital nutrients and so hardy that U.S. farmers seldom have to spray it with pesticides. In Maine a special variety called tartary is grown in the St. John River Valley.

Corn: *Corn was here when the explorers landed. Stoneground cornmeal, complete with germ, makes great quickbreads and cornmeal-mush dishes (see* **Polenta**). *Most commecially milled cornmeal is degermed and therefore less nutritious. Corn has always been a Maine staple.*

To avoid a grainy texture when adding cornmeal to a bread recipe, mix cornmeal with cold liquid, bring to a boil, and cool before further mixing.

Corn is wonderful as a vegetable, as flour, and as grits. Popcorn is a special variety grown for its popping qualities. Cornstarch is used as a thickener for gravies, sauces, and soups.

Millet: *Millet flour is low in gluten but good for flatbreads such as chupattis. Toasting before milling brings out a nutty flavor. The grain is alkaline and nutritionally rich.*

Whole millet is delicate, tiny, light, and very digestible. It's good cooked rather like rice for breakfast or dinner, and it cooks faster.

Oats: *Oats grow well in Maine. Seldom made into flour, they are more commonly cut and rolled and then they combine well with other grains for bread. (Substitute for up to a third of the flour in a wheat-bread recipe.) Oats contain an antioxidant which keeps bread fresh longer.*

Steel-cut oats are uncooked. They're chopped with rotary-type cutters and may then be rolled. Rolled oats are lightly steamed and then flattened.

Oats can be purchased whole or cracked, and make good cereal, as well as being a delicious component of cookies, casseroles, and soups as well as burgers and loaves. (See Index for suggestions.)

Rye: *Rye thrives in Maine because it enjoys a cool climate. It can be bought both whole and flaked (like rolled oats). Rye flour has less gluten than wheat flour so rye bread is heavier. Dark rye flour contains more protein and other nutrients than the light or medium varieties. Rye is also cooked whole in soups, and rye flakes can be used like oatmeal in other dishes. With good reason, rye has long been considered an especially healthful grain.*

Note: Rye sometimes harbors a fungus when growing that causes the grains to swell up and become black. The fungus contains a toxin called ergot which in the past has caused epidemics of a nervous disorder, St. Anthony's Fire.

Triticale: *Triticale is a grain hardly known in Maine, probably because it's so young in an evolutionary sense. It's a hybrid of wheat and rye, and is probably higher in protein than either parent–a balanced protein close to that in eggs and meat. Though lower in gluten than wheat, it makes a very nice raised bread, but its gluten is worn out by too much kneading. Whole, it can substitute for rice with longer cooking. It can be purchased at most health food stores.*

Wheat: *Wheat grows well in Maine. It produces the only flour with enough gluten in it to make beautifully risen bread. Next to oats, it contains the largest amount of usable protein of all grains, but it's low in one amino acid called lysine, a so-called "limiting acid" whose absence prevents the other eight essential amino acids from being fully*

used by the body. Combined with beans or flours which contain lysine, however, the protein of whole-wheat flour is complete.

I recommend adding about fifteen percent by weight of a legume flour (such as soy) to wheat. It not only increases usable protein but helps loaves retain moisture. Bean flour can be made by grinding about a quarter-cup of beans at a time in a heavy grain mill. Garbanzo bean flour, very popular in India, and lima bean flour offer additional leavening action. Soy beans are oily and gum up the best mills, so it's wise to purchase soy flour. Blend it with the liquids when making bread in a proportion of two tablespoons per seven-eighths of a cup flour. If you like it a lot, you can add up to twenty percent of total flour weight. Soy flour causes heavy browning, so baking temperature can be reduced about twenty-five degrees. You can also add up to thirty percent **peanut flour** *or fifteen percent* **sunflower seed flour**, *both easily ground in your blender.*

The easiest way to combine wheat with legumes, of course, is simply by serving whole-wheat bread with peanut butter; or **Pocket Bread** *with* **Hummus** *(a garbanzo bean and tahini spread).*

I also like to include lecithin granules. Lecithin, extracted from soybeans, is an emulsifying, antispattering, and stabilizing agent, and is a natural preservative. It gives bread a finer, less crumbly texture.

Whole-wheat berries keep fresh for many years. They

can be cooked like rice, using more water, or sprouted. They can also be purchased flaked.

Although most Americans will have no trouble, whole grains including wheat pose a problem for ill-nourished people. Bran, that outer covering of wheat and rice kernels, contains phytic acid, a phosphorus compound, which combines with essential minerals such as calcium, iron, and zinc to carry them out of the body. The refining of flour (and the polishing of rice) may remove this bran, but it also removes many other vital nutrients as well. Therefore, refined flour has some advantages over whole-grain flour which retains much of the phytic acid. The ideal wheat flour is one known in India for centuries: some of the bran is removed, about ten percent of the whole grain, but the germ and all other nutrients remain intact.

The best bread flour is milled from **hard wheat,** *either red winter or red spring. It's higher in protein and gluten than soft wheats, and the amount increases in northern latitudes.* **Spring wheat,** *planted in spring and harvested in fall, can either be hard or soft.*

Storing Whole Grains
Buying grains in bulk is a traditional method for saving money, and they are easy to store. Whole-grain flours should be stored in the refrigerator or freezer, as their oils quickly become rancid. Ideal safe storage conditions are a temperature of 40° F and a moisture content of twelve percent or less. The best

»

method is to store whole berries and grind them only when you need flour.

Bulgur wheat and pasta are traditional methods of grain storage which need no refrigeration. But even precooking does not ensure protection against insects. To protect grain from bugs or to kill them, either freeze it at 0°F for four days, or heat it in a 130-150°F oven for twenty to thirty minutes, spreading it no more than three-quarters of an inch deep and leaving the oven door slightly ajar to prevent overheating. Stir occasionally to ensure even exposure to heat. Store in airtight containers such as tightly capped jars, cans, or plastic bags.

Sprouted grain will spoil in a week or so. The best method of saving what is left is to dry it in the oven.

Breads

Whole-grain bread, to many Maine cooks, is one splendid aspect of a high-quality lifestyle. Bread not only smells good and raises the spirits of everyone around, but tastes superb and is grand for your body.

A few pointers about baking bread with whole grains, though:
1. Don't knead "till satiny and elastic." Whole-grain dough remains sticky, and does not become satiny and elastic as will a refined white-flour dough. If you were to add enough flour to make your dough nonsticky, you would end up with hard, tough bread. Greasing with butter (not oiling) one's hands often solves the problem.

2. Do flour your bread board with unbleached white flour. Kneading is definitely easier and you don't incorporate as much flour into the dough as you would by flouring the board with whole-grain flour (see **Bread Kneading**).
3. The best flours for bread-making are the hard, red spring wheats because they're high in gluten, which causes the bread to rise and hold its shape. They contain slightly more protein than good winter wheats. Soft wheats can be either spring- or winter-grown, contain weak gluten, and are good for pastries, cookies, and so on. Pastry wheats are lower in protein but have a light starchy core good for pie crusts, cakes, and similar goods.
4. **Do** be choosey about your baking pans. My favorite measures nine by four by six inches— an old black tin once owned by my great-great-grandmother. It bakes bread evenly and perfectly every time. Never wash your pans—grease well each time with butter or a mixture of oil and liquid lecithin. Pans will season as you bake.

Fats for Baking Pans
Baked goods tend to stick to oiled pans but not to greased ones. Therefore, I suggest using butter. I recommend it because the flavor is unsurpassed and it is a natural grease. If the use of highly saturated, cholesterol-rich butter disturbs you, however, combine liquid lecithin half-and-half with sunflower seed oil and coat your pans with that. Store in the refrigerator.

Yeasts
Yeasts of a different variety from ordinary baking yeast are often used to enhance the nutrition of bread (and other foods). Primary and brewer's yeasts, however, are usually made with the same kind of organism: **Saccharomyces cerevisiae**. All the yeasts are high in B vitamins.

Primary yeast is grown for its own sake (in other words, not as a by-product), usually on a base of molasses.
Nutritional yeast is a valuable primary yeast with a cheesey flavor grown with **Saccharomyces cerevisiae** in a molasses solution. It contains all the essential amino acids.
Baker's yeast is a type of primary yeast used as a leavening agent in bread-making.
Torula yeast is a type of primary yeast made with another organism: **Candida utilis**. It can be grown on industrial wastes (as in paper-making). Torula contains less chromium than brewer's yeast and other primary yeasts.
Brewer's yeast is recovered as a by-product of the brewing process.

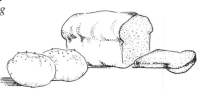

Much wonderful bread takes kneading. But have you ever done it with a three-year-old asking, "Why, Mama?" and grabbing at the dough until you have none left, while a two-year-old is hanging around both your legs doing the same thing? This unkneaded bread recipe is a response to all those harried moms who must turn out gastronomic delights without the chef's most essential ingredient—the opportunity to think one thought through. This moister dough takes longer to bake and will not rise so high.

Busytime Bread

(3 loaves)

6 cups vegetable stock or whey
6 tablespoons dry baking yeast
6 tablespoons Date or Raisin Butter (optional) OR 3 tablespoons maple syrup
9 cups whole-wheat bread flour
3 teaspoons sea salt (optional) and/or 3 teaspoons kelp powder
3 tablespoons dried, crumbled herb of choice
2 1/4 cups sunflower seeds
3/4 cup wheat germ
3/4 cup non-instant low-fat powdered milk
6 tablespoons brewer's or nutritional yeast

1. Warm stock to about 105-115°F. (Use bean-simmering stock, whey from making chenna, cottage cheese, or yogurt, vegetable liquor or just plain water.) Divide between three medium-large mixing bowls.
2. Add two tablespoons baking yeast and two tablespoons fruit butter or one tablespoon maple syrup to each bowl. Allow yeast to begin bubbling while you measure out flour.
3. Add two cups flour to each bowl and beat. Use an electric mixer if you have one—it's easier on the arms and quicker.
4. Add one teaspoon salt (if desired) and one tablespoon dried herbs to each bowl. Mix again.
5. To each bowl add three-quarters of a cup each of whole wheat flour and sunflower seeds, a quarter cup each of wheat germ and powdered milk, and two tablespoons brewer's or nutritional yeast. Use part rye flour or any cereal or cooked grain, if desired. Mix well by hand. This dough is going to be much moister than kneaded bread, so don't be upset by its looks. Set in a warm place, free of drafts, covered with a damp towel. Allow to rise about forty-five minutes.
6. Preheat oven to 375°F. Using a spoon, mix each bowl's dough around as much as your arms can stand, then pour into baking pans. Bake for sixty to eighty minutes. Test with a toothpick (if pulled out dry, it's done) or by removing bread from pan and knocking the bottom (a good hollow "thunk" means done). Return to oven, in or out of pan, if necessary.

The following recipe makes two loaves which are very high in usable protein. If you lack any of the flours, substitute what you wish or double up on some. If you prefer to use fresh yeast, the best water temperature is 80-85°F.

Many-Grain Bread

(2 loaves)

1/3 cup pitted, chopped dates or chopped raisins OR 1/4 cup maple syrup
1 cup warm (105-115°F) water, stock, or whey from making yogurt, cheese, or tofu
1 tablespoon dry baking yeast
1 1/2 cups warm water (110-115°F)
1 egg
4 cups whole-wheat flour
1 tablespoon lecithin granules (optional)
1 teaspoon sea salt or 1 teaspoon kelp flakes
2 tablespoons sesame seeds (rinsed and drained well)
1/4 cup rolled oats
1/4 cup cornmeal
1/2 cup rye flour
1/4 cup soy flour
1 tablespoon brewer's or nutritional yeast (optional)
1-2 cups unbleached white flour for kneading
oil, milk, or beaten egg for glazing bread

1. Purée dates or maple syrup in one cup warm liquid in your electric blender. Add baking yeast. Allow to work and bubble.
2. Add one and a half more cups warm water and blend with egg.
3. Pour into a large bowl and mix in two cups whole-wheat flour and remaining ingredients except white flour for kneading and oil/milk/beaten egg for wash. Stir well. Set in a warm place to rise for thirty minutes. (A heating pad set at about 90°F often speeds up the process.)
4. Add one to two more cups whole-wheat flour and mix well again.
5. Pour one full cup of un-bleached white flour onto board and turn dough out directly onto it. Knead about ten minutes, adding more flour as necessary (usually one cup). When two cups of white flour have been incorporated, grease your hands with butter if they need greasing and continue kneading about five minutes to develop gluten.
6. Place in an oiled bowl in a warm place to rise till double in bulk, about forty minutes. Punch down. Let rise till double in bulk again (thirty to forty minutes), then form into loaves. Fill greased baking tins half full.
7. Brush top of each loaf with oil, milk, or an egg beaten with a little water. Let rise till nearly double,

Bread Kneading

"Kneading bread," someone once said to me, "is good for the soul"—and I do enjoy it. But it takes a knack which comes most easily from watching another do it. I remember with such joy those hours spent watching mother's hands and breathing the heavenly aroma of Saturday morning bakings.

*It's difficult to describe kneading, but let's just say that you turn your still-sticky dough out onto a thickly-floured bread board or marble slab (my choice), then gingerly flour it and push it around with both hands until you can really begin to knead—a process of leaning down into it, pushing it away with the heels of your palms, then pulling it forward with your fingers and pushing away again until all flour is incorporated and the mass is no longer sticky. Grease your hands if necessary and knead until you obtain something resembling a giant spongy puffball. Remember that whole-grain dough will remain slightly sticky, be far firmer than white-flour dough, and will **not** shine.*

about twenty minutes. Preheat oven to 425°F.

8. Bake for ten minutes at 425°F, then reduce heat to 375°F and bake for thirty to forty minutes. When done, remove loaves from pans and cool on their sides on a rack.

Yeasted Whole-Grain Banana Bread

(2 large loaves)

*Banana bread is usually a quickbread made with baking powder, but it can be yeasted as well. This recipe makes two **large** loaves. Using yeast to raise bread makes the nutrients more available and the bread more digestible, and baking powder is high in sodium unless you buy or make a special low-sodium variety.*

3 chopped, pitted dates OR 1 teaspoon maple syrup
1 cup lukewarm water (85-105°F)
1 tablespoon dry baking yeast
1 1/2 cups lukewarm water
2 bananas, mashed
2 eggs
1 cup non-instant low-fat powdered milk
1 tablespoon lecithin granules (optional)
1 tablespoon nutritional yeast
2 tablespoons cinnamon
6-8 cups whole-wheat bread flour
1 1/2 cups white flour for kneading
1 egg whisked with 1/4 cup water or milk, for brushing

1. Purée dates or maple syrup in one cup warm water in blender. Add baking yeast, blending at low speed. Pour into a large bowl.
2. Combine lukewarm water with bananas, eggs, milk powder, lecithin if desired, nutritional yeast, and cinnamon in blender. Add to yeast solution.
3. Add three cups whole-wheat flour to liquid mixture and stir in well to make a "sponge." Cover and allow it to rise one hour.
4. Fold in three more cups whole-wheat flour till dough comes away from sides of bowl. If you can't mix it all in well, don't worry. Turn out onto a floured board and knead, adding unbleached white flour as needed, for ten to fifteen minutes till dough is smooth. Grease your hands as necessary.
5. Place in a large greased bowl, cover with a moist cloth, and let rise fifty minutes in a warm, draft-free spot.
6. Punch down. Let rise forty minutes. Shape into loaves, place in pans and let rise a further twenty minutes. Brush loaves with egg wash and bake at 350°F for forty-five minutes to one hour. Remove from pans and cool loaves on their sides on a rack.

Note: Two apples may be substituted for the bananas for variation.

Cheese Bread

(3 large loaves)

3 cups milk (soy or
    dairy) or whey
1/3 cup Date Butter OR
    1/4 cup maple syrup
1 tablespoon sea salt OR 2
    teaspoons flaked kelp
2 tablespoons dry baking
    yeast
1 cup tepid water (85°F)
2 well-beaten eggs
3 cups finely shredded
    cheese
5 cups whole-wheat
    bread flour
5 cups unbleached white
    flour
3 tablespoons
    nutritional yeast
1-2 cups unbleached
    white flour for
    kneading

1. In a medium-sized
saucepan, scald milk (150°F)
and let cool to 90°F. If using
whey, simply heat to about
90°F. Add sweetener of
choice and salt or kelp.

2. In a large bowl dissolve
yeast in the water and let rest
ten minutes. Stir in the
cooled milk mixture.
3. Add eggs and cheese.
4. Sift three cups each whole-
wheat and unbleached flour
with nutritional yeast three
times, and beat into the
liquid mixture thoroughly
with a rotary beater. Sift
remaining flours together,
and beat in with a spoon.
5. When dough is really
stiff, turn out onto white-
floured board and knead
until springy and firm.
6. Place in an oiled bowl,
cover with a damp towel,
and let rise in a warm spot
till doubled in bulk. Punch
down. Shape into loaves
and half-fill well-greased
pans. Be sure dough touches
ends of pans as well as sides
to help support the rising
dough. Preheat oven to
375°F.
7. Let rise again till doubled
in bulk. Bake at 375°F until
bread tests done, about forty-
five minutes.

*Here is a light but
rich loaf which rises
nearly to the sky. If
you want to make
especially nutritious
bread, put a
tablespoon each of
soy flour, non-
instant, low-fat,
powdered milk, and
wheat germ in the
bottom of your
measuring cup, then
fill to the one-cup
mark with flour.*

Cuban Bread

(l small loaf)

1 cup warm water
1 tablespoon Date Butter
    OR maple syrup
1 tablespoon dry baking
    yeast
1 teaspoon sea salt
1/4 teaspoon powdered
    vitamin C, or about
    500 mg (optional)

1 tablespoon brewer's
    yeast (optional)
about 3 cups
    whole-wheat flour

1. In a medium-sized bowl
mix sweetener of choice with
warm water and baking
yeast, and stir till yeast
dissolves.

*A small loaf to go
with a meal is
always delightful,
especially if it's
rather like crisp
French bread.*

2. Add salt, vitamin C powder, and brewer's yeast if desired, and stir well.

3. Add whole-wheat flour, one cup at a time, stirring hard after each cup. Knead slightly with greased hands.

4. Place dough in a greased bowl and allow to rise till doubled in bulk, one to one and a half hours. You can set the bowl into a pan of hot water to speed up this rising.

5. Knead well. Roll dough back and forth to make a long, narrow log, or make a rectangle and roll up tightly, lengthwise, sealing seam and ends by pinching. Place on a cookie sheet and allow to rest five minutes, covered with a dry towel. With a very sharp knife, slash loaf diagonally three times, about a quarter-inch deep, before baking.

6. Place in a *cold* oven. To make a very crusty crust, put a pan of hot water on the bottom of the oven. Set heat at 400°F. Bake till medium-brown, about thirty minutes, and oil the crust if you like.

Note: For variation, after adding two cups flour, mix in about three-quarters of a cup grated cheese. Add more flour or water as necessary for correct kneading texture.

Irish Soda Bread

(1 loaf)

For Irish Soda Bread variations, add one cup currants or raisins to dry ingredients. Or omit cardamom and substitute one teaspoon crushed caraway seeds.

**2 cups whole-wheat
    bread flour**
1/2 teaspoon sea salt
1 teaspoon baking soda
**1/8 teaspoon ground
    cardamom (optional)**
**2 heaping tablespoons
    nutritional yeast**
1 egg, lightly beaten
**1 cup yogurt thinned to
    cream consistency OR
    buttermilk OR milk
    soured for a half
    hour with 1
    tablespoon vinegar**

1. Sift all the dry ingredients into a medium-sized bowl and pour any sifted-out bran back into the bowl.

2. In a smaller bowl beat together the wet ingredients. Add gradually to the dry. (This will look rather like yeast-bread dough.) Blend with hands to work all the flour in. If too dry, add a little buttermilk; if too wet, more flour.

3. Knead on a floured board for about five minutes. Shape into a flat, round loaf about an inch-and-a-half thick and place on an oiled baking sheet. Cut two parallel slashes about a half-inch deep in the top. Bake at 375°F till well browned for about thirty minutes.

Dinner Rolls

(12 rolls)

1 1/3 cups milk
2 tablespoons butter
(optional)
2 tablespoons dry baking
yeast
1 tablespoon maple
syrup (optional)
1 egg
1/2 teaspoon sea salt
3 1/2 cups whole-wheat
bread flour

1. In a medium-sized saucepan heat milk and butter to lukewarm.
2. Add yeast and maple syrup, and allow yeast to work.
3. Beat egg slightly in a small bowl. Add salt, and combine with the milk/yeast.
4. Sift flour into a large bowl. Drop bran back into bowl after sifting.
5. Mix wet into dry ingredients. Turn out onto a floured board and knead ten minutes. Place in a large oiled bowl, turning to coat all sides. Cover with a towel and allow to rise three hours in a warm, draft-free place.
6. To form into rolls, make one-inch balls and dip tops into melted butter or oil. Arrange three in every well of a greased muffin tin. Let rise again half an hour or until they are *very* light.
7. Bake at 400°F about twenty minutes. Remove from pans when done and cool on a rack.

Usually whole-wheat rolls become heavy and hard the next day—but these dinner rolls will actually stay light and fresh.

Sourdough Starter

3 cups warm water
1 tablespoon dry baking
yeast
3 cups unbleached white
flour

1. Sprinkle yeast over water in a large glass bowl and allow to soften and bubble about ten minutes.
2. Add flour, one cup at a time, and stir with a wooden spoon until well blended.
3. Cover and set in a warm (85-100°F) place, on your heating pad if necessary, for forty-eight hours. Stir several times with a wooden spoon. By the end it should have changed from a heavy, doughy texture to a thick and bubbly one, and it should smell sour.

To store: Cover with plastic wrap and refrigerate. I prefer a stone crock with its own cover.
Before using: Mix well and allow to warm up at room temperature for at least two hours, or overnight if possible.
After use: Replenish with equal amounts each of warm water and unbleached white

*Sourdough was a Maine favorite for generations before it went west. Because sourdough action is killed by both metal and cold, always use wooden spoons, glass or crockery bowls, and sour in a warm place (85-100°F). Be sure to leave **plenty** of air space in the bowl—the starter expands! An electric heating pad can help maintain an even temperature.*

flour and stir well. Set in a warm spot for several hours, then store as above.

When not used: Throw half the starter away once a week and add one and a half cups each warm water and unbleached flour. Mix well and set in a warm spot for several hours till bubbly and active.

Most important: If it doesn't act properly, *throw it out.*

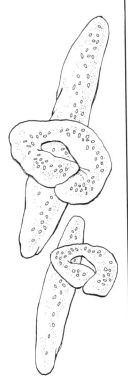

Sourdough Loaves

(2 loaves)

1 cup Sourdough Starter
1 cup unbleached white
    flour
1 cup warm water
1 tablespoon dry baking
    yeast
1/2 cup warm water
1/2 teaspoon maple
    syrup
1 teaspoon grated lemon
    rind (optional)
1 teaspoon sea salt
2 cups unbleached white
    flour
2 cups whole-wheat
    bread flour
1 cup wheat germ
2 tablespoons
    nutritional yeast
3 tablespoons cornmeal
oil or melted butter
    OR egg wash

1. *The night before,* mix up a sponge in a glass bowl by combining starter with one cup each unbleached flour and warm water. Remember to use a wooden spoon. Cover with a moist towel and place in a warm spot (85-100°F).

2. *In the morning,* mix baking yeast with half a cup warm water, maple syrup, and lemon rind, in a large glass or crockery bowl, using a wooden spoon. Allow yeast to dissolve and work for about five minutes.

3. Using a wooden spoon, combine sponge with yeast mixture, and add salt, two cups each unbleached and whole-wheat flour, wheat germ, and nutritional yeast. When dough becomes too difficult to mix with a spoon, turn out onto a board well-covered with unbleached white flour, and knead about ten minutes or until slightly elastic and smooth.

4. Place in a well-oiled bowl, turning once to grease, and cover with a moist towel. Allow to rise in a warm place (85-100°F) until doubled, about one hour.

5. Punch down and turn out onto a lightly floured board. Knead two minutes. Cut in two and shape into long thin loaves.

6. Thoroughly butter a large cookie sheet. Sprinkle lightly with cornmeal. Arrange loaves on pan so

»

that they measure about ten inches long. Brush with oil, melted butter, or an egg wash. Cover with a damp towel. Place in a warm spot about forty-five minutes or until risen a bit less than double. When almost doubled, slash top twice with a sharp knife.

7. Place in a *cold* oven and set heat at 425°F. Bake for twenty to twenty-five minutes. For a soft crust, brush again with oil, butter, or an egg wash. Cool on a wire rack.

Lemon-Baked Bird

(6-8 servings)

For stuffing:
**2 cups small whole-
    wheat bread cubes
1 medium-sized onion,
    diced
1-2 stalks celery, diced
    (including leaves)
1 teaspoon dried thyme
    or 2 teaspoons fresh
    thyme
2 teaspoons sea salt
freshly ground black
    pepper
2 heaping tablespoons
    plus 1 teaspoon
    finely chopped fresh
    parsley
1/4 cup plus 2
    tablespoons freshly
    squeezed lemon juice
7 tablespoons extra-
    virgin olive oil
    (optional)
boiling water**

**1 (6-pound) roasting hen
1 lemon quarter
6 tablespoons melted
    butter
1/4 teaspoon shoyu**

1. Combine bread cubes, onion, celery, thyme, one teaspoon salt, pepper to taste, two heaping tablespoons parsley, two tablespoons lemon juice, and a tablespoon of olive oil. Add enough boiling water and mix so that texture resembles hamburger.
2. Rinse gutted and prepared fowl with boiling water quickly. Pat dry with a paper towel. Rub all over with a quarter of a fresh lemon.
3. For a basting sauce, melt butter in a small saucepan and combine with remaining six tablespoons olive oil, one teaspoon sea salt, pepper to taste, a teaspoon of finely chopped fresh parsley, a quarter cup of freshly squeezed lemon juice, and shoyu.
4. Stuff fowl and truss legs and wings. Using a pastry brush, coat bird with the basting sauce. Lay on an open rack and bake at 300°F for thirty minutes. After that, baste every fifteen minutes for an hour and a half to two hours, until legs

Poultry

When I was a child, the Pekin ducks, bathing in the dust just below my little bedroom window, announced the day. But that was nothing compared to the Rhode Island Red rooster in the henyard. Loud but basically benign, he strutted his stuff, kept his harem in line, and ultimately provided a Thanksgiving feast which I would not attend.

There are health reasons for eating home-grown fowl in preference to red meat, and free-ranging birds rather than "factory" birds, whose meat may be tainted with growth hormones and pesticide residues. Poultry fat is less saturated than that of red meat, and much of it occurs in the skin, which can be peeled off and discarded, or given to the dog.

move easily when pressed, and clear liquid oozes from any fork pricks. (Or insert a meat thermometer into stuffing near tail. When it reads 185°F, the bird is done.)

Allow to rest ten minutes before carving.

Serve with vegetables in season, a leafy green salad, and potatoes of choice.

Dinosaurs didn't utterly disappear. Those that lived on turned into our present-day feathered companions.

Dinosaur for Dinner

(6 servings)

1 broiling chicken
1 lemon
2 tablespoons clarified butter
2 tablespoons extra-virgin olive oil
1/2 teaspoon cinnamon
1/4 teaspoon allspice
sea salt
freshly ground black pepper
2 cups home-canned tomatoes OR 2 very large, ripe tomatoes, peeled
1/2 cup dry white wine
1/4 cup finely chopped fresh parsley
1 heaping teaspoon fresh rosemary
1 heaping teaspoon fresh basil
1 heaping teaspoon fresh thyme
2 garlic cloves, minced

1. Select a broiling chicken and cut off legs at body. Separate lower part from thigh by cutting through joint. Cut off wings at body-joint.
Using both hands, break back bone, separating top from lower body. Halve top section by cutting through breast bone with a strong, sharp knife.
Remove all skin by holding meat with a paper towel and grasping skin with another. Pull it off. Rinse quickly with boiling water and pat dry. Then rub chicken parts all over with a cut lemon.
2. Heat butter and olive oil in a heavy cast-iron wok or pan. Sprinkle chicken pieces with equal amounts of cinnamon, allspice, salt, and pepper. Brown until golden.
3. Remove and pour out fat. Return chicken to pan and add remaining ingredients. Cover and simmer over low heat until tender, about thirty minutes.

Serve with potatoes, polenta (see Glossary), or spaghetti, cooked vegetables in season, and a tossed salad.

Remember that light chicken meat is leaner and lower in cholesterol than dark meat.

Remember also never to cut your fowl on your vegetable cutting board. Bacteria from the fowl can contaminate vegetables. Keep a separate meatboard instead.

Chicken and Whiskey

(6 servings)

1 broiling chicken
1 lemon
4 tablespoons butter
2 tablespoons sunflower
    seed oil
1/4 cup whiskey
1/2 cup stock or water
2 tablespoons chopped
    shallots
1/4 cups chopped celery
2 small tart apples,
    peeled, cored, and
    chopped
1/2 teaspoon dried
    thyme
1/2 cup heavy cream (or
    substitute)
1 teaspoon arrowroot
1 teaspoon freshly
    squeezed lemon juice
sea salt to taste
cayenne
1 scant tablespoon
    chopped fresh
    tarragon or parsley
    for garnish

1. Cut up broiler. Remove skin as in preceding recipe. Rinse quickly with boiling water and pat dry. Rub all over with a cut lemon.
2. Heat two tablespoons each of butter and oil in a skillet and sauté chicken pieces until golden brown on all sides. Remove chicken pieces for a moment to discard fat, then return them to skillet.
3. In a long-handled metal ladle heat whiskey slightly. Hold ladle over chicken and light whiskey with a match. (Hold well away from your body.) Begin to pour it *slowly* over chicken, a little at a time, shaking pan back and forth continuously until whiskey burns itself out. Then add stock or water.
4. In a small skillet, melt remaining two tablespoons butter. Sauté shallots, celery, and apples. When wilted, add thyme. Add to pan of flamed chicken and broth. Bring to a boil, reduce heat to low, and cover. Cook till chicken is tender, about thirty minutes.
5. Remove chicken and arrange on a heated platter. Boil down remaining sauce to half a cup and strain it through a sieve into a small saucepan. Whisk in cream and arrowroot. Bring to high heat and simmer, whisking, till slightly thickened. Add lemon juice, salt to taste, and a dash of cayenne. Pour over chicken and sprinkle with chopped fresh tarragon or parsley.

Serve with vegetables in season and rice.

Many of the Maine French are descended from people who came from Normandy. A friend of mine tells a story about walking down a Parisian street at the close of World War Two. He was speaking Canadian French with a companion when he suddenly realized he was being followed by an unassuming little man. He stopped, inquired why, and the gentleman replied: "But sir! You are speaking three-hundred-year-old Norman. I am a professor at the Sorbonne." That, of course, began a great friendship.

This recipe is based on classic braised Norman chicken.

Rabbit

If one's diet includes meat, there is none better than rabbit. It is nearly fatless. Maine has many a rabbitry these days, but if you come from a family of hunters, wild rabbit may be yours. Snowshoe hares or cottontail rabbits are best in the winter after a summer of feeding and bud nibbling.

Wok'd Hare
(4-6 servings)

1 (2-pound) hare or 2 small cottontail rabbits
3 cups water
2 tablespoons vinegar
1 teaspoon sea salt
2/3 cup unbleached white flour
freshly ground black pepper, about 20 grindings
2 tablespoons extra-virgin olive oil
2 tablespoons butter
1 medium-sized onion, chopped
1 clove garlic, minced
2 heaping tablespoons chopped fresh parsley
1/4 teaspoon each minced fresh basil, marjoram, and rosemary
1/8 teaspoon powdered cloves
1 cup dry white wine
1 teaspoon sea salt

1. Wash and cut up game as you would chicken (see **Dinosaur for Dinner**). Place in a glass bowl and pour the water, vinegar, and one teaspoon salt over it. Marinate one hour.
2. Drain, rinse, and dry meat well with a paper towel. Roll in a shallow bowl in flour seasoned with black pepper.
3. Heat a heavy cast-iron wok or casserole, and add oil and butter. Sauté rabbit bits until golden, then remove and discard all but one tablespoon fat. Add onion and garlic and sauté till limp. Add remaining ingredients.
4. Return rabbit to wok or casserole and simmer two hours, stirring often.

Serve with potatoes, rice, polenta, or pasta, and cooked vegetables in season.

Note: You may substitute two pounds chicken legs and thighs.

Mimi Carpenter, an artist friend, was blessed with a Belgian mother who is an artist with "lapin." Here's a marvelous recipe for rabbit with prunes. Remember to marinate the prunes well ahead of time.

Rabbit with Prunes
(6 servings)

12-16 pitted prunes
1/3 cup cognac
1 (4-pound) hare or 2 smaller rabbits
3-4 cups water (optional)
2 tablespoons vinegar (optional)
1 teaspoon sea salt (optional)
2/3-1 cup unbleached white flour
freshly ground black pepper, about 20 grindings
3 tablespoons butter
3 tablespoons sunflower seed oil
1/4 cup cognac

»

1 large onion, coarsely
    chopped
3 cups water
1 cup sweet red wine
1/2 teaspoon dried
    thyme
2 heaping tablespoons
    chopped fresh
    parsley
1 tablespoon freshly
    squeezed lemon juice
1 teaspoon maple syrup
sea salt to taste
chopped fresh parsley
    for garnish

1. In a small bowl marinate prunes in one third of a cup of cognac for three hours.
2. Wash and cut up rabbit as you would chicken. If wild, place in a glass bowl, and pour the water, vinegar, and one teaspoon salt over it. Marinate one hour. Rinse with fresh water. If domestic, omit the marination and simply rinse with fresh water. In either case, drain and dry meat well with a paper towel. Roll pieces in a shallow bowl of flour seasoned with black pepper.
3. Heat butter and oil in a heavy cast-iron wok or pot and sauté rabbit bits until brown on all sides. (Tongs are handy for this.) Transfer to a lightweight skillet.
4. In a long-handled ladle, heat a quarter cup cognac. Set it aflame and dribble it slowly over the rabbit, moving skillet constantly. Set aside for a few moments.
5. Pour off all but one tablespoon oil from wok or heavy pot. Add onion and sauté till limp. Then add three cups water, wine, thyme, and parsley, and stir well. Return rabbit to pot and nestle it securely under cooking liquid. Cover tightly, reduce heat, and simmer two hours. (The long, slow cooking time blends the flavors.)
6. Add marinated, pitted prunes, cover and simmer one more hour.
7. When ready to serve, remove rabbit and place on a heated platter. Taste sauce and adjust seasonings by adding lemon juice, maple syrup, and sea salt (if necessary). Sauce should be slightly sweet-sour, rich with wine, yet tart. Pour it over the rabbit and sprinkle with parsley.

Serve with potatoes, rice, or pasta, vegetables in season, and tossed green salad.

Oysters

Mother never considered herself a good cook, but she was. "I'm too much in a hurry!" she'd say. But her kitchen was scrupulously clean and she paid attention to what she was doing. No oyster stew can match hers, and of course Mother used fresh oysters which she had to shuck–quite a procedure. Here's how:

Shucking Oysters

Place your fresh oyster on a chopping block and break off enough of the protruding lip to be able to insert a knife blade. Slide the blade against the flat side of the shell to sever the adductor muscle. This will relax the oyster and you can then pull the flat side of the shell off. Next, cut the oyster body from the rounded shell side.

Mussels

When I was a child, mussels in Maine were something you tried not to step on at the shore. In recent years, however, they've become a culinary delicacy. The largest and most handsome come from saltwater mussel farms. These fat, meaty, cultivated mussels have thin »

Oyster Stew

(4-6 servings)

**1 quart freshly shucked
   oysters
1/4 cup clarified butter
1 quart milk
unbleached white flour
sea salt
freshly ground black
   pepper
1/2 cup non-instant
   low-fat powdered
   milk mixed with 1-2
   tablespoons
   arrowroot (optional)
chopped fresh parsley
   for garnish
a few drops angostura
   bitters**

1. *The day before cooking,* clean oysters by placing in a colander and pouring cold water gently over them.
2. Melt butter in a skillet. Pat oysters dry and dredge in white flour seasoned with salt and pepper. Shake off excess.
Sauté oysters in butter until edges *just begin* to curl.
3. Scald milk. Add oysters and season with salt and black pepper to taste. Set aside and allow flavors to mellow at least a day.
4. If you prefer a thicker stew, whisk in powdered milk and arrowroot before heating to serve. Heat to piping hot but *do not boil.*

Serve sprinkled with finely chopped fresh parsley, a few drops of angostura bitters, and pilot crackers.

Julia's Simple Steamed Blue Mussels

(2-4 servings)

**about 24 mussels
1 tablespoon chopped onion
1 garlic clove, crushed
1/2 teaspoon *crumbled*
       thyme (not powdered)
freshly ground black pepper
1 teaspoon finely chopped
       fresh parsley
1 cup white wine**

1. Wash mussels and remove beards.
2. Place in a kettle with remaining ingredients, cover, and heat.
3. When steam rises, remove from heat and shake pot vigorously, so that mussels change position. Return to heat. When liquid rises, repeat shaking.
4. When it boils up a third time, mussels should be done to perfection and shells open.

Serve in bowls with hot broth as a side dish for dunking and drinking.

Julia's Marinated Mussels

(4 servings)

2 cups cooked and
drained mussel
meats
1 cup strained mussel
broth
1 carrot, peeled and
sliced
2 onions, thinly sliced
4 garlic cloves, mashed
1/8 teaspoon allspice
1/4 teaspoon crumbled
dried basil or 1/2
teaspoon finely
chopped fresh basil
1/4 teaspoon crumbled
dried tarragon or 1/2
teaspoon finely
chopped fresh
tarragon

1 bay leaf
freshly ground black
pepper
pinch cayenne
1 cup dry white wine or
vermouth
2 tablespoons extra-
virgin olive oil

1. Cook enough mussels to
obtain two cups meats.
2. Place in a glass or ceramic
container and refrigerate for
twenty-four hours with
remaining ingredients.

Drain and serve on greens or
alone, with a tiny dollop of
Whipped Cottage Cheese
flavored with lemon juice
and sea salt.

*These mussel recipes are
thanks to Julia Myers, upon
whose hospitable back porch
I enjoyed my first taste of the
civilized variety of this
shellfish.*

*"To me," says Ed Myers, "a
mussel stew is the finest
concoction. The ideal
atmosphere is by the
woodstove at eleven in the
morning, after five or six
hours of duck hunting in a*

*snowstorm. The stew is
followed by a one and a half
hour nap, after which
follows duck hunting to
dusk, and then coming in
wet and chilled to the bone
for more stew. It is preferable
not to have shot any ducks,
so there are no delays after
putting the decoys away and
oiling up the fowling piece
against the salt spray."*

*shells and cook more
quickly than their
wild cousins. They
are washed clean for
shipping and lack
pearls–those
romantic, tiny stones
that can crack a
tooth.*

*If you do collect your
own, clean carefully.
Scrub well with a
brush in several
changes of water. If
they're very dirty,
allow them to soak
for two hours in cold
water to cover, with
a third of a cup salt
and a tablespoon of
cornmeal per gallon
of water. This will
help disgorge sand.
Then scrape off the
beards, rinse, and
drain under cold
water.*

*Ed Myers, who
operates Abandoned
Farm, Inc. in
Walpole, says
mussels (like
oysters) are best
enjoyed during
months with R's in
them. "All mollusks
build up gonad until
spawning time,
usually mid-May for
ours. After much
weight loss post-
spawning, it may
take two or three
months to recover to
a satisfactory meat
yield. But they are
okay to eat anytime,
as long as you don't
expect perfection."
Leftovers can be
pickled and kept for
a month. A score or
two of little ones
make a great
omelette aux
moules.*

Winter

Winter in Maine! Trees glistening with frost, fields swaddled with snow, children out skiing–and those deep old cellars walled with granite, dirt-floored, lined with sand-filled boxes of root vegetables, bags of onions, crocks of pickles, sauerkraut, eggs in waterglass, salted pork, smoked herring; and all those shelves of sparkling canned goods. The picture is more modern now– Maine's cellars and kitchens are stocked with freezers full of summer harvest, though shelves remain bright with jellies and jams.

The new Maine cuisine features many ideas less favored in the good old days– such as using low-fat sauces or the oriental stir-fry method, instead of traditional, heavy deep-frying. Still, traditional vegetables provide midwinter sustenance, and winter fare remains rich in root vegetables and all that can easily be preserved or frozen from summer's abundance.

Maine Protein

Mainers have always been devoted to "making do." Farms in the old days were mostly self-sufficient, their traditional diet consisting mainly of whole grains and garden vegetables. Meat was eaten, too—but such meat! Nothing commercial today can match the taste of those free-ranging chickens or the hog butchered in December to be hung, frozen, in the shed.

More people today are becoming vegetarian, concerned with "getting off the top of the food chain." It's easy to obtain enough protein without meat, but it requires a basic understanding of protein complementarity.

Protein consists of about twenty-two amino acids, of which eight or nine are "essential" in that our bodies can't produce them. The essential amino acids exist in equal proportions in meat, fish, dairy products, and eggs—so we can eat these foods singly and obtain "complete protein." They do supply all the essential amino acids but not in equal proportion.

Plant foods also contain all of the essential amino acids, but in varying amounts depending on the plant. Whole grains, legumes, nuts, and seeds vary as sources of protein (with the exception of soybeans and soybean products such as tofu, which have complete protein); they are high in some amino acids and low in others—and if one of the essential amino acids is in short supply, it limits the extent to which the others can be used.

But this lack is easily remedied. Combining grains and legumes produces a high-quality protein because grains are rich in the amino acids beans lack, and vice versa. Beans and grains complement each other.

Beans and Other Legumes

Treat legumes with respect. Don't use baking soda for soaking (it destroys B vitamins), and don't add salt (it toughens beans by attracting water away from them). In fact, salt, fat, or molasses prolong cooking time. When legumes are simmered, vitamins and minerals pass into the water, so never throw it out. Cook beans over low heat to prevent protein from becoming tough, just as in meat cooking, and remember that beans can be "baked" on top of the stove more cheaply and quickly than in an oven if you have a heavy cast-iron pot. Add a crumbled bit of kelp to the bottom of a bean pot before cooking to make richer gravy and, according to some people, to help make beans more digestible. In puréeing beans, it's easier to sieve or mash while still hot.

Cooking Dried Beans

Note: 1 cup dry beans yields about 2-2 1/2 cups cooked beans.
1. Clean beans carefully. Pour from hand to hand and discard any moldy or discolored ones, stones, and dirt lumps. Wash thoroughly and drain in a colander.
2. Place in a large bowl, cover with three times as much water, and soak overnight. Soaking shortens cooking time and aids digestibility.

Soybeans may ferment, so soak them in the refrigerator. (Note: If you don't have time to soak overnight, add dried beans slowly to three times as much boiling water, so the boil does not stop, and cook two minutes. Remove from heat, cover tightly. Soak two hours and continue as follows.)
*3. When ready to cook after soaking, bring to a boil. Reduce heat and simmer one or more hours (or till skins peel slightly if blown upon), then drain and proceed with baking (see **Saturday Night Baked Beans**). Or don't drain but continue cooking beans with herbs, onion, garlic (optional) till tender. Add more boiling water if necessary. Add sea salt only when beans are tender (see **Seasoned Stovetop Beans** or **Simple Cooked Dried Beans**). Cooked beans can be used in casseroles, loaves, burgers, soups, marinades, or whatever you fancy.*

Flatulence

If gas results from eating beans (and it will be a problem especially for those just adopting a whole-grain/legume diet) try the following:
1. Be sure to soak beans overnight. This helps a little in breaking down the starches which cause the trouble.
2. Cook beans thoroughly.
3. Add summer savory to bean recipes. This helps some people. Hot, spicy flavorings (such as chili peppers) may also aid by stimulating digestion.
4. Choose your bean carefully: red kidney, soy, and fava (broad beans) are more difficult to digest than others. Garbanzos, adukis, and

lentils seem to be gentler to the system.
*5. Or try sprouting beans first in a glass jar (see **How to Sprout Seeds, Whole Grains, and Legumes**). This eliminates most of the gas-producing starches and shortens cooking time considerably. It also increases protein content.*

Bean Recipes (and Accompaniments)

Saturday night in Maine was always baked bean night, just as Friday meant fish. Yellow-eye, Jacob's cattle, and the lovely red kidney beans were–and remain–great favorites. Here's a new version of the old classic.

Saturday Night Baked Beans

(6-8 servings)

3 cups red kidney beans
1 medium-sized onion, sliced thin
2-3 medium-sized tart winter apples, cored and sliced
freshly ground black pepper (optional)
1 teaspoon (or more) dried mustard
1 teaspoon dried summer savory (whiz in blender for instant powder)
1/2 cup maple syrup (optional)
enough simmering water to barely cover

1. *On Friday night*, pick over beans carefully, removing any small stones. Rinse clean and soak overnight in a big bowl with about three times as much water.
2. *On Saturday morning*, put soaked beans in a big pot with just enough fresh water to barely cover and bring to a boil. Lower heat and simmer until skins start to peel when you blow on them. When ready, drain beans and save water.
3. Place beans in a large ceramic bean pot (preferably well-seasoned), and add remaining ingredients in the order listed.
4. Bake, covered, in a 300°F oven all day, adding *hot* stock as necessary; or if you

are boiling down maple sap, use boiling sap.

Serve with **New Downeast Cole Slaw** and **Aunt Mae's Steamed Brown Bread**.

Note: On stormy days or days when a storm is "brewing," beans will "cook away,"or dry up much faster than on clear days, so watch them. The secret to really good baked beans is *long and slow* simmering in just enough liquid to cover but not drown them.

Note again: If unexpected company arrives for dinner, take down a home-canned jar of shell beans (such as cranberry beans), pop them into a bean pot, season as above, and bake for an hour in a 325°F oven.

Yellow-Eye Down-Maine Baked Beans

(6-8 servings)

3 cups yellow-eye beans
1 medium-sized onion,
    sliced thin
1 carrot, chopped in
    medium-fine pieces
    OR 2 medium-sized
    apples, peeled and
    sliced
2 teaspoons powdered
    mustard
freshly ground black
    pepper
1 teaspoon dried
    summer savory
    (whizzed in blender
    till powdery)

1 teaspoon cumin
    powder
1 teaspoon coriander
    powder
1 tablespoon maple
    syrup
1 tablespoon brandy
enough simmering
    water to cover

Follow directions one through four for **Saturday Night Baked Beans**, adding boiling water as necessary.

Serve with the customary **New Downeast Cole Slaw**, **Aunt Mae's Steamed Brown Bread**, and pickles.

Some people prefer their beans savory rather than sweet. The yellow-eye bean has always been a down-Maine favorite.

Aunt Mae's Steamed Brown Bread

(6 servings)

1 cup unbleached white
    flour
1 cup whole-wheat bread
    flour
1 cup yellow cornmeal
1 teaspoon baking soda
1 teaspoon sea salt
2 cups sour milk
1/2 cup molasses
1 cup raisins or currants

1. Sift dry ingredients into a medium-sized bowl and add the sifted-out bran.
2. Mix sour milk with molasses in a large measuring cup. (To sour, add one tablespoon vinegar to one cup milk and let it rest a while.)
3. Combine the two mixtures, and add raisins or currants.
4. Pour immediately into well-buttered, cylindrical baking tins. Fill about half full. The batter will rise. Cover with buttered foil, and tie around top edge with string or seal with tape.
5. Place on a trivet in a deep kettle and add boiling water to come about two inches up sides of cans. Cover kettle and bring to a boil. Reduce heat to simmer and steam for three and a half hours. As the water steams away, add more boiling water to

Saturday night baked beans were always served with hot, steaming brown bread. My Aunt Mae concocted this one, raised with sour milk and baking soda. I often wondered why so many old-fashioned recipes called for sour milk until I realized two things: country folk usually had more milk than could be kept fresh, and baking soda, reacting with an acid, can raise dough. (Today's baking powder has made baking soda obsolete, unless one prefers the old-time taste.)

keep the level up. You might have to weight the cans at first. A saucer with a rock on top makes a good weight. The loaves get heavier as bread becomes solid. When done, remove from pans and cool on a rack. If they seem too moist, pop them into a 375°F oven for ten minutes–no more.

Serve hot with **New Downeast Cole Slaw** and **Saturday Night Baked Beans** or **Yellow-Eye Down-Maine Baked Beans**.

Simply Super Skillet Corn Bread

(6 servings)

Corn bread is a quickbread of long-standing in Maine– the Indians made the first version. It's delicious for breakfast, lunch, or supper. Many a grandmother must have cooked hers in the big cast-iron skillet on top of the cast-iron stove as mine did. It's especially good with beans, and the combination yields complete protein.

1 cup plus 2 tablespoons cornmeal
2 teaspoons double-acting baking powder
1/2 teaspoon baking soda
1/2 teaspoon sea salt
1/4 cup whole-wheat or rye flour
1 tablespoon nutritional yeast
1 1/4 cups buttermilk OR 1 1/4 cups milk soured for 1/2 hour with 2 tablespoons cider vinegar
2 large eggs, beaten lightly
2 tablespoons sunflower seed oil
2/3 cup blueberries (optional)

1. Preheat oven to 450°F. Set aside two tablespoons cornmeal. Sift the rest of the dry ingredients together into a medium-sized bowl. Return any sifted-out bran.
2. Stir in buttermilk or sour milk and add eggs. Heat a ten-inch iron skillet over high heat for one minute. Add oil and heat fifteen seconds. Sprinkle skillet with two tablespoons cornmeal and allow to brown slightly. Spoon in batter. (Sprinkle in blueberries if desired.)
3. Bake in the upper third of a preheated 450°F oven for ten minutes, or till it's firm in the center and pulls away slightly from skillet sides. Cut into wedges or squares. (I have a square cast-iron skillet which is particularly good for this corn bread.)

Serve for breakfast, lunch, or dinner with hearty fare.

Seasoned Stovetop Beans

(4-6 servings)

1 cup red kidney (or
other) beans
2 cloves garlic, minced
2 bay leaves
freshly ground black
pepper
1 small onion, chopped
fine
(a) 1/4 green bell
pepper, chopped
3 inches celery stalk,
chopped
1 teaspoon powdered
fennel (optional)
1/2 teaspoon dried
thyme (optional)
1 teaspoon powdered
summer savory
OR (b) 1 teaspoon dried
oregano
1 teaspoon dried basil
1 teaspoon dried thyme
1/4 teaspoon cayenne
(optional)
sea salt to taste

1. Pick over beans, rinse
quickly, and soak overnight
in three times as much water
(or use the late-to-cook
method described under
number two in **Cooking
Dried Beans**). Place in a
saucepan with just enough
boiling water to cover.
2. Add garlic, bay leaves,
black pepper, and onion.
Then add remaining
ingredients (a) or (b).
3. Simmer till beans are
tender, two to three hours
(or about a half hour for
sprouted beans). Add more
hot water as necessary to
keep it even with beans.
When tender, remove cover
and allow liquid to simmer
until it's half gone. The
result will be beans in a
creamy gravy.
4. Store, covered, in
refrigerator. For "refried"
beans, simply mash. You
can also "curry" beans by
adding **Simple Garam
Masala** to taste.

Serve as a side dish with a
whole grain to produce
complete protein, in tacos,
as enchilada stuffing with
other ingredients, and in
loaves and burgers.

*For people with no
time to cook, beans
are especially
appropriate: all one
need do is set them to
soak and, the next
day, cook them on
top of the stove.
They require no
stirring and little
clock-watching.
Kept on hand in the
refrigerator, they
provide the basis for
dishes such as tacos,
enchiladas, bean
burgers, casseroles,
and loaves.*

Cuban Black Beans

(6-8 servings)

1 1/2 cups black turtle
beans
1 bay leaf
3 cloves garlic, smashed
with the broad side
of a knife blade
1/4 teaspoon cayenne or
to taste
1 chopped green bell
pepper
1 medium-sized onion,
chopped
2 tablespoons vinegar or
freshly squeezed
lemon juice

*Black beans are such
wonderful-looking
gems! Cooked
simply, they
provide a tasty dish.
Combined with
brown rice they
produce a complete
protein.*

2 tablespoons extra-
   virgin olive oil
2 teaspoons maple syrup
sea salt to taste
freshly ground black
   pepper
6 tablespoons finely
   chopped scallions for
   topping
2 finely chopped
   tomatoes for topping
2-3 tablespoons finely
   chopped fresh
   parsley for topping
1 lemon quarter per
   diner for garnish

1. *The day before*, pick the beans over carefully, removing any dirt, stones, or imperfect beans. Wash and soak overnight.

2. *The next day*, combine beans, bay leaf, garlic, cayenne, and enough water to cover the beans in a heavy kettle. Cover and bring to a boil. Reduce heat and simmer until beans are tender, two to three hours, adding boiling water as necessary to keep them covered.

3. One hour before serving time, stir in remaining ingredients, except the toppings and garnish. Allow to simmer, uncovered, till half of the water is absorbed and vegetables are tender but not mushy. What you are aiming for is beans and vegetables in a creamy gravy.

Serve several tablespoons of beans to each diner over heaps of brown rice and topped with one tablespoon finely chopped scallions or chives, two or more tablespoons chopped tomatoes, one teaspoon finely chopped parsley, and as much freshly squeezed lemon or lime juice as each diner desires. Freshly made **Cuban Bread** complements this dish beautifully.

Simple Cooked Dried Beans

(4-6 servings)

1 cup cranberry or pinto
   beans
2 tablespoons extra-
   virgin olive oil
3-4 chopped scallions
sea salt to taste
7-10 grindings of black
   pepper
2 tablespoons finely
   chopped fresh
   parsley

Cranberry and pinto beans are quick cookers. They make a lovely small side dish with any meal.

1. Soak beans overnight in three times as much water or use the late-to-cook method described under number two in **Cooking Dried Beans**.

2. In the morning, drain, and place in a heavy kettle with boiling water to cover. Simmer until tender. Drain well and save liquid for soups or breads.

3. Place in a hot ceramic serving bowl and add remaining ingredients.

»

Serve as a side dish with twice as much whole grain for complete protein, tomatoes if possible, any other vegetable in season, and fresh rolls.

Elizabeth's Red Kidney Beans and Endive

(4 servings)

3 cups cooked red kidney beans (see Seasoned Stovetop Beans)
1 cup finely chopped onion
3 large cloves garlic, minced
2 tablespoons extra-virgin olive oil
freshly ground black pepper
1 teaspoon kelp powder or crumbled kelp
1 teaspoon sea salt (optional)
2 tablespoons dry sherry
2 cups rinsed, coarsely chopped curly endive

1. *The day before,* cook one and a half cups beans (see **Seasoned Stovetop Beans**) to yield three cups cooked beans.
2. *Before dinner* the next day, sauté onions and garlic in olive oil till limp. Use a large skillet or heavy wok.
3. Add beans and their gravy, remaining ingredients; cover, and simmer about ten minutes till well blended and hot. You may need to add a bit more water.

Serve hot with fresh rolls, **Simply Super Skillet Corn Bread**, or **Corn Crêpes**, and a small tossed salad.

Note: Substitute finely chopped kale for endive for variation.

Beans can also be cooked with greens. The basic recipe for this comes from a beloved neighbor of mine, a Mainer of many generations.

Chili Con Tempeh

(6 servings)

1 cup dried red kidney beans
4 cups cold water
1 tablespoon butter
1 tablespoon sunflower seed oil

1 pound tempeh, crumbled (see Glossary)
2 tablespoons water
1 1/2 cups chopped onion
1 1/2 cups chopped green bell pepper
3 tablespoons minced garlic

Chili is an American favorite and here is a meatless but authentic-tasting version. Chili worshippers exchange recipes and taste slowly and judgmentally in the manner of wine connoisseurs. This recipe appears long, but it is simple to prepare—and I think the most serious of chili judges will approve. Begin preparing it two days before you plan to serve it.

2 canned jalapeno
    peppers (or to taste),
    drained and chopped,
    including juice and
    seeds OR
2 fresh chopped
    Hungarian wax
    peppers
2 tablespoons chili
    powder
2 1/2 teaspoons ground
    cumin
2 bay leaves
sea salt to taste
freshly ground black
    pepper
3 1/2 cups vegetable or
    chicken stock
6 cups Italian plum
    tomatoes, chopped
    (well drained if
    canned)
1 cup tomato paste
1 cup beer

1. *The night before*, pick
over beans, wash carefully,
and soak overnight in water.
2. *In the morning*, add
enough water to cover
soaked beans by one inch.
Bring to a boil and simmer,
partially covered, till beans
are just tender.
3. Heat butter and oil in a
very large skillet or heavy
cast-iron wok and sauté
tempeh till browned.
Remove tempeh to a bowl.
4. In the same skillet sauté
onion and pepper in two
tablespoons water till limp.
Add garlic and cook three
minutes, stirring.
5. Add tempeh, hot peppers,
chili powder, cumin, bay
leaves, salt, and black pepper.

Simmer two minutes. At
this point, you may need to
transfer it to a larger pot.
6. Add stock, tomatoes, and
tomato paste. Simmer,
stirring as it thickens, two
hours or till thick.
7. Add drained, cooked
kidney beans and simmer
ten minutes. Chill
overnight.
8. Discard bay leaves. Add
beer, stir, and reheat.

Serve in large heated serving
bowls with separate bowls of
sour cream, yogurt, or
unsweetened **Whipped
Cottage Cheese**, minced
scallions, minced zucchini.

Corn Crêpes

(16 crêpes)

2 cups water
1/2 teaspoon sea salt
1 teaspoon maple syrup
    (optional)
2 tablespoons
    nutritional yeast
1 cup yellow cornmeal
1/2 cup milk

1. Bring water, salt, and maple syrup to a boil.
2. Combine nutritional yeast and cornmeal in a medium-sized bowl and pour in the boiling water. Whisk thoroughly. Add milk and whisk again. (It should have the consistency of thick cream.) Allow to sit ten minutes.
3. Pour dollops of two tablespoons each onto a well-seasoned, well-oiled hot griddle–the hotter and more seasoned the griddle, the thinner and lacier the cakes. (They'll splatter!) Place dollops far enough apart so crêpes don't run together. They should spread to be four inches across and exquisitely thin, with "holes" (not quite through) on one side. Cook till golden brown on the bottom. Pushing a thin, wide, metal spatula underneath, turn, and cook till second side is browned. Stack them to keep warm.

Serve in great crisp heaps, drizzled with pure maple syrup and interlaced with yogurt and squirts of freshly squeezed lemon juice.

(Note: With fresh fruit such as raspberries, blackberries, blueberries, or strawberries they make a wonderful dessert or summer breakfast. They are also good as finger breads with chili, and make fine little tortillas for a taco lunch.)

Tamale Pie

(6 servings)

1 tablespoon extra-virgin
    olive oil
1/2 cup chopped onion
2 cloves garlic, minced
2 cups cooked pinto or
    kidney beans, well
    mashed (see Simple
    Cooked Dried Beans)
1/4 cup sliced ripe
    olives
    OR mushrooms
1/2 cup fresh corn or
    home-canned corn
    OR 1 medium carrot,
    shredded
1/2 cup finely chopped
    green bell pepper
1/4 cup chopped fresh
    parsley
1/2 cup chopped celery,
    leaves and all
1 teaspoon sea salt
freshly ground black
    pepper

Tamale pie is another dish of Mexican origin which fits beautifully into Maine's local cuisine. It provides complete protein, and is a meal in itself. And in Maine, corn and beans have been at home from Indian days.

2 teaspoons chili
   powder
4 tablespoons tomato
   sauce
1 1/2 cups stone-ground
   yellow cornmeal
1 teaspoon sea salt
2 1/2 cups cold water
1/4-1/2 cup grated
   cheddar cheese

1. In a heavy-bottomed pot sauté onion and garlic in olive oil till limp. Then add and mix together well beans, vegetables, one teaspoon each salt and chili powder, black pepper, and tomato sauce, and simmer till mixture is hot.
2. Whisk together cornmeal, one teaspoon each salt and chili powder, and water in a medium-sized saucepan. Cook over medium heat till cornmeal thickens and comes to a boil. Stir constantly with a wire whisk.
3. Spread two-thirds of the cornmeal over the bottom and sides of a well-buttered ten-inch pie pan. Pour in the bean mixture. Spread the remaining cornmeal mush on top and sprinkle with a quarter cup grated cheddar cheese. Bake in a preheated 350°F oven thirty to fifty minutes, or till the crust is browned and insides are hot.

Serve with fresh salad and fruit for dessert.

Soups

Bean soups are popular and nutritious, especially if suitably herbed. Onions and garlic are essential ingredients, and when combined with other traditional, native-American vegetables— tomatoes, squash, and corn—Mainers can enjoy this classic winter soup.

All-American Soup
(8 servings)

6-12 cups water
1 1/2 cups dried cran-
   berry or navy beans
   OR 3 cups shelled fresh
   (or canned) cranberry
   beans
1 1/2 cups chopped
   onion
2 cloves garlic, minced
6 medium-sized
   tomatoes, peeled,
   seeded, and chopped
   OR 4 cups canned
   tomatoes, partially
   drained and chopped
1 1/2 teaspoons dried
   basil, crumbled
1 teaspoon dried
   oregano, crumbled
freshly ground black
   pepper
1 pound winter squash
   (such as a buttercup
   or butternut), peeled,
   seeded, and cut into
   small cubes equaling
   about 2 cups
1/2 cup corn kernels, cut
   from 1 large ear of
   fresh corn if possible
2 teaspoons sea salt
1 tablespoon nutritional
   or brewer's yeast

1. If using dried navy or cranberry beans, *the night before* clean beans carefully and set to soak in three times as much water.
2. *In the morning*, bring six cups water to a boil in a heavy kettle. Add drained »

beans slowly to the boiling water. Reduce heat and simmer until nearly done, about forty-five minutes. (If using canned shelled beans, simply heat through with the water.)

3. While beans cook, simmer onion, garlic, tomatoes, basil, oregano, and black pepper till onions and tomatoes are limp.

4. Add this tomato sauce to beans along with squash. Simmer till both squash and beans are done, about half an hour.

5. Stir in remaining ingredients and simmer five minutes.

Serve in large soup plates topped with a dash of a hot pepper sauce with a hearty tossed salad and **Simply Super Skillet Corn Bread** or fresh whole-wheat bread.

Curried Red Lentils

(6 servings)

1 cup red lentils
2 tablespoons sunflower seed oil
2 medium-sized onions, chopped
1 teaspoon poppy seeds
1 teaspoon cumin powder
1 teaspoon Hungarian paprika
1 teaspoon turmeric powder
1 teaspoon coriander powder
1/8 teaspoon powdered cloves
1 teaspoon cinnamon
freshly ground black pepper
4 cloves garlic, minced
about 2 cups water
1/2 teaspoon sea salt

1. Rinse lentils quickly.

2. In a skillet heat oil and sauté onions till limp. Add poppy seeds, spices, and garlic and fry about one minute until spices are browning.

3. In a medium-sized saucepan combine lentils with water and salt. Bring to a boil and simmer on medium heat till tender. This won't take long (perhaps fifteen to twenty minutes).

4. Just before serving, stir spice/onion paste into lentils and mix well.

Serve as a side dish with brown rice, other whole grain, or pasta (for complete protein), a vegetable curry, chupattis, or puris.

Lentils

As in many other parts of the world lentils are a staple in India where, along with other legumes and pulses, they are regularly served with a whole grain to create complete protein. Americans tend to think of lentils as being flat, green legumes similar to split peas–and sometimes they are. But they also come in other colors, and their flavors are distinctive, if subtle. There are about five major types–some that resemble split peas in shape and size, others that are small and black. Our native split peas can be substituted in many recipes.

Sadie's Lebanese Lentils
(6-8 servings)

2 tablespoons extra-virgin
   olive oil
1 medium-sized onion,
   chopped fine
2 cups greenish-brown
   lentils
1 teaspoon sea salt
some freshly ground
   black pepper
1/2 teaspoon powdered
   cinnamon
4 cups water
juice of 1 1/2 lemons,
   freshly squeezed
2 (or more) cloves
   garlic, minced
1 packed cup chopped
   fresh parsley
2 lemons, quartered, for
   garnish

1. In a heavy cast-iron wok or saucepan heat olive oil and sauté onion till limp.
2. Wash and pick over lentils. Mix into onion and add salt, pepper, cinnamon, and water. Bring to a boil over high heat. Reduce heat, cover, and simmer about thirty minutes, or until lentils begin to get tender.
3. Add lemon juice, garlic, and parsley. Continue to simmer a few minutes, covered, until the lentils are very tender.
4. Lentils should be poured onto a plate and allowed to set. To make soup, advises Sadie, add lots of lemon juice.

Serve garnished with lemon quarters, accompanied by heaps of rice, barley, or pasta, a tossed salad, cooked vegetables in season, and yogurt.

Split Peas

Green split pea soup is a Maine favorite. The following recipe is definitely the best I've ever tasted. To increase flavor, simmer split peas till done, add vegetables, and immediately set dish aside to cool overnight. The following day, bring to a simmer, get the vegetables barely done, then add the remainder. But at the very least, begin making the soup early in the afternoon!

Split Pea Soup
(6-8 servings)

2 cups dry green split
   peas
5 cups water
2 teaspoons sea salt
1 bay leaf
1 cup diced onion
3 cloves garlic, minced
1 cup diced celery
1 small potato, cubed
2 cups diced carrots
1/4 cup port
1/4 teaspoon powdered
   mustard
1/4 teaspoon dried
   thyme

1 tablespoon nutritional
   yeast
3 tablespoons red wine
   vinegar or freshly
   squeezed lemon juice
1 cup chopped ripe
   tomatoes OR
   home-canned
   tomatoes, drained
1/4 cup freshly chopped
   parsley

1. *Early in the afternoon,* combine peas, water, salt, and bay leaf. Bring to a boil, lower heat and simmer, covered, until tender–about one hour.

»

2. One hour before dinner, add onion, garlic, celery, potato, and carrots, and simmer till vegetables are barely done.
3. About ten minutes before serving, add wine, mustard, thyme, nutritional yeast, vinegar or lemon juice, tomatoes, and parsley.

Serve with warm whole-grain bread and a tossed salad.

Spiced Pressure-Cooked Soybeans
(6 servings)

2 cups soybeans
2 tablespoons sunflower seed oil
3 medium-sized onions, chopped fine
3 garlic cloves, minced
2 cups thick canned tomatoes, chopped
1 cup finely chopped dates or raisins
1 tablespoon maple syrup
1 tablespoon shoyu
1/2 teaspoon allspice
1 tablespoon sea salt
1/4 teaspoon cayenne
1/4 cup cider vinegar OR 1/2 cup freshly squeezed lemon juice

1. Sort soybeans and wash.

Pressure-cook them according to directions on cooker.
2. Meanwhile, make the sauce. Heat oil in a heavy-bottomed enameled saucepan and sauté onions and garlic till limp. Add remaining ingredients and simmer, stirring, till dates are dissolved. If you want a sweeter dish, add more finely chopped dates or raisins.
3. Add cooked soybeans to sauce and simmer thirty minutes. The longer beans and sauce blend, the better the flavor.

Serve with a tossed salad and whole-grain bread, or over rice, other whole grain, or pasta, with steamed root vegetables.

Slurried Soy Casserole
(8 servings)

3/4 cup uncooked soybeans
1 1/2 cups water
1/2 cup bulgur wheat
1 cup boiling water
2 green bell peppers, chopped
1 (12-inch) stalk celery including tops, diced
4 medium-sized fresh ripe tomatoes,

Soybeans
In China and Japan the soybean is supreme, appreciated in its own right as well as being turned into tofu, tempeh, miso, and shoyu (see Glossary).

Soybeans contain all eight essential amino acids, which means they provide a complete protein as well as other vital nutrients. Called "the meat without a bone" in China, they're one of the oldest crops grown, first mentioned in Chinese records a little after 2000 B.C.

If you're allergic to dairy products, soybeans may be the food for you. They can be made into any number of items from "cheese" to "milk" to... paint! They are bland, accepting seasoning heartily. There are several varieties of soybeans, from the oilseed type (most commonly grown in America) to special tofu varieties, and colors vary from green to black to tan. Cooking times vary as well. If you purchase commercial oilseed soybeans from a farmer's supply store, the price will be cheaper because you'll be buying in bulk. But be sure that the beans are not treated with mercury or other poison.

To cook dry soybeans, simply soak them overnight in three times as much water, then simmer two to two and a half hours, or pressure-cook for a shorter period of time. Sprouting also lessens cooking time.

When pressure-cooking soybeans, observe instructions carefully, especially regarding the vent— soybean hulls can cause clogging.

chopped OR 2 cups
canned tomatoes,
drained thoroughly
1 1/2 cups chopped
onion
2 or more garlic cloves,
minced
1/4 cup chopped fresh
parsley or cilantro
3 tablespoons tomato
paste
1 teaspoon sea salt (or to
taste)
freshly ground black
pepper to taste
1/8 to 1/4 teaspoon hot
pepper sauce
1 teaspoon powdered
cumin
1 teaspoon dried basil
1 cup shredded cheddar
cheese

1. *The night before*, pick over beans and wash. Soak in four times as much water.

2. *The next day*, purée soaked, drained soybeans in blender with one and a half cups water, until smooth (resulting in about two cups).

3. Soak bulgur wheat in boiling water for fifteen minutes. Drain if any water remains.

4. In a large bowl combine all the remaining ingredients (except cheese) with puréed soybeans and soaked bulgur.

5. Place the mixture into a large, well-buttered casserole. Sprinkle cheese on top. Bake in a 375°F oven, covered, for forty-five minutes. Remove cover and bake fifteen minutes more.

Serve with shoyu, and a simple tossed salad of greens and sprouts.

Soylami

(1 small 4-cup loaf)

Here's a steamed "salami" which my family swears by. It makes a fine addition to cold salad platters and sandwiches, and can be served hot with gravy.

1 cup tan soybeans
1 small onion
2 large garlic cloves
4 tablespoons tahini
4 tablespoons
nutritional yeast
1/2 cup rolled oats
1 teaspoon kelp powder
2 tablespoons Dijon
mustard
1/2 teaspoon fennel
seed, whizzed in
blender
1 teaspoon freshly
ground black pepper

2-3 teaspoons sea salt
(or to taste)
3 teaspoons dried
oregano
1/2 teaspoon cayenne
1 teaspoon powdered
allspice
2 tablespoons finely
chopped fresh
parsley
1 slightly beaten egg
3 tablespoons milk to
moisten, if necessary

1. *The night before,* pick over beans and soak overnight.

2. *The next day,* grind beans

»

and onion through the fine-tooth cutter of a meat grinder and place in a large bowl.

3. Add remaining ingredients and mix well with your hands. Consistency should be like hamburger.

4. Fill one *well-buttered* four-cup coffee can or long, thin loaf pan nearly to top. (For a butter substitute see liquid lecithin and oil mixture, page 174.) Cover with aluminum foil, tie tightly with a string around edge (or use an elastic). Place on a rack in a kettle with water up to one inch from top of can/pan. Cover kettle, bring to boil, and simmer two and a half hours. When steamed enough, remove from kettle. (Check by inserting a knife–if it comes out clean, it's done.) Allow to cool completely. Remove from container.

Serve hot, sliced, and topped with gravy (see **Mushroom Gravy**) or white sauce, and accompanied by such vegetables as carrots, steamed greens, and salad. Or serve cold, sliced, with a tossed salad and a whole-grain dish. Or use in sandwiches.

Jean Ann's Soybean Sausages

(22 sausages, or 6-8 servings)

2 cups cooked soybeans
    OR sprouted soybeans,
    steamed 5
    minutes
1 large onion, peeled
    and quartered
3/4 cups fine
    whole-wheat bread
    crumbs
1 egg, beaten slightly
2 tablespoons chopped
    fresh parsley
1 teaspoon sea salt
freshly ground black
    pepper
1 teaspoon dried sage or
    dried thyme
1 teaspoon dried
    oregano

2 cloves garlic, minced
2 teaspoons soybean
    broth
unbleached flour OR
    finely ground
    breadcrumbs for
    coating
2 tablespoons sesame or
    extra-virgin olive oil
2 tablespoons clarified
    butter

1. Finely grind soybeans and onion in a meat grinder.

2. In a large bowl mix them together well with all but last three ingredients. Shape into little rolls like sausages about two and a half inches long. Dredge each roll in unbleached flour or finely ground breadcrumbs.

3. Sauté over medium heat

Soybean Sausages

Folks in Maine and elsewhere are turning soybeans into familiar dishes. Take sausages. Soybean sausages can be sautéed or baked, and seasoned to suit your mood. The sausage mixture can also be used to stuff cabbage, Swiss chard, or grape leaves.

for about five minutes, turning frequently, in oil and butter. Or bake for half an hour on a greased cookie sheet in a 350°F oven.

Serve with **Mushroom Gravy**, noodles, tossed salad, and/or cooked vegetables, and fruit for dessert.

Note: For variation, season the sausages with one teaspoon dill seed or three teaspoons chopped dill weed in place of thyme and oregano. Serve with dill-seasoned **Laban** (see Index) and top with chopped hard-boiled eggs.

In Maine where the growing season is short but often quite hot, the butterbean variety of green soybean grows very well. Developed for cooking in the fresh shell stage, it is superior in flavor, nutrition, and yield to lima beans, which are not adapted as well to northern growing conditions. Green soybeans are easily digested and well suited to canning and freezing.

Fresh Green Soybeans

Harvest pods when beans are plump. For easier shelling, rinse pods and steam or boil in a covered pot about five minutes. Flush with cold water and shell by popping beans out of pods and back into pot. Steam or boil shelled beans fifteen minutes or to taste.

Serve as a side dish with any meal as you would peas or lima beans.

Dried green soybeans, unlike their famous tan cousins, are more akin to dried peas or lima beans: they don't have to be soaked before cooking. In fact, cooking time is only about one hour.

Dried Green Soybeans

(4 servings)

1 cup dried green soybeans (carefully rinsed)
any herb you fancy
about 4 cups water

1. Place all ingredients in a heavy cast-iron (or other) pot.
2. Simmer one hour or till tender.

Serve with a whole grain, potatoes or pasta, and a crisp salad.

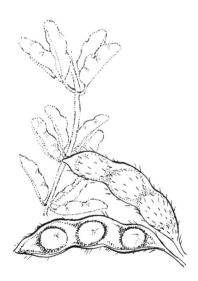

Tofu

*Tofu is Asia's meat. In fact, it has often been called "the meat of the field" because it's made of soybeans and delivers protein comparable to that found in fish. In Maine tofu is available in two forms: **doufu**, the firm Chinese variety; and **tofu**, the softer Japanese type. It can be made very soft, when it's called the **silken** custard type. Stocked by most local supermarkets as well as health food stores, tofu tastes extremely bland to Westerners–but its very blandness is its strength, for it easily absorbs other flavors.*

Making tofu at home is about as time-consuming and as complicated as bread-making, and the product (like home-made bread) is far superior to the purchased kind. I was first introduced to it by friends–we enjoyed a long, surprising evening watching mere soybeans come to a foam, turn into milk, and ultimately solidify into "meat." The taste was fine and sweet.

After that I set out on the trail of tofu-making, reading all that I could en route . What resulted, as always, was my own version. My tofu is firm. It takes less water and more epsom salts than some other tofu recipes. When finished, the cake is heavier and grainier than most. I reminded myself, the first time around, of what it might have been like for an old Chinese housewife discovering tofu for the first time. There was no art to it, no highly refined phrases, no "wine-tasting" attitude such as one finds in Japan. It was hot, hard work ending with solid "meat."

So here is "meat without a bone"–a firm, bland, whitish cake of rather cheesey stuff that you can slice, eat as is with a little shoyu, fry, or knead to produce wild and wonderful spinoffs.

There is a substance in raw soybeans, antitrypsin, which negates a good part of the usable protein. Adequate cooking destroys it. Note that both the tofu and okara (a nutritious by-product of making tofu) offered below are thoroughly cooked. You don't have to worry about steaming tofu before use, although you may cook it in any variety of ways. And okara can go directly into burgers. The actual work involved in the following recipe takes about an hour and a half.

Kitchen Sink Tofu

(1 sixteen-ounce cake)

2 cups dry soybeans equals 6 cups soaked soybeans
about 12 cups hot water
1 heaping tablespoon epsom salts in 1/4 cup warm water

1. Use beans not more than one year old. Pick over, discarding any dirt or imperfect specimens, and wash two cups of them.
2. Place in a large bowl with enough *cold water* to cover, about three inches over the top. Soak overnight, for four to five hours in summer; seven to ten in winter. Or pour boiling water over rinsed beans and soak two to four hours. (These beans will be wrinkle-free and have a flat, not concave, inner surface when ready.)
3. Split a bean after soaking overnight. If the inner surface is uniform-ly creamy and flat, it's ready. If concave and darker yellow, it's not. (Save the soak water for house plants only.)
4. Rinse beans well three times.
5. In a large pot bring twelve cups water to the boil. Purée two cups

soaked beans with three cups boiling water in blender about three minutes (don't overheat blender). Place a towel over the top so you don't get splashed and burn yourself. Pour purée into a very large, heavy-bottomed kettle. Repeat process two more times till all beans have been puréed.

6. Using a rubber spatula, scrape down sides of blender and add purée to kettle. Rinse the blender with a half cup *boiling water* and add to the pot.

7. Over medium heat, bring purée to a boil (fifteen to twenty minutes). It may foam up suddenly. *Simmer twenty minutes*, stirring a lot, to destroy the trypsin inhibitor.

8. Lay a twenty- by twenty-inch square of fine cheesecloth in a colander and set it over a big bowl. Pour in the purée. Gather the four corners, twist to close any openings, and squeeze out as much liquid as possible. Then press with a potato masher or sturdy glass jar to squeeze out the rest.

9. When most of the milk is squeezed out, loosen cheesecloth, shake the okara (the mealy substance inside),

open the cheesecloth, and pour in one cup *boiling water*. Close cheesecloth and squeeze again. Repeat if necessary with up to three cups water.

10. You have now produced soy milk. Save the valuable okara and store, covered, in the refrigerator for use in breads, soy meats, soups, burgers, and all sorts of goodies. (See the Index for recipes.)

11. Two large, nesting stainless-steel mixing bowls and a wok ring, if available, are perfect for what follows. Pour soy milk into a large stainless-steel mixing bowl set on a wire rack inside a still larger stainless-steel bowl. Set both on a wok ring. Fill outer bowl with water to come three inches up sides of inner bowl. Bring soy milk to a slow, rolling boil (212°F). If you don't have such bowls or a wok ring, use a large heavy kettle over moderate heat and stir often to prevent sticking.

12. As the soy milk cooks you will note a thin film developing on top as happens with dairy milk. This is called *yuba*, a highly prized delicacy in Japan. Remove and eat with a little shoyu sprinkled on top. (The Japanese use it in cooking.)

13. Once soy milk has come to a boil, remove from heat and immediately add your epsom salts dissolved in water. Stir in evenly and thoroughly with a wooden spoon.

14. Stop the milk from moving by holding the spoon upright. Remove and wait five to ten minutes till milk curdles well. You should have "white clouds floating in a yellow sky."

15. Set a wooden tofu box, or a colander lined with one layer of moistened cheesecloth, over a large, flat pan. Gently ladle curd into cloth-lined tofu box or colander. (Save whey for bread-making, soups, and so on.)

16. When whey has mostly run through, fold the cheesecloth over the curds and place a three- to five-pound weight on top. Drain about fifteen minutes for soft tofu, longer for firm tofu.

17. When tofu is firm, fill a sink or pan with cold water, sink box into it, and push tofu (in its cheesecloth) out the bottom. If you used a colander, lift the tofu-filled cheesecloth into the cold water. Allow the tofu to rest about ten minutes, then gently pull cloth off underwater.

»

18. Slide tofu onto a dish to use immediately, or store, covered with cold water, in the refrigerator in a closed container. It will keep about a week if you change water daily.

19. Wash all dishes, box, and cloths immediately in *cold* water. The tofu box ought to be sweetened with lemon juice and placed in the sun until dry. If soy milk sticks to kettle, bring two tablespoons bicarbonate of soda and four cups water to a boil in it. The kettle should come clean. An overnight soak with bleach to cover the bottom of the kettle is also helpful.

Note: Other coagulating agents can be used to solidify soy milk into tofu. Try two teaspoons coarse nigari (seawater minerals) in one cup water OR five table-spoons cider vinegar or lemon juice in one cup water.

Tips: (1) If you purchase tofu, drain off the water. If used within twenty-four hours, don't bother to add new water. If saved for later use, cover each day with fresh cold water and refrigerate.

(2) If tofu needs freshening because you've kept it so long that it shows signs of spoiling, drop it into one quart boiling salted water, remove from heat, and allow to rest two to three minutes. Drain and store as above.

Tofu Cutlets
(6 servings)

1 (16-ounce) fresh cake tofu
1 tablespoon clarified butter
1 tablespoon extra-virgin olive or sunflower seed oil

1. Drain tofu for fifteen to thirty minutes in a colander over a container.
2. If soft, place on a towel, top with a small cutting board or plate, and press with about three pounds weight for thirty minutes. Firm tofu doesn't need this.
3. Slice into six half-inch-thick pieces. (Save the rest for another dish.)
4. Heat butter and oil in heavy skillet and sauté tofu over moderate heat until golden on both sides. Salt to taste (optional) before serving.

Serve with a tossed salad, brown rice, and cooked vegetables.

Note: Good garnishes for **Tofu Cutlets** are thinly sliced scallions, chopped chives, grated ginger root, Dijon mustard, grated carrot and cucumber, chopped hard-boiled eggs, miso, freshly squeezed lemon juice, shoyu, sesame tahini seasoned with miso (see Glossary), and/or freshly squeezed lemon juice, **Laban**, or **Tomato Sauce**.

The simplest and quickest way to serve tofu is in cutlet form. The contrast between the crusty exterior and the smooth interior is delightful. Accompanied by salad greens and rice, dinner is easier than a hamburger meal.

Or serve as you would burgers on **Burger Buns**. For an open-face sandwich sprinkle grated cheese on top, and pop under the broiler till melted.

Tofu with Noodles

(4-6 servings)

1 8-ounce cake firm
    tofu
1/4 cup shoyu
1 tablespoon sunflower
    seed oil
1 tablespoon clarified
    butter
1 medium-sized onion,
    sliced thin
2 cups mushrooms,
    sliced
1/4 cup finely chopped
    bell pepper
1 cup Laban
1/4 cup white wine or
    dry sherry
2 tablespoons tomato
    sauce
freshly ground black
    pepper
1/2 teaspoon maple
    syrup (optional)
2 tablespoons finely
    chopped fresh parsley

1. Drain tofu well. (If using soft tofu, press for fifteen minutes under a three-pound weight.) Cut into slices about two inches long, a quarter-inch thick and half-inch wide.

2. Pour shoyu into a shallow bowl and dip tofu in it. Drain. .

3. Warm wok and heat oil and butter.

4. Sauté tofu over moderate heat until brown on all sides. Set aside.

5. Stir-fry onions, mushrooms, and pepper three minutes. (See **The Wok**.)

6. Make **Laban** in a small saucepan. Add wine, tomato sauce, salt, and pepper. If it is very tart, add maple syrup. Cook a little bit longer to make it as thick as thick cream.

7. Add to vegetables and return sautéed tofu to wok. Simmer all together one to two minutes or until just heated through.

Serve hot, sprinkled with two tablespoons finely chopped fresh parsley, accompanied by one pound of cooked whole-grain noodles (preferably homemade).

Tofu Kebabs

(6 kebabs)

1 (16-ounce) cake firm
    tofu
komé miso (see
    Glossary)
12 small button
    mushroom caps
    (save stems for other
    dishes)
12 cherry tomatoes
green or red bell pepper,
    cut into 6 (1-inch)
    bits
6 small onions
1/2 cup shoyu
6 tablespoons white
    wine
6 tablespoons maple
    syrup
1 teaspoon grated fresh
    ginger root
3 garlic cloves, minced
1/2 teaspoon Dijon
    mustard

1. Drain firm tofu. (If using soft tofu, be sure to press it with three pounds for thirty minutes.) Cut crosswise into two slices one inch thick.
2. Spread slices on both sides with a thin layer of komé miso. Then cut into one-inch cubes. You will have twelve.
3. Parboil onions for one minute in boiling water and peel.
4. Cut pepper into six one-inch chunks.
5. In a medium-sized bowl, make a marinade by combining shoyu, wine, maple syrup, ginger root, garlic, and mustard. Add onions, tomatoes, peppers, and mushrooms, and marinate for at least one hour.
6. Soak six bamboo skewers in water for fifteen minutes. Arrange on skewers in the following order: mushroom, tofu cube, tomato, pepper, onion, mushroom, tofu, and tomato. Broil six inches below preheated broiler two minutes for the first side. Turn with a spatula, baste with marinade, and broil one minute on the second side. Repeat for remaining two sides. Use your judgment and remove from heat when vegetables and tofu are cooked but not overcooked.

Serve on a bed of brown rice or pasta, with side dishes of remaining marinade for dipping, a small raw salad, and warm rolls or chupattis.

Note: The above marinade of shoyu, wine, maple syrup, ginger root, garlic, and Dijon mustard is excellent for use with poultry or fish.

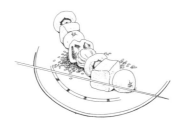

Tofu and Brown Rice Casserole

(6 servings)

There are a number of steps to the following one-dish meal, but the result is well worth it–and it's especially good for company.

2 cups water or
    vegetable stock
1/2 teaspoon sea salt
    (optional)
1 cup brown rice
1 tablespoon sunflower
    seed oil
1/2 cup chopped
    scallions or 1 small
    onion, chopped
1 3/4 cups sliced
    mushrooms (about 6
    ounces)
1 tablespoon finely
    chopped red bell pepper
    OR 1 tablespoon
    chopped pimento
2 tablespoons clarified
    butter
1 1/2 cups firm tofu
    cubes (cut into
    1/2-inch cubes)
1 cup nutritional yeast
1 teaspoon sea salt
1/4 cup toasted
    sunflower seeds
1 tablespoon shoyu
2 tablespoons sliced
    black olives
    (optional)
2 cups finely chopped,
    cooked spinach (10
    ounces, raw)
    OR any home-canned or
    frozen green of
    choice
3/4 cup shredded jack or
    cheddar cheese
3/4 cup shredded
    cheddar or bleu
    cheese

1. In a one-quart saucepan bring salted water or stock to a boil. Add rice, cover, and simmer forty-five minutes or till tender. Remove from heat, uncover, and cool slightly.

2. Heat oil in a skillet and sauté scallions, mushrooms, and (if used) red bell pepper till limp. Remove to a plate.

3. In the same skillet heat the butter. Toss the tofu cubes in a bowl with the nutritional yeast and one teaspoon sea salt. Sauté the coated tofu in the butter until golden on all sides. Set aside.

4. With a fork, mix sunflower seeds, pimento (if used), and olives lightly into the rice. Spread evenly in a well-buttered, seven-and-a-half- by eleven- by two-inch baking pan.

5. Arrange spinach, tofu, jack, or cheddar cheese over the rice layer. Place sautéed mushrooms and scallions on top. Sprinkle with shredded cheddar or bleu cheese. Bake, uncovered, at 350°F till browned and hot, about thirty minutes.

Serve with tossed salad and fresh rolls.

Tofu Balls

(6-8 servings or 54 balls)

1 1/2 pounds soft tofu
1 teaspoon sea salt
2 large cloves garlic,
    minced
1 tablespoon freshly
    grated lemon peel
1 heaping tablespoon
    fresh parsley, finely
    chopped
1/8 teaspoon freshly
    grated nutmeg
1/2 teaspoon dried
    thyme or 1 teaspoon
    fresh, finely chopped
    thyme
1 teaspoon nutritional
    yeast
freshly ground black
    pepper to taste
1 egg, slightly beaten
2 cups dry, finely
    ground whole-wheat
    bread crumbs
2 or more tablespoons
    clarified butter
2 or more tablespoons
    sunflower seed oil
4 cups cubed winter
    squash (such as
    buttercup)
1 cup chopped onion
1 medium-sized white
    potato, cubed
3 heaping tablespoons
    celery leaves and
    stalk, diced finely
2 cups water
1 teaspoon sea salt
1 clove garlic, minced
2 tablespoons cornstarch
    OR arrowroot
    dissolved in 1 cup
    water
1/8 teaspoon nutmeg

2 lemons, quartered, for
    garnish
1-2 tablespoons finely
    chopped fresh
    parsley, for garnish

1. Place tofu in a sieve and drain fifteen minutes. Then twist and squeeze hard in a towel or cheesecloth.
2. Transfer to a medium-sized bowl and knead with fingers for three or four minutes until soft and smooth.
3. To tofu add one teaspoon salt, two cloves garlic, lemon peel, parsley, nutmeg, thyme, nutritional yeast, and black pepper. Knead two or more minutes, then mix in egg. Shape tofu into "meatballs" one inch in diameter. Whiz dried breadcrumbs in blender until fine. Then roll tofu balls in crumbs.
4. Heat butter and oil in a heavy skillet and sauté tofu balls over moderate heat until golden on all sides. (You may have to add additional butter and oil before finishing all fifty-four balls.) Remove from pan and set aside.
5. To make a gravy, combine squash, onion, potato, celery, two cups water, one teaspoon salt, one clove garlic, and black pepper in a heavy saucepan. Simmer until all vegetables are tender (about twenty minutes), then purée in blender with dissolved arrowroot or cornstarch till

velvety. (Do in two batches if necessary.) Result should be five cups thick sauce. Return to saucepan, bring to a boil stirring constantly, and adjust thickness with water if necessary to make a creamy gravy.

6. Add tofu balls and one-eighth teaspoon nutmeg, and simmer very gently over very low heat at least an hour. Do not stir if possible.

Serve sprinkled with freshly chopped parsley, on brown rice, noodles, or other whole grain, with a green salad and lemon quarters for each diner.

Note: For variety, add tofu balls to **Carrot Nut Soup** and simmer as above.

Okara

Okara is the sediment collected in your cheesecloth during the first stages of tofu-making–a side-effect that makes the process doubly worthwhile. It's a wonderfully versatile, nutritious food, fine for burgers, loaves, casseroles, or, as in this case, to make a type of "bologna."

Okara Bologna

(making 1 tofu cake yields 4 cups okara)

2 cups okara
1 cup whole-wheat flour
1/2 cup wheat germ
1/2 cup nutritional yeast
1 teaspoon kelp powder
2 tablespoons Dijon mustard or 1 teaspoon dry mustard
1/2 teaspoon fennel seeds, whizzed a moment in blender
1 teaspoon freshly ground black pepper
1/4 cup shoyu
3 teaspoons dried oregano
1-2 teaspoons sea salt
1/2 teaspoon (or more) cayenne
3 cloves garlic, minced
2 teaspoons allspice
about 3/4 cup soy or dairy milk OR water

1. In a medium-sized bowl combine all ingredients, except milk or water, and mix well.

2. Add just enough milk or water to make a stiff dough. Knead in bowl with hands to mix thoroughly.

3. Press into a well-buttered four- by six- by two-inch loaf pan, a twelve-ounce cylindrical baking tin, or several sausage-shaped, oven-proof glasses or cups. Cover with foil and tie down tightly with string or an elastic band. Stand container(s) on a rack in a baking pan of boiling water and bake at 350°F for forty-five minutes. Or stand containers on a rack in a large kettle. Pour in hot water to within an inch of the okara container's top. Bring to a boil, then lower heat, and simmer one and a half hours.

4. Remove from kettle or pan. Set on a rack and allow to cool till firm. Remove "bologna" by inverting and shaking.

Serve thinly sliced in sandwiches; as a cold cut on a tray of cheese slices and vegetables; or fry in a little

»

butter and serve hot with a gravy; or cube for spaghetti and "meatballs."

Note: Instead of steaming, make patties of the mixture and sauté. Okara from the tofu recipe is precooked and can therefore be used directly.

Tempeh Chips
(4-6 servings)

(a) 1/2 cup water
1 teaspoon sea salt
1/2 teaspoon powdered coriander
1 clove crushed garlic

(b) 1/4 cup freshly squeezed lemon juice
1/4 cup water
1 teaspoon sea salt
1-2 cloves crushed garlic

(c) 1/2 cup water
1 1/4 teaspoons Garam Masala
1 teaspoon sea salt

1 (10- or 12-ounce) tempeh cake
3 cups peanut oil

1. Choose ingredients (a), (b), or (c) for marinade and combine in a small bowl.
2. Cut tempeh cake into slices an eighth of an inch thick. Soak in marinade of choice ten minutes. Drain on a towel and pat dry.
3. Warm wok (see **The Wok**) and heat oil to 350°F. Slide in tempeh slices and fry about two minutes or till crisp and golden brown. Drain.

Serve immediately with brown rice, other whole grain or polenta, vegetables in season, and the dipping sauce from **Tofu Kebabs**.

Tempeh Burgers
(3 servings)

1 (10-ounce) rectangular tempeh cake cut into 3 pieces, each measuring about 2-by-3-by-1/2-inch
(a) 2 tablespoons minced onion
1 tablespoon maple syrup
1/2 teaspoon sea salt
1 cup water

(b) 1 cup water
1 1/4 teaspoon Simple Garam Masala
1 teaspoon sea salt

2/3 cup white unbleached flour
1 egg, slightly beaten
1/4 cup cornmeal
2 tablespoons nutritional yeast
3 cups peanut oil

Tempeh
Unlike some bean products, tempeh (see Glossary) doesn't cause flatulence. It appears to keep the intestinal tract healthy, and is reported to prevent dysentery. Usually made from split soybeans, it can also be made from grains and other legumes. It's most commonly available commercially in ten- or twelve-ounce flat, rectangular cakes.

Tempeh Chips are an excellent way to cook this wholesome product. But tempeh can also be cubed and quickly deep-fried or used in place of tofu for kebabs (see Tofu Kebabs). Or tempeh cakes may be cut into three pieces and sautéed to make straightforward "hamburgers."

Tempeh burgers are absolutely delicious and can be served in the usual manner on a bun with ketchup, mustard, onions, pickles, or whatever you fancy. Simmering before quickly deep-frying makes them succulent and tender.

1. Combine the tempeh and (a) or (b) in a small saucepan. Bring to a boil, then turn heat to low and simmer, uncovered, twenty minutes.
2. Remove tempeh from pan and cool on a rack till dry. Then dip into flour, egg, and cornmeal mixture; return to rack, and allow to dry a minute or two.

3. Heat wok and add peanut oil. Heat to 350°F. Deep-fry tempeh slices about two minutes or till golden brown. Drain quickly.

Serve on **Burger Buns** with one tomato slice, lettuce, and the usual condiments of mayonnaise, ketchup, mustard, or relish as desired. An open-face burger is perhaps best.

Grains

*Unrefined whole grains are nutritious and **very** tasty. From corn to wheat to rice, they've been the staples of traditional cuisines since people began farming. Combined with legumes, whole grains offer a diet rich in complete protein and complex carbohydrates. When left in its nutritious whole form, grain fuels the body and provides it with many crucial vitamins and minerals as well as bulk and protein.*

New Maine cooks know that "organically grown" grains (raised on land fertilized with compost and manure, as opposed to commercial chemical fertilizers) are richer in nutrients as well as being free of pesticides, herbicides, and fungicides. Buy these if you can—they are available in health food stores, or, for a lower price, from food co-operatives.

Cooking Whole Grains

1. Rinse whole grain of choice quickly in cold water. Drain well in a strainer.
2. Bring liquid to a boil in a heavy-bottomed kettle (or a double-boiler, which is superb for cooking grain) and add a quarter- to a half-teaspoon sea salt per cup of grain (optional).
3. Pour grain slowly into specified amount of boiling liquid so that boiling does not stop, and stir as you pour. This keeps each grain or particle separate and shortens cooking time.
4. Lower heat, and simmer, tightly covered, till all water is absorbed–twenty to sixty minutes. Add boiling water and simmer longer if necessary.
5. Remove lid and simmer ten minutes longer. Don't stir, or grain will become gummy.

Rule of thumb: One part raw grain yields about two and a half parts cooked. One cup raw grain yields four to six half-cup servings.

Note: Cornmeal must always be mixed with cold liquid first.

Specific Simmering Time for Whole Grains

Amount of Water, Milk, or Stock	1 Cup Grain	Cooking Time	Yield
2 cups liquid	**Amaranth** (toasted seeds are good for cereal)	15 minutes	3 1/2 cups
2 cups liquid	**Brown barley** (whole grain; also comes flaked)	50 minutes	3-3 1/2 cups
2 1/4 cups liquid	**Buckwheat groats** (cook like rice; or use toasted groats to make kasha)	15 minutes	4 cups
2 cups boiling water	**Bulgur** (already precooked by steaming and cracking; comes in fine to coarse grinds)	Pour boiling water over and let stand 10-30 minutes. Drain.	2 cups
4 cups cold liquid	**Coarse cornmeal** (as used in polenta)	25-45 minutes	3 cups
2 cups lukewarm water	**Couscous** (precooked semolina)	Let set 10 minutes. Fluff with fork.	4 cups
2 cups	**Cracked wheat** (not precooked)	25 minutes	2 1/2 cups
3 cups	**Millet** (swells enormously)	30 minutes	4 1/2 cups
3 cups	**Wild rice**	50 minutes	5 1/4 cups
2 cups	**Long-grain brown rice**	45-60 minutes	3 cups
2 cups	**Short-grain brown rice**	45 minutes	3 1/2 cups
2 1/4 cups	**Whole oats** (oat groats; (also comes rolled or cut)	55 minutes	2 cups
3 cups (drain after cooking)	**Whole rye berries** (also comes flaked)	1 hour	2 1/2 cups
3 cups (drain after cooking)	**Whole-wheat berries** (see bulgur and cracked wheat; also comes flaked)	1 1/2 hours	2 1/2 cups

Note: Soy grits can be cooked with any grain to boost protein quality.

Barley
(4-6 servings)

Barley can replace rice in any recipe. It is highly nutritious and filling—wonderful winter fare. It also makes a fine salad.

1 cup whole (hulled)
    brown barley
3 cups hot water
1 bay leaf
1 teaspoon dill seeds
    (optional)
1 teaspoon sea salt
1 teaspoon finely grated
    lemon rind
1 tablespoon finely
    chopped fresh
    parsley

1. Rinse barley quickly. In a large skillet, over moderate heat, toast barley, stirring constantly, about five minutes or until dry and slightly brown.
2. Add hot water and next three ingredients. Cover tightly, reduce heat to very low, and simmer until all moisture is absorbed, about forty-five minutes. Add more hot water if necessary.
3. Stir in grated lemon rind and garnish with parsley.

Serve with half as much legume for complete protein or with fish and cooked vegetables.

Barley Salad
(4 servings)

Pearled barley, though less nutritious than brown, makes a fine salad.

2 cups water
1 teaspoon sea salt
1 cup rinsed pearled
    barley
1/4 cup scallions, diced
1-2 heaping tablespoons
    chopped fresh dill
    weed
freshly ground black
    pepper
1 teaspoon grated lemon
    rind (optional)
1 recipe My Favorite
    Salad Dressing mixed
    with half as much
    yogurt
more dill weed and
    Hungarian paprika
    for garnishes

1. Bring water and salt to boil. Add barley slowly so boil does not stop.
2. Reduce heat, and cook till tender, about thirty minutes.
3. Cool, then add remaining ingredients. Bind nicely with salad dressing.

Serve mounded on greens, garnished with more dill and a dash of paprika.

Kasha

(4 servings)

2 eggs
2 cups buckwheat groats
    (hulled)
4 cups boiling water
2 teaspoons sea salt
    (optional)

1. Lightly beat eggs in a small bowl. Stir in groats.
2. Pour egg-coated groats into a hot, ungreased skillet, and stir around till grains are dry, separate, and toasted. (Don't burn.)
3. Add boiling water and salt. Stir and cover. Reduce heat to low, and simmer thirty minutes.
4. Remove cover and allow any remaining liquid to evaporate.

Serve as a side dish to anything from tempeh (see Glossary) to fish, with a tossed salad or cooked greens and vegetables in season. **Red Cabbage Delicious** complements it beautifully.

Note: For variation, add one and a half cups finely diced carrot, onion, celery, sunchokes, and mushrooms to kasha during cooking; or sauté vegetables, add to cooked kasha along with one tablespoon dry sherry or dry white wine, and season with sea salt and freshly ground black pepper to taste.

Buckwheat Groats

Early Americans ate a lot of nutritious buckwheat both as flour and as groats (or whole seeds). But kasha is originally a northern European classic. Leftover, it's wonderfully well suited for filling peppers or cabbage leaves, or for making **Kasha Meatloaf.**

Baked Indian Pudding

(4 servings)

2 cups milk
1/3 cup stone-ground
    yellow cornmeal
1/2 cup molasses
1/2 teaspoon sea salt
1/2 teaspoon cinnamon
1 1/2 teaspoons
    powdered ginger
1/2 teaspoon finely
    grated lemon rind
1 beaten egg
2 cups milk

1. In a double boiler over boiling water, whisk together two cups milk, cornmeal, and molasses. Cook for twenty minutes, stirring occasionally.
2. Add salt, cinnamon, ginger, and egg. Scald the remaining two cups milk and add.
3. Pour into a well-buttered two-quart casserole, and bake uncovered at 250°F three hours. Allow to rest from fifteen to twenty minutes before serving.

Serve hot with ice cream. (Lemon sherbet or vanilla are best.) In the old days it was garnished with thick cream, plain or whipped. **Crème Fraîche** would also be fine.

Note: For variation, add a quarter cup of raisins.

Cornmeal

Cornmeal was a staple in our house. Mother made cornmeal mush, muffins, and innumerable sheets of thin, crisp johnny cake.

And how well I remember enjoying that hot, sticky mass of Baked Indian Pudding when I was a child! I present it here in all its glory, a recipe cooked by my grandmothers, aunts, and mother, if adapted a bit to suit the modern palate.

Millet

Millet is a high-quality food rich in vital nutrients, including vitamin B-17. It's easily digested and, being bland, helps to heal gastrointestinal problems. It's quick and easy, and an excellent food for babies as well as adults.

Simple Millet with Curried Gravy

(4-6 servings)

for the millet:
5 cups water
2 cups rinsed millet
1/2 teaspoon sea salt (optional)

for the gravy:
1 cup yogurt
3 cups water
    OR 3 cups buttermilk
2 tablespoons sunflower seed oil
1/2 teaspoon mustard seed (black or yellow)
1/2 teaspoon cumin seed
1 teaspoon fenugreek seed
3 whole cloves
1 (1-inch) stick cinnamon
1/2 teaspoon sea salt
1 teaspoon powdered ginger
1 teaspoon turmeric
1 teaspoon powdered coriander
1/4 teaspoon Hungarian paprika
1/2 teaspoon (or more) cayenne (optional)
2 tablespoons cornstarch or arrowroot
1/4 cup water
1 teaspoon honey or maple syrup (optional)

1. Bring five cups water to a boil in a medium-sized saucepan. Add salt and millet slowly without stopping the boil.
2. Simmer over low heat about twenty-five minutes. Remove from heat, remove cover, and let rest five minutes. Fluff with fork.
3. To make gravy, combine yogurt and three cups water or buttermilk.
4. Heat oil in a heavy skillet. Add mustard seed, cumin, and fenugreek seed, cloves, and cinnamon stick, and heat, stirring constantly, until the mustard seeds hop.
5. Pour in the diluted yogurt, and whisk in one-half teaspoon salt, ginger, turmeric, coriander, paprika, and cayenne if desired. Allow to simmer twenty minutes over low heat.
6. Then add cornstarch or arrowroot dissolved in a quarter cup water, bring to a boil, cook one minute or until it thickens, and remove from heat.
7. Just before serving add sweetening if desired.

Serve millet topped or mixed with the gravy, accompanied by sprouts, sunflower seeds, chopped apples and celery, cooked greens, and other vegetables in season, raw or cooked.

Jenny's Rice

1. Wash brown rice quickly.
2. Soak in a saucepan with water to cover for as long as is convenient–thirty minutes to all night.
3. When ready to cook, measure depth of water by placing your little finger vertically into pot until fingertip touches top of rice and water just reaches first knuckle, or slightly beyond if your finger is very short.
4. Bring to a boil.
5. Lower heat immediately, and cover.

6. Simmer until done, about forty-five minutes.

Check rice. Serve when tooth-tender. Water should be soaked up with little "holes" appearing in the surface. If rice tastes tough and you're out of water, add more boiling water and continue simmering.

Note: Spices such as cumin and turmeric or grated lemon rind may be added while cooking, as well as cinnamon and diced, dried fruits.

Rice

Rice isn't grown in Maine, but it has become an enormously popular staple of modern American cooking. There are numerous methods for cooking rice, but I favor this one offered by my Korean friend, Jenny Kim.

Jenny uses white rice, which has a tradition of long standing in the orient. White rice, its outer coverings removed, has obviously lost nutrients, most particularly B vitamins, but it also keeps better than brown rice, and causes less intestinal gas.

However, New Maine cooks prefer brown rice. Of the hundreds of strains of rice, the long-grain variety cooks up the driest. Short-grain rice is less expensive and has a higher protein yield. Though cooking it seems to require more of a knack, it can be very fluffy. Basmati, a high-grade variety that is naturally light-colored even without milling, and fluffier than most brown rice, is considered the "queen of rice." It has a particularly pleasant, nutty flavor.

Burgers

*One of the nicest things about cooking beans and grains is that leftovers are never a problem. In fact, they're welcomed. Combined–in burgers or loaves–they produce a whole protein that easily replaces hamburger and meatloaf. Mainers, like all Americans, eat a lot of hamburgers. Grain and legume burgers are just as quick, often have a similar texture, are tasty, and are becoming increasingly popular. They make hearty winter eating. Try **Burger Buns**, **Sunflower/ Navy Bean Burgers**, and **Red Lentil Burgers** as well as the following recipes.*

Note: Combining bean burger mixture with the hands is the method of choice to ensure success.

Also note: Beans vary in their moisture content due to age and cooking time. Thin any mix with yogurt or bean stock, and thicken any mixture with rolled oats.

Basic Bean Burgers
(10 burgers)

2 cups leftover cooked beans, drained well (black turtle, pinto, and navy are especially good)
1 cup leftover cooked brown rice, oat groats, or whole barley
1 large Spanish onion OR 1 cup chopped scallions
3 cloves garlic, minced
1 teaspoon sea salt (optional)
freshly ground black pepper
1 teaspoon dried thyme
1 teaspoon dried oregano
1 teaspoon dried basil
1 tablespoon brewer's or nutritional yeast
1 teaspoon kelp powder
1/4 cup non-instant, low-fat powdered milk (optional)
1/4 cup wheat germ (optional)
1/2 cup sunflower seeds
1 large egg, slightly beaten

1 egg whisked with 1 teaspoon cold water
1 cup sesame seeds
2 tablespoons extra-virgin olive oil
2 tablespoons clarified butter

1. Grind beans, rice, and onion in the fine cutter of a meat grinder. (Chop scallions if you use them.)
2. Combine with garlic, salt, pepper, herbs, yeast, kelp, milk powder, wheat germ, sunflower seeds, and one beaten egg. Mixture should be the same consistency as hamburger.
3. Make patties three inches in diameter, and dip into egg whisked with a teaspoon of water. Then dip into sesame seeds, and sauté gently over medium heat, about seven minutes per side in olive oil and butter.

Serve on a slice of whole-grain bread or a **Burger Bun** with lettuce or alfalfa sprouts, slices of tomato and cheese, and **Yogurt Tahini Dressing**. Or serve hot with potatoes, steamed or pickled vegetables, and sprouts.

Soyburgers
(6 burgers)

2 cups cooked soybeans (1 cup dry soybeans)
1 egg, slightly beaten
1/4 cup whole-wheat bread cubes

1/2 stalk celery, diced
1/2 cup grated carrot
2 cloves garlic, minced
1/2 cup diced onion
1/2 teaspoon dried marjoram
1/2 teaspoon dried sage

»

1/2 teaspoon dried
    summer savory
1 teaspoon dried thyme
freshly ground black
    pepper
1/2 teaspoon sea salt
    (optional)
1 cup unbleached white
    flour for dredging
2 tablespoons extra-
    virgin olive oil
    (optional)
2 tablespoons clarified
    butter (optional)

1. Grind soybeans through the fine cutter of a meat grinder.
2. Combine with remaining ingredients except oil, butter, and flour.

3. Shape into patties three inches in diameter.
4. Dredge with flour and sauté in olive oil and butter in a skillet till golden on each side. OR omit dredging and bake in a 350°F oven for about ten minutes on each side, turning once.

Serve for lunch on **Burger Buns**, topped with grated cheddar cheese, sliced onions and mushrooms, sliced tomato, and strips of green bell pepper. Or serve for dinner with green salad, a cooked whole grain, pasta or potatoes, and steamed or marinated vegetables in season.

Bean Oat Burgers

(6 burgers)

1 1/2 cups any type
    cooked beans with
    their cooking liquor
1 cup rolled oats
1/4 cup chopped walnuts
1/2 cup finely chopped
    onion
2 tablespoons brewer's
    or nutritional yeast
1/2 teaspoon dried
    thyme
1/2 teaspoon dried
    oregano (optional)
1/2 teaspoon dried basil
    (optional)
1/2 teaspoon sea salt
freshly ground black
    pepper

1 large garlic clove
1 egg
1 cup unbleached white
    flour for dredging
    (optional)
2 tablespoons extra-
    virgin olive oil
    (optional)
2 tablespoons clarified
    butter (optional)

1. Grind drained beans through the fine cutter of a meat grinder.
2. Combine with remaining ingredients except oils and flour. Allow to rest ten minutes. Consistency should resemble hamburger. If too wet, add rolled oats. If too dry, add bean liquor

as necessary.

3. Shape into patties three inches in diameter. Dredge with flour and sauté in olive oil and butter until golden brown on both sides. OR omit dredging and bake in a preheated oven at 350°F for about fifteen minutes on the first side, and ten on the other.

Serve on a **Burger Bun** with the traditional condiments or as cutlets with tomato sauce, grated parmesan or romano cheese, a tossed salad, and any marinated or steamed vegetables in season.

Oatburgers 'n Gravy

(9 burgers)

Meat 'n Gravy is one of the great American staples and has been so in Maine for generations. But the New Maine cook goes light on the saturated fat that traditional gravies rely upon. Fortunately, there are vegetarian gravies, which are delicious served with grains.

2 1/4 cups water or stock
1/4 cup shoyu
2 1/4 cups rolled oats
1/2 cup finely chopped onions
1/4 cup nutritional yeast flakes
1/2 cup sunflower seeds or chopped walnuts
1/4 cup sesame seeds, rinsed and drained
3 garlic cloves, minced freshly ground black pepper
1 cup unbleached white flour for dredging (optional)
2 tablespoons extra-virgin olive oil (optional)
2 tablespoons clarified butter (optional)
1 recipe Mushroom Gravy

1. In a medium-sized saucepan bring water or stock and shoyu to a boil. Lower heat and add oats. Cook about five minutes. Remove from heat.

2. Add remaining ingredients and mix well.

3. When cool enough to handle, form into patties three inches in diameter, dredge in flour, and sauté in oil and butter until well-browned on both sides. OR omit dredging and bake on a greased cookie sheet in a 350°F oven, ten minutes on each side, turning once.

Sunflower Burgers

(6 burgers)

1-1 1/2 cups sunflower
    seeds
1/2 cup grated carrot
1/2 cup diced celery,
    leaves and all
2 tablespoons diced
    onion
1 tablespoon finely
    chopped fresh
    parsley
1 tablespoon diced green
    bell pepper
1/8 teaspoon dried basil
1 tablespoon nutritional
    yeast
1 tablespoon shoyu
    (optional)
2 eggs, slightly beaten
1/2 teaspoon sea salt

1. Preheat oven to 375°F.

Grind enough sunflower seeds till moderately fine in blender to produce one and a half cups sunflower seed meal.

2. In a medium-sized bowl combine with the rest of the ingredients and mix well.

3. On a well-buttered baking sheet spoon two heaping tablespoons of mixture into patties two and a half inches in diameter. Flatten with spatula, and smooth edges. Bake about ten minutes on one side, five minutes on the other, or until browned.

Serve for lunch on a **Burger Bun** or in a tortilla with steamed greens and any other vegetable, stored or in season.

Sunflower burgers don't hang together well before cooking, but the result is delicious.

Cheese-Nut Whole-Grain Loaf

(6-8 servings)

2 cups finely ground
    walnuts
2 cups grated sharp
    cheddar or other
    cheese
2 cups cooked whole oats,
    barley or short-grain
    brown rice
3 cups chopped onions
4 beaten eggs
1 teaspoon sea salt
2 tablespoons
    nutritional yeast
2/3 cup sunflower seeds
1 teaspoon caraway seeds

1/2 teaspoon celery
    seeds (optional)
parsley for garnish

1. Combine all ingredients in a medium-sized bowl.

2. Spoon into a well-buttered ten- by four- by three-inch loaf tin. Press in lightly, and smooth top. Bake at 350°F for forty minutes, or until a knife comes out clean. Cool on a rack at least fifteen minutes before removing.

Serve cold or with **Hot Cheese Sauce** or **Laban**, and sprinkle with parsley. Also serve with lightly steamed vegetables and a tossed green salad.

Loaves

Along with burgers, meatloaves have always been popular with people on a budget or with those who enjoy simple, homey cooking. Nut and grain loaves are a complementary combination—tasty and satisfying. Quick to prepare, they are both economical and packed with protein.

Kasha Loaf

(6 servings)

4 cups leftover Kasha
1 cup finely chopped
    onion
1/2 cup finely chopped
    celery
1 teaspoon sea salt
freshly ground black
    pepper
1 teaspoon dried thyme
    or marjoram
1 teaspoon celery seeds
2 tablespoons
    nutritional yeast
1 cup grated sharp
    cheddar cheese
2-3 lightly beaten eggs,
    depending on size
vegetable stock or
    whey, if necessary

1. Mix all ingredients together, except stock or whey. Consistency should be like hamburger. If too dry, moisten with stock or whey.
2. Spoon rather firmly into a well-buttered ten- by four- by three-inch loaf pan. Smooth top. Bake at 325°F for forty-five minutes to an hour. Test by inserting a knife–if it comes out clean, the loaf is done. Allow to cool ten to fifteen minutes before removing from pan.

Serve hot or cold with **Mushroom Gravy** or **Hot Cheese Sauce**. Crisp potatoes and a salad would round out the meal beautifully.

Lentil Carrot Cheese Loaf

(6-8 servings)

4 cups sprouted lentils
    (see Sprouting Chart)
4 eggs, slightly beaten
1 teaspoon sea salt
1 teaspoon dried thyme
freshly ground black
    pepper
1/4 cup red or green bell
    pepper, chopped fine
3 tablespoons diced
    onion
1/2 cup grated carrot
1/2 cup diced celery
1 cup grated sharp
    cheddar cheese
1 cup whole-wheat bread
    crumbs
2 tablespoons extra-
    virgin olive oil

1. Grind lentil sprouts through the coarse cutter of a meat grinder. Mix together with remaining ingredients.
2. Press gently into a well-buttered loaf tin. Brush with olive oil. Bake thirty minutes at 350°F.

Serve doused with **Carrot Lemon Sauce**, with a whole grain, and steamed vegetables in season.

Carrot Lemon Sauce

(1 cup)

1 cup cooked carrots
1/4 cup freshly squeezed
    lemon juice
1/2 teaspoon sea salt
1/2 teaspoon dried
    thyme
1 cup water
1 tablespoon cornstarch
    or arrowroot
1 tablespoon finely chopped
    fresh parsley

1. Purée in blender till smooth.
2. Pour into small saucepan, bring to boil and cook, stirring, for one minute. Add parsley.

Serve over **Lentil Carrot Cheese Loaf**.

Wheat Meat

(6-8 servings)

1 2/3 cups high-gluten
    wheat flour (see Wheat
    under Whole-Grain
    Flours)
8 cups water

1. About two hours before dinnertime mix flour and half a cup water (or more) in a small bowl with a wooden spoon. Knead lightly to form a soft ball. Place into a bowl, cover, and allow to rest thirty minutes.
2. In a large saucepan bring remaining six cups water to a boil. On a wet board, using a wet knife, slice the gluten dough into bits about three-quarters of an inch thick. Drop into the boiling water, lower heat, cover, and cook for thirty minutes. (They will swell to about three times their initial size.) Drain in a colander and allow to cool. When cool enough to handle, squeeze gently to remove excess water. Refrigerate, covered, up to one week.

Serve thinly sliced, marinated, and fried in any stir-fry (for example, **Wheat Meat With Broccoli** and **String Beans and Wheat Meat Stir-Fry**).

Note: Wheat meat requires marination or cooking in a well-seasoned sauce.

Gluten "Meat"

Gluten is the protein part of wheat flour. It makes bread stick together. It can also be separated from starch by washing and turned into a vegetarian "meat" often used in oriental cuisines. The process is lengthy; however, there's another method which uses the whole grain without rinsing. Being devotées of "waste not want not," Maine cooks may prefer it. And it's far easier!

Gravies and Sauces

*Traditional gravies and sauces are often based on a flour roux rich in butter. The following are based on cornstarch, arrowroot (which can be added directly to hot ingredients without lumping), or puréed vegetables or beans. (See also **Simple Millet with Curried Gravy**, **Carrot Lemon Sauce**, and **Arrowroot Lemon Egg Sauce**.)*

*To make a purely vegetable gravy, delete cheese, nuts and mushrooms from the **Hot Cheese Sauce** recipe and substitute one teaspoon dried thyme, a half cup puréed, cooked carrots, squash, potatoes, peas, or beets, one or two tablespoons freshly squeezed lemon juice, and a pinch of nutmeg.*

Note: When preparing vegetables the important thing is to retain as many vitamins and minerals as possible. Many should be served raw, or steamed until just tender, or cooked slowly in milk. Save cooking liquor for sauces, to preserve any vitamins which have escaped.

Mushroom Gravy
(about 2 cups)

1 1/4 cups cold vegetable stock or water
2 tablespoons shoyu
2 tablespoons cornstarch or arrowroot
1 medium clove garlic, minced
1 tablespoon sunflower seed oil (or less)
1/4-1/3 cup sliced mushrooms
1 tablespoon freshly squeezed lemon juice
freshly ground black pepper
1/4 cup finely chopped fresh parsley

1. Combine stock or water with shoyu, cornstarch, and garlic in a large measuring cup.
2. Heat oil in skillet, and sauté mushrooms until limp.
3. Pour liquid mixture into skillet, and bring to a boil over medium heat, stirring. Simmer about one minute, or until clear and somewhat thickened. Then add remaining ingredients.

Hot Cheese Sauce
(2 1/2 cups)

2 cups milk (soy or dairy)
2 tablespoons cornstarch or arrowroot
1/2 teaspoon sea salt
freshly ground black or white pepper
1/8 teaspoon powdered cloves
3/4 cup grated sharp cheddar cheese
2 tablespoons finely chopped walnuts (optional) OR 1/4 cup sliced mushrooms, lightly sautéed in butter (optional) OR 1 heaping tablespoon finely chopped fresh parsley (optional)

1. Place first five ingredients in a small saucepan. Bring to a boil, whisking constantly, and cook about one minute or until thick. Add cheese and whisk till creamy and thick, only a matter of moments.
2. Add either walnuts or mushrooms or parsley, as desired, before serving.

Navy Bean Sauce
(2 cups)

1 cup hot dairy or soy
    milk OR liquor from
    cooking vegetables
1 cup cooked navy beans
1/2 teaspoon sea salt
freshly ground black
    pepper
1 teaspoon dried thyme
    or other herb
dash of powdered cloves
1 tablespoon finely
    chopped fresh
    parsley (optional)

Purée all ingredients except parsley together until smooth. Add parsley before serving. Reheat if necessary.

Laban
(1 cup)

1 cup yogurt
1 egg white
1 tablespoon cornstarch
    or arrowroot powder
1/2 teaspoon sea salt (or
    to taste)

1. Combine all ingredients together in a small saucepan.
2. Using a whisk, cook over high heat, stirring gently and constantly *in one direction only* till mixture begins to bubble.
3. Lower heat and cook gently, stirring constantly till smooth and creamy: about two minutes.

Serve *hot* over soymeat, burgers, loaves, tofu cutlets, fish, poultry, eggs, or vegetables. It's especially good heaped into big, freshly baked potatoes and spiked with toasted sesame seeds or **Shoyu Sunnies** and chopped parsley. Or *cool* for use as a salad dressing.

Laban can be seasoned to taste with a pinch of nutmeg or cloves, tahini, Dijon mustard, miso (see Glossary), grated cheese, a tablespoon dry white wine, saké (see Glossary), dry sherry, grated ginger root, hot pepper sauce, any herbs of choice including mint, chopped tofu, or chopped hard-boiled eggs.

Most sauces are too fatty, heavy with eggs or cream, or floury. This classic Middle Eastern low-fat yogurt sauce takes only two minutes to prepare and makes the tastiest gravy you can imagine.

Sprouts

By October, frosts are a nightly occurrence in Maine. Tomato vines, zucchini and pepper plants are black and limp. Winter squash and pumpkins lie exposed. It's time to thresh beans and enjoy the rows of canned goods on cellar shelves.

Though a few endive plants may survive, only kale is still happy, and garden salads are a thing of the past. But there are ways and means of bringing summer greens indoors—dandelions and Belgian endives in boxes, celery and chard plants in greenhouse pots, late plantings of lettuce and Chinese vegetables on windowsills.

And there's another method of maintaining marvelous salad nutrition without going to the grocery store. With warmth and moisture, in containers inside darkened cupboards, whole grains, seeds, and whole dried peas and beans spurt into life and thrust out eager tendrils, becoming rich in nutrients. As if by magic, vitamins and protein levels increase. In short, sprouts are a wonderful winter food. They can be added to salads, sandwiches, soups, dips, casseroles, omelets, muffins, or almost anything. Alfalfa is the most popular; wheat grass is considered therapeutic; and there are spicy types such as radish, cress, cabbage, and fenugreek.

How to Sprout Seeds, Whole Grains, and Legumes

Day 1

Wash a one-quart wide-mouth glass jar with a hot, soapy bleach solution to sterilize it, and rinse well. Rinse seeds, grains, or beans well in cool water; then place in the jar.
Nearly fill with tepid water, or add about four times seeds' volume of water.
Cover with a square of cheesecloth held on with a rubber band, or a commercially obtainable plastic mesh or wire cap. Soak overnight unless noted otherwise in the sprouting chart.

Day 2

Drain off soak water. Save for houseplants or, with the exception of that from soybeans, for cooking stock. Rinse with tepid (65-75°F) water. Drain well. Store in a dark, warm (60-75°F) cupboard.

Day 3

Rinse twice (or more) and drain well as above. Continue for as many days as necessary.

Last Day

Rinse sprouts in cold water briefly to disentangle and to rinse off seed cases. Drain well. Place in sun a few hours to green, if suitable, before refrigerating.

Store in covered containers in the refrigerator.

Alternative Sprouting Method

Make a cheesecloth bag with a string for closing at the mouth. Simply dip sproutables into water and out again, letting bag hang over sink while it drips.

Spicy Salad Sprouts: Combine alfalfa, radish, cabbage, and red clover.

Sunflower Legume Sprouts: Combine sunflower seeds, lentils, whole peas, aduki beans, mung beans, and garbanzo beans.

Sprouting Chart

Note: Be certain to buy only untreated seeds for sprouting.

tbl=tablespoon(s) qt=quart(s) c=cup(s) greened=set in the sun to allow leaves to green up

What to sprout	Sprout length when ready	Amount sprouted/ yield	Days needed to sprout	Number of daily rinses required
Seeds/Nuts				
Alfalfa[1]	1-2" greened	2-3 tbl = 1 qt greened	3-5	2
Almonds[2]	1/8-1/4"	1/2 c = 3/4 c	3-4	2-3
Unhulled sesame seeds	length of seed	1/2 c = 2 c	3	3-4
Flax	1-2" greened	1 1/2 c = 2 c	4	2-3
Red clover[3]	1 1/2"	1 tbl = 1 c	5	2
Hulled sunflower	no longer than seed[4]	1 c = 2 1/2 c	2-5	2
Hulled pumpkin or winter squash	1/4"	1 c = 2 c	3-5	2-3
Corn	1/2 - 1"	1 c = 2 c	3-6	2-3
Fenugreek	1/4" greened	1/4 c = 4 c	4-5	1-2
Garden cress[5]	1 1/2" greened	1 tbl = 1 1/2 c	3-4	2
Cabbage[6], cauliflower, turnip, collards, broccoli, brussels sprouts, kale, kohlrabi, mustard, beets, chard, endive, lettuce:				
	1-1 1/2" greened	1 tbl =1-2 c	3-5	2
White radish[7], celery, dill:				
	1/2-1"	1 tbl = 1-2 c	3-4	2

[1] Soak only four to six hours. On third day pour into a colander in a water-filled bowl and allow unsprouted seeds to wash away. Return to jar for further sprouting. (To grow a "field" of it, sprout in a flat basket on wet paper towels.) Set in the sun when nearly mature to green. Some folk advise against eating excessive amounts of alfalfa because, like at least four hundred other kinds of plants, it contains saponins. Saponins are a group of toxic materials, some of which can foam like soap in water and kill fish. So-called primitive tribes have used them for food gathering, and they are rumored to damage red blood cells. Eat in moderation.

[2] Sprout on a moist towel.

[3] It's possible to grow a field of this in a basket too.

What to sprout	Sprout length when ready	Amount sprouted/ yield	Days needed to sprout	Number of daily rinses required
Whole Grains				
Buckwheat groats	1/4-1/2"	1 c = 3 c	2-3	1
Wheat berries	1/2" or shorter	1 c = 3 1/2-4 c	2-7	2-3
Millet	1/4"	1 c = 2 1/2 c	3-4	2-3
Rice	seed length	1 c = 2 1/2 c	3-4	2-3
Rye	seed length or 1-1 1/2" and allow to green	1 c = 3 1/2 c	2-3	2-3
Oats[8]	seed length	1 c = 2 c	3-4	2-3
Barley	seed length	1/2 c = 1 c	3-4	2-3

Whole Dried Beans and Peas
(In general, bean sprouts should be steamed a few minutes before eating to destroy trypsin, a protein-inhibiting enzyme.)

What to sprout	Sprout length when ready	Amount sprouted/ yield	Days needed to sprout	Number of daily rinses required
Soybeans[9]	1/4 - 1"	1 c = 4 c	3-6	every 3 hours
Lentils	1/4 - 1/2"[10]	1/2 c = 3 c	3-4	2
Aduki beans	1" or shorter	1/2 c = 2 c	3-5	4
Garbanzo[11]	1/4 -1"	1 c = 3 c	3-6	4-6
Whole peas	length of seed	1 1/2 c = 2 c	3-5	2-3

[4] If longer it gets bitter.

[5] Sprout a field of it on paper towels in a pan or basket. Do not soak. Place on a moist towel, sprinkle with water, cover with another moist towel, and dampen three times a day. Set in the sun when nearly mature to green.

[6] Sharp flavor if too old.

[7] Allow to grow to an eighth of an inch. Set in the sun when nearly mature to green.

[8] Don't presoak. Sprout on towels.

»

Mung beans[12]	1/2 - 3"	3/4 c = 4 c	3-6	3-4
Navy beans	tiny sprout	1 c = 2 c	4	2
Jacob's cattle	tiny sprout	1 c = 2 c	5	2

Lima beans, marrow, kidney, red pinto, cranberry, haricot, fava, black, great northern white, blackeye peas[13]:

	best at 1/4"	1 c = 2-4 c	3-5	3-4

[9] Soak twelve to sixteen hours. Rinse at least three times a day–up to five or six times. Sprout at 55-65°F. Don't eat raw. Steam five minutes or so, and don't use soak water except for house plants.

[10] Less nutritious if grown longer.

[11] Soak twelve to sixteen hours and rinse five or six times per day. Sprout at 55-65°F.

[12] Soak a minute when rinsing. Grow in the dark at warmer temperature.

[13] Taste like fresh peas.

Winter Salads

Winter salads can be very satisfying. Many New Maine cooks will have shelves of delicacies such as pickled beets and dilled string beans, along with sand-coddled root vegetables (plus deep red and saucy green cabbages) in the cellar; potted celery and Chinese vegetables on the windowsill; and sprouted beans and seeds on kitchen shelves. So imaginative salads in midwinter need not be a problem.

Cold-loving Chinese greens, (such as nozaki Chinese cabbage, kyona, or Chinese pac choi) are easy to grow in a chilly greenhouse in temperatures between 32 and 60°F. I also suggest Batavian endive, kale, collards, kohlrabi, buttercrunch, and salad-bowl lettuces, bunching onions, shallots, and Indian summer spinach. Seeds should be planted during hot fall days when they will sprout readily. A healthy celery plant brought into the greenhouse from the garden will also continue growing.

Winter Dandelion Salad
(4 servings)

4 cups winter dandelion greens (see next page), coarsely chopped
1 hard-boiled egg
1 clove garlic, minced
4 tablespoons extra-virgin olive oil
1 1/2 tablespoons red wine (or other) vinegar
1 tablespoon chopped fresh parsley
1/2 teaspoon sea salt

Carrots are one of the most important winter vegetables. Dug fresh from protecting winter soil (which doesn't freeze in Maine under a heavy two-foot mulch of hay), they're always favorites for "dippers" and delicious as a finely grated salad. In fact, many root vegetables make excellent salad ingredients.

Winter Vegetable Platter
(6-8 servings)

1/4 small fresh turnip, cut into matchsticks
2 carrots, cut into matchsticks
3 sunchokes, peeled, sliced, and marinated in lemon juice and water
1/4 celeriac root, cut into matchsticks and

freshly ground black pepper
1/4 cup grated daikon radish (optional)

1. Wash greens, dry well, and chop coarsely.
2. Mash together the hard-boiled yolk, garlic, and olive oil. Add vinegar, parsley, salt, and pepper. Toss in sliced hard-boiled egg white and daikon.
3. Add dandelion greens, and toss till each leaf is coated with dressing.

dipped into freshly squeezed lemon juice
slices of 1 tart apple, dunked quickly into freshly squeezed lemon juice
1/2 cup Classic Pickled Beets
1/2 cup Dilled Beans
2 Pickled Pink Eggs, sliced
1 cup shredded red cabbage, sprinkled with 2 teaspoons Japanese umeboshi vinegar
1 cup cubed feta cheese
dip of choice

On a large round platter, arrange vegetables and feta in pie-shaped sections.

Serve with a chenna dip such as **Chenna Herb Garlic Spread or Dip** or **Hot Chenna Dip.**

Winter Salad Platter

(4-6 servings)

1 cup Classic Pickled
    Beets
1 cup alfalfa sprouts
1 cup finely grated
    carrot, plain or
    dressed
1 cup sprouted aduki
    beans, sunflower
    seeds, lentils, or
    marinated beans for
    garnish

1. Arrange vegetables in pie-shaped wedges on a large platter, leaving a circular area clear in the center. Carrot can be served plain or mixed with a little minced onion and sprinkled with lemon juice before adding to the platter.
2. In the center, place sprouted aduki beans, sprouted sunflower seeds or lentils, or cooked, marinated beans.

Serve with a bowl of yogurt-based salad dressing, flavored with such herbs as your windowsill produces.

Beet and Carrot Salad

(6 servings)

2 medium-sized,
    well-washed firm
    beets (2 cups
    shredded)
2 medium-sized,
    well-washed carrots
    (2 cups shredded)
1 small onion, diced
2 heaping tablespoons
    diced celery stalk
    (optional)
1/2-2/3 cup My Favorite
    Salad Dressing
chopped chives for
    garnish (optional)
1/4 cup coarsely chopped
    walnuts for garnish
    (optional)
2 cups alfalfa sprouts

1. Without peeling, finely grate beets and carrots.
2. Combine in a bowl with onion, celery, and a half cup salad dressing. You may need a bit more.

Serve sprinkled with chives and walnuts on a platter, surrounded with alfalfa sprouts.

A low-fat alternative dressing :
1 cup thick yogurt
1 teaspoon grated lemon
    rind
2 tablespoons freshly
    squeezed lemon juice
1/2 teaspoon dried
    tarragon, crumbled
    between the palms
1/2 teaspoon sea salt
2-3 drops hot pepper
    sauce

Wild plants, such as Maine's ubiquitous dandelion, can also enhance winter salads. Late in November, before the ground freezes hard, dig up twenty or more dandelion plants and clip the leaves off to within one inch of the roots. Place roots in a tightly made, deep wooden box filled with sand. Put the box in a dark corner in the cellar, and water it every three days. Pale greenish-yellow leaves should grow to salad length in two to three weeks. Keep cutting and watering these greens for two to three crops of salad makings. This process is rather like that for Belgian endive.

Note: Dressings and salad condiments may be found in the Summer section—see Index.

During a Maine winter, nothing is so satisfying to the eye as the color red! Beets are always a delight, but one can easily tire of cooked or pickled beets before spring. Root-cellared beets, still firm and tender, can be enjoyed raw. A rich, oily salad dressing is really the tastiest binder. For folk on a low-fat diet, however, I suggest a low-fat alternative.

Midwinter Salad

(6 servings)

2 cups shredded,
      well-washed
      unpeeled carrot
1 cup shredded red
      cabbage
1/3 cup raisins
1 cup chopped apple,
      dipped into fresh
      lemon juice
2/3 cup My Favorite
      Salad Dressing

Arrange everything attractively on a large flat platter. Bind with as much **My Favorite Salad Dressing** as necessary. If a low-fat dressing is preferred, substitute the one suggested with the **Beet and Carrot Salad** recipe, omitting the tarragon.

Apples always make wonderful winter salads. We store red delicious because they keep so well and taste so good. Dipping peeled apple flesh in lemon juice prevents it from going brown.

Minted Apple Salad

(6-8 servings)

6 crisp apples
3 cups finely shredded
      green cabbage
1/2 cup currants or
      raisins
1/2 cup coarsely
      chopped walnuts
1 heaping tablespoon
      chopped fresh mint
3/4 cup thick yogurt
2 tablespoons freshly
      squeezed lemon juice
1/2 teaspoon sea salt
1 tablespoon finely
      chopped fresh mint
      (or 1 teaspoon dried,
      crumbled well)

1. Wash apples, peel if sprayed, and chop coarsely. Dip into freshly squeezed lemon juice.
2. Combine apples, cabbage, currants, walnuts, and one tablespoon fresh mint in a large bowl.
3. In a separate bowl, combine yogurt, lemon juice, salt, and one tablespoon mint. Add enough to the salad to bind it nicely.

Serve on leafy greens or surrounded by alfalfa sprouts.

Oil-less Marinated Beans

(2 cups)

1 cup navy or garbanzo
    beans
2 cups boiling water
2 cloves garlic, minced
2 tablespoons chopped
    onion to taste
1 bay leaf
1 tablespoon fresh
    summer savory,
    finely chopped, OR 1
    teaspoon dried
    summer savory
    OR 1 tablespoon fresh
    basil, marjoram,
    thyme, or fennel,
    finely chopped, OR 1
    teaspoon dried herb
    of choice
1/8 teaspoon cayenne OR
    3-4 drops hot pepper
    sauce (optional)
freshly ground black
    pepper
1 teaspoon sea salt
1/2 cup vinegar or
    freshly squeezed
    lemon juice

1. Pick over beans and rinse.
2. In a heavy pot pour beans into boiling water, and add garlic, onion, herbs, and cayenne.
3. Simmer two to three hours, or until done but still fairly firm. Drain well while still hot.
4. Immediately add pepper, salt, and vinegar or lemon juice. Allow to marinate till well-seasoned. Chill and store, covered, in a cold place.

Serve sprinkled with finely chopped fresh parsley; scattered over any leafy salad; or piled in the center of a large tray of other vegetables or on top of greens, topped with finely chopped fresh parsley, herbs of your choice, and surrounded by black olives and cherry tomatoes.

Beans are wonderful salad ingredients, either by themselves or sprinkled over anything else. Marinated and kept in the cold cellar or refrigerator, they're handy for quick additions. Serving them with a whole grain yields complete protein.

Many Bean Salad

(4 quarts. Simply halve for a smaller batch)

1 cup garbanzos
1 cup red kidney beans
1 cup green soy beans
2 cups extra-virgin olive
    oil OR 1 cup olive oil
    plus 1 cup
    sunflower seed oil

1 1/4 cups cider vinegar
4 tablespoons honey
4 garlic cloves, minced
2 teaspoons sea salt
1/4 teaspoon cayenne (or
    more to taste)
2 teaspoons dried basil
1 quart yellow string beans
1 quart green string beans
3/4 cup diced carrots,
    lightly steamed

One of the classic bean dishes—beans marinated in a pungent vinaigrette—has always been a favorite in Maine. I first tasted it in a tiny restaurant, whose cook had duplicated her mother's recipe for bean salad. Here is my version, sweetened with honey instead of white sugar, and with some additions Mummy hadn't dreamed of. Make it in quantity—it stores very well in the refrigerator or in a cold cellar.

**1/2 cup pitted black
olives, sliced**
**1/2 cup chopped
pimentos**
**3/4 cup (or more) sliced
Bermuda onion**

1. Cook dry beans by adding
to roughly boiling water
with a pinch of salt, which
toughens them slightly and
prevents mushiness; then
simmer till tender, one to
two hours. (If you substitute
other varieties, be sure to
cook together only those
which have similar cooking
times. Otherwise, cook in
separate pots.)

2. Meanwhile, combine oil
and vinegar in a large bowl,
and add honey, garlic, salt,
cayenne to taste, and basil.
3. Drop hot, well-drained
beans into marinating sauce.
They'll soak up the flavor.
4. Bring home-canned string
beans to a boil, then simmer
for fifteen minutes (to
destroy any threat of
botulism). If you use fresh
beans, simply cut into bite-
sized bits, and simmer till
barely tender. Add to the
marinade along with
remaining ingredients, and
chill.

*Broccoli and
cauliflower make
winter salads which
are always a treat,
both nutritionally
and to the palate.
This platter is
especially fine for
company. Prepare
half a day in
advance.*

Broccoli/Cauli-flower Platter

(6 servings)

4 cups broccoli florets
4 cups cauliflower florets
2/3 cup cider vinegar
**1 1/3 cups extra-virgin
olive oil or
sunflower seed oil**
**1 1/2 teaspoons sea salt
(or to taste)**
**freshly ground black
pepper**
3-4 cloves garlic, minced
**2 medium-sized onions,
thinly sliced**
**2 tablespoons diced
pimento for garnish**

1. Bring two inches of water
to a boil in a heavy pot. Set
broccoli florets into a colander over the water. Steam
till tender. Do the same for
the cauliflower.
2. Combine the vinegar, oil,
salt, pepper, and minced
garlic to make a marinade.
3. As each colander is
finished, place the hot
vegetables into separate
bowls with one sliced onion
each, and *immediately* pour
half the marinade over each
one. Allow vegetables to
marinate at least half a day.
They'll come out gleaming,
satisfying to both eye and
palate.

Arrange on a very large
platter, sprinkled with
pimento.

Yogurt Marinated Vegetables

(4-6 servings)

4 large carrots, cut diagonally in 1/4-inch slices
1 small head cauliflower broken into 1 cup small florets (fresh or frozen)
1 cup broccoli florets (fresh or frozen)
1 cup small mushrooms
2/3 cup yogurt
1/4 cup Tarragon Vinegar
2 tablespoons freshly squeezed lemon juice
1 garlic clove, minced
1 1/2 tablespoons Dijon mustard or 1 teaspoon powdered mustard
1 teaspoon sea salt (or to taste)
freshly ground black pepper

1. Bring two inches of water to a boil in a large pot. Steam all vegetables separately until just tender, six to eight minutes for carrots, cauliflower, and broccoli, about one minute for mushrooms.
2. Whisk together the remaining ingredients in a large bowl.
3. As you remove each vegetable, drop it gently into the marinade. Stir lightly.
4. Marinate overnight.

Serve on a platter with black olives and tomatoes if available, and possibly **Falafel** balls, sautéed tofu cubes, or cubed feta cheese.

Greek platters of marinated vegetables, reeking of lemon juice, garlic, and olive oil, are absolutely beautiful. These are marinated in yogurt. Prepare one day in advance.

Pasta

Italians have always understood good basic food. Seizing upon the American tomato, pepper, and zucchini, they've invented dishes Italy now takes for granted. And when Italians moved into Maine, they brought their pasta, tomato, pepper, and zucchini dishes with them.

Pasta, of course, is made from flour, usually wheat. It has the unenviable reputation of being "fattening." This is erroneous. By itself, pasta is a complex carbohydrate and is rich in protein and essential amino acids if made of whole-grain flours. It is always low in fat—heavy, oily sauces, butter, and cheese add the calories.

Pasta comes in about fifty different varieties, which include the best-known ones—spaghetti and macaroni—along with more exotic cousins such as tagliarini, vermicelli, fettucine, gnocchi, orzi, rigatoni, lasagna, maccheroncelli, mostaccioli, pennini, and rigati.

The finest Italian pasta is always made of semolina, a refined flour from hard spring wheat rich in gluten—in America, usually durum wheat. Commercial whole-wheat pasta is made with whole durum flour mixed with hard and soft wheat flours and sometimes with vegetables and eggs. Recent "health-food" pastas have appeared in a rainbow of combinations: artichoke whole-wheat pasta; spinach pasta; buckwheat and whole-wheat pasta; corn pasta; rice, soy, and wheat pasta; Japanese buckwheat noodles (soba); and so forth.

Good pasta comes from the kettle firm and smooth with no starchy residue, unlike some moping, limp, whitish productions from supermarket shelves, which can easily become gummy. So buy only Italian semolina pasta or pastas made from whole grains.

Tomato Sauce is a perfect blanket for any pasta. Fresh herbs added last give an appetizing and attractive touch of greenery. Spiral pastas are particularly good with sauce because they hold so much.

I learned about cooking spaghetti from a modern Roman. Here are his instructions.

General Notes on Pasta Cooking

1. Pasta should be cooked *al dente*, a famous Italian phrase indicating some resistance when the teeth bite in.
2. Pasta is always cooked in a large kettle of rapidly boiling, generously salted water (about two tablespoons per gallon of water), so it can swim freely.
3. It must be closely watched and occasionally stirred to prevent sticking.
4. Most pasta will cook in about eight minutes, but must be tested when almost done to prevent overcooking.
5. When the pasta is just tender (*al dente*), remove kettle from heat. Add about three cups cold water to stop the cooking.
6. Pour pasta into colander, and drain thoroughly, tossing a little to be sure all the water is out.

Cooking for Guests

If you're planning to cook a lot of pasta as well as other dishes, and need to be flexible about dinner time, cook pasta hours before you need it, but remove from water slightly underdone. Drain and wash thoroughly with cold water in colander. Set aside. Close to dinner time, heat a kettle of salted water. Sink pasta, in colander, into boiling water about twenty seconds. Then lift out, drain well, and sauce.

Eating Pasta

In Italy pasta is served as the first course, straight from the stove, followed by salad. This allows the pasta to be eaten at its best.

Serving Spaghetti

1. Have all ingredients at hand before combining and serving. Ladle a little sauce onto a long, shallow ceramic platter

»

which has been heated in the oven.

2. Place about half of the hot, well-drained pasta on top of the sauce.

3. Spoon about a third of the remaining sauce over the pasta.

4. Turn the pasta over and over with a tablespoon and fork as if you were tossing a salad.

5. Add the rest of the pasta and another third of the sauce.

6. Finally, spoon on the remaining sauce and serve *at once*. Pass grated parmesan or romano cheese at table.

Eating Spaghetti

1. Don't cut it! Hold a fork in your right hand and a soup spoon in the left.

2. Let the tip of the spoon rest lightly on top of the pasta and pick up about three strands of pasta with your fork tines.

3. Bring your fork to the bowl of your spoon and turn it slowly away from you, winding the pasta around. You now have a compact mouthful.

Carlo's Simple Spaghetti

(4-6 servings)

3/4 pound pasta
6 tablespoons butter
6 tablespoons freshly grated parmesan or romano cheese
2 heaping tablespoons finely chopped fresh parsley OR cilantro (optional)

1. Cook pasta until *al dente*. Drain well.

2. Return to hot (now empty) saucepan with remaining ingredients. Cover and shake pasta quickly until nicely coated.

Serve immediately on a very hot platter and eat at once, followed by salad and fresh bread.

Note: For variations, add a half cup chopped chives or scallions; sauté three or four minced garlic cloves in six tablespoons extra-virgin olive oil till golden, for about one minute, and add to pasta instead of butter; or add ten chopped anchovies.

Macaroni with Tempeh and Prunes
(6-8 servings)

1 pound whole-grain
    macaroni or spiral
    pasta
6 tablespoons extra-
    virgin olive oil
10 ounces tempeh, cut
    into 3/4-inch cubes
1 medium-sized onion,
    diced
2-3 garlic cloves, minced
3 1/2 cups tomato sauce
1/2 teaspoon powdered
    cinnamon
1/4 teaspoon nutmeg
1/4 teaspoon allspice
1/2 cup dry red wine
1 teaspoon sea salt
freshly ground black
    pepper
16-20 pitted dried prunes
grated parmesan cheese
    for garnish

1. Cook macaroni till *al
dente.*
2. Heat three tablespoons oil
in skillet or two-quart heavy-
bottomed kettle. Add
tempeh and sauté till
browned on all sides.
Remove and set aside.
3. Heat three more
tablespoons oil and sauté
onion and garlic till limp.
4. Return tempeh and add
remaining ingredients,
except prunes, and simmer
about thirty minutes.
5. Add prunes and simmer
another thirty minutes,
stirring often. Add parsley.

Serve over hot pasta and
pass parmesan at the table.
Complement with a tossed
salad.

*Lasagna is an all-
time favorite—
perfect for parties
because you can make
it ahead of time,
freeze it, and then
bake it at medium
heat for about two
hours just before
dinner.*

Lazy Time Lasagna
(6-8 servings)

Filling
2 tablespoons extra-
    virgin olive oil
1 medium-sized onion,
    chopped
2-3 cloves garlic, minced
2 1/2 cups spinach,
    Swiss chard, or any
    other green

2 1/2 cups low-fat
    cottage cheese or
    ricotta
2 large beaten eggs
1 teaspoon sea salt
plenty of freshly ground
    black pepper
1 teaspoon dried
    oregano or twice as
    much fresh oregano
1 teaspoon dried basil or
    twice as much fresh
    basil

»

1/4 cup chopped fresh
parsley
1/2 cup grated cheddar
cheese

1. Heat oil in a skillet. Add
onion and garlic and sauté
until limp.
2. Wash spinach or other
green, drain well, and chop
fine.
3. Combine onions and
garlic with chopped greens
in a large bowl, and add
remaining filling
ingredients.

Pasta
1 tablespoon sea salt
2 tablespoons extra-
virgin olive oil
1 pound whole-wheat,
spinach, soy, or
artichoke lasagna
noodles

1. To a big pot of water, add
one tablespoon of salt and
two of oil. Bring to a boil
and add pasta slowly so
boiling does not stop and
lasagna noodles are not
broken.
2. Return to a rolling boil,
and cook until pasta is done
(eight to ten minutes). Drain
in a colander and rinse with
cold water until pasta is no
longer starchy. It should be
clean and not stick together.

Assembly
2 tablespoons butter
3 1/2 cups well-seasoned
tomato sauce
1 cup freshly grated
parmesan or romano
cheese

1. Butter a nine- by thirteen-
inch lasagna pan thoroughly.
In the bottom, spread eight
tablespoons tomato sauce.
2. Arrange a layer of lasagna
noodles, overlapping
slightly, then two and a
quarter cups of the cheese
and greens mixture. Spoon
over three-quarters of a cup
of tomato sauce.
3. Top with another layer of
pasta, the rest of the cheese
mixture, three-quarters of a
cup tomato sauce. End with
the remaining lasagna
noodles and tomato sauce.
4. Sprinkle the parmesan or
romano cheese over the top,
and bake at 350°F for about
forty-five minutes or until
the sauce is bubbling and
cheese is browned slightly.

Serve very hot with a tossed
salad and fresh bread.

Note: If you prefer a thicker
cheese filling, add another
cup ricotta or cottage cheese,
a half cup more of chopped
greens, and a quarter cup
more grated cheddar.

Italians consider pasta and beans peasant food, but to my mind this recipe is "family gourmet."

Pasta e Fagioli

(6-8 servings)

1 1/2 cups dried navy beans (equals 3 cups cooked beans)
6 cups water
2 1/2 teaspoons sea salt
1 bay leaf
2-3 cloves garlic
1/3 cup plus 2 tablespoons extra-virgin olive oil
3 carrots, chopped fine
2 stalks celery, chopped fine
1 large onion, chopped fine
1 teaspoon sea salt
1 teaspoon dried oregano leaves
1/2 teaspoon dried basil
3-4 medium-sized peeled tomatoes, cut into large chunks (OR 4-5 cups drained canned tomatoes)
2 cups vegetable or soy elbow macaroni (equals 3-4 cups cooked macaroni)
1/4 cup chopped fresh parsley for garnish
grated parmesan or romano cheese for garnish

1. Pick over beans, wash, and soak overnight.
2. The next day, place beans and water in a heavy kettle with one and a half teaspoons salt, bay leaf, garlic, and one-third of a cup olive oil. Simmer till beans are tender, two to three hours. Drain. Save cooking liquor.
3. Heat two tablespoons oil in a heavy casserole and sauté carrots, celery, onion, one teaspoon salt, oregano, and basil till onion is limp.
4. Add tomatoes, cover, and simmer fifteen minutes.
5. In a separate pot cook macaroni until tender (eight to ten minutes).
6. Drain and combine cooked beans and pasta with sautéed vegetables. Add about half of the reserved bean liquor (or enough to make it moderately moist but not soupy). Cover again, and simmer about fifteen minutes. Add more sea salt and freshly ground black pepper to taste.
7. Turn out onto a large hot platter and sprinkle with chopped fresh parsley.

Pass a bowl of grated parmesan or romano cheese at table, and serve with tossed salad and fresh bread.

Macaroni and Tomato Soup

(6-8 servings)

1 tablespoon extra-virgin
    olive oil
1 medium-sized onion,
    diced
3 cloves garlic, minced
1 quart canned tomatoes,
    home-grown if
    possible
2 cups buttercup squash,
    cubed
1 large carrot, diced
1/2 cup chopped bell
    pepper
1 well-washed, unpeeled
    medium-sized
    potato, cut into
    3/8-inch
    cubes
1/2 small savoy (or
    other) cabbage,
    shredded (4 cups)
1 cup cooked navy (or
    other) beans
1 teaspoon dried oregano
1 teaspoon dried basil
1 teaspoon sea salt, or to
    taste (optional)
freshly ground black
    pepper
2 tablespoons
    nutritional yeast
1 tablespoon crumbled
    kelp
1/2 teaspoon carraway
    seeds
1 quart home-canned
    string beans, or
    purchased variety, if
    necessary

1 tablespoon komé miso
    (see Glossary)
    dissolved in 1/2 cup
    hot water
1 cup elbow macaroni,
    broken spaghetti, or
    other small pasta of
    choice
1/4 cup dry sherry or
    vermouth (optional)
1/4 cup finely chopped
    fresh parsley for
    garnish
grated parmesan or
    romano cheese for
    garnish

1. Heat oil in a large, heavy soup pot. Sauté onion and garlic until limp.
2. Add vegetables (except string beans), herbs, salt, pepper, yeast, and kelp. Add liquid from the jar of string beans along with one to two and a half cups water (as necessary). Allow to simmer till squash is thoroughly mushy and seasonings have blended well. Then add string beans and simmer another fifteen minutes.
3. During the last ten minutes of cooking, add miso broth to the soup. Simmer till noodles are *al dente*, about ten minutes.
4. Add sherry or vermouth.

Serve very hot, garnished with freshly chopped parsley and grated parmesan or romano cheese, and accompany with fresh bread.

This list of ingredients may seem long, but cooking couldn't be easier. And results couldn't be tastier. This is a homey soup just right for a cold winter's evening, friends, and a roaring fire.

Noodles

Making your own pasta, even without the aid of a pasta machine, is easy.

To Cook Homemade Noodles

(for 6)

1. Bring four quarts water to a boil with one tablespoon sea salt and one tablespoon olive oil.
2. Drop in one pound of noodles, unthawed if they were frozen. Stir lightly.
3. Cook, uncovered, till al dente, about two to three minutes. Drain well.

Serve topped with **Hot Cheese Sauce***, garnished with parsley, and accompanied by a huge tossed salad, fresh bread, and vegetables in season.*

Fresh Whole-Wheat Egg Noodles with Herbs

(2 pounds)

3 1/2 cups whole-wheat flour
1/2 cup toasted wheat germ
4 large eggs
6-12 tablespoons water
1 cup finely chopped fresh herbs such as parsley (optional)

1. Mix flour and wheat germ together in a large bowl. Make a deep well in the center.
2. Break the eggs into a small bowl and beat lightly with a fork. Stir four tablespoons water into the eggs and pour into the well in the flour. Using a circular motion, draw flour in from the sides of the well. Then add two more tablespoons water and continue mixing until all flour is moistened. Add more water, a tablespoon at a time, up to twelve if necessary. Add herbs if you care to at this point.
3. When dough becomes thick, use your hands to mix it and form a ball. Knead on a board lightly floured with unbleached white flour till smooth, about six or seven minutes.
4. Flour the ball of dough lightly and place under an inverted bowl to rest for thirty minutes.

5. Return it to the floured board and knead five or six times. Then cut into eighths. Roll and cut one portion at a time as follows: Roll into an eight- by ten-inch rectangle about one-sixteenth of an inch thick. Turn and dust both sides with white flour to prevent stickiness. Lay each rectangle on a lightly floured board or waxed paper to rest, about ten minutes, till dough feels rather leathery. Starting at the narrow end, roll up each rectangle loosely, jelly-roll fashion. Cut into strips three-eighths of an inch thick.
6. Uncurl the strips. Hang them over a large wooden dowel for about sixty minutes. Don't let them get brittle by overdrying. "Leathery" describes the way they should feel.
7. Cook immediately after drying, or store in plastic bags in the refrigerator for up to two days (or freeze for up to one month).

String Bean Sauce

(3 cups)

1 quart string beans,
    drained, OR fresh
    cooked string beans
sea salt to taste
freshly ground black
    pepper
1 cup cottage cheese
1 tablespoon freshly
    squeezed lemon juice
freshly grated nutmeg
hot milk as necessary

1. If beans are home-canned, simmer for fifteen minutes. Drain.
2. Purée three cups hot beans with salt, pepper, cottage cheese, and nutmeg till thick and velvety. (Cover blender top with a towel to prevent burning yourself.) Thin, as necessary, with hot milk.

A delicate low-fat sauce for pasta can be made with string beans (either fresh or canned).

Sesame Egg Noodles

(1 pound)

1/4 cup sesame seeds
2 eggs plus 1 egg yolk
1 teaspoon shoyu
1/4 cup milk (soy or
    dairy)
about 2 cups whole-
    wheat flour

1. Grind sesame seeds in a blender until you have a half cup of sesame seed flour.
2. In a bowl whisk together the eggs, shoyu, and milk. Add all of the sesame flour and enough of the whole-grain flour to make a stiff dough.
3. Knead slightly and form into a ball. Place the ball on a lightly floured bread board and divide in half. Roll each half very thin and allow to rest for twenty minutes.

Dust with flour lightly and roll up like a jelly-roll—loosely—and slice into strips of any width you please. (I prefer quarter-inch widths.)
4. Unroll the strips (cut into short lengths if you please), and hang over a wide dowel to dry, or allow to dry unrolled and lying on your board, for at least two hours.
5. Cook immediately (see below); or store for up to two or three days in the refrigerator, well wrapped; or freeze for up to a month.

Fresh Sesame Noodle Dinner

4 quarts vegetable stock
OR water
1/4 cup shoyu
1 tablespoon sesame
seed oil
1 recipe Mushroom
Gravy
1 teaspoon powdered
ginger
1/2 teaspoon maple
syrup
3 chopped green onions,
tops and all
1 cup diced cooked fish,
poultry, chopped
hard-boiled eggs, OR
cooked navy beans
(optional)
2-3 tablespoons finely
chopped fresh
parsley OR cilantro

1. Bring the stock or water to a boil in a large kettle. Add shoyu and sesame oil. Drop in the noodles and cook until *al dente*, about six to seven minutes.
2. While noodles are cooking, make up the **Mushroom Gravy**. Add ginger and maple syrup.
3. Pour the sauce into a large, hot, shallow ceramic serving dish. Drain the noodles well, add them to the sauce, and toss gently with the onions, optional ingredients, and finely chopped parsley or cilantro.

Serve immediately with a tossed salad and fresh bread.

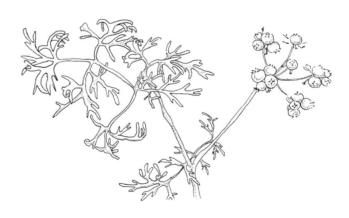

Stir-Fried Noodles and Bean Sprouts

(4 servings)

1 pound fresh noodles,
  cooked and drained
2 tablespoons sesame or
  sunflower seed oil
1 (1-inch) piece ginger
  root, finely grated
1 garlic clove, minced
4 tablespoons shoyu
3 cups mung bean
  sprouts
4 green onions cut into
  1-inch lengths
1/8 teaspoon maple
  syrup
8 ounces firm tofu, cut
  into 1/2-inch cubes

1. Heat wok, and then add oil. Stir-fry ginger root and garlic one minute or less (see **The Wok**).
2. Add shoyu, bean sprouts, onions, maple syrup, and tofu. Lower heat, toss gently, and cook about four minutes. Add noodles and stir-fry briefly.

Serve with a crisp tossed salad.

Tofu Crêpes

(14 crêpes)

3/4 cup nutritional
  yeast flakes
1 cup unbleached white
  flour
1 cup whole-wheat
  pastry flour
1/2 teaspoon
  double-acting baking
  powder
1 teaspoon sea salt
  (optional)
3 1/2-3 3/4 cups water
2 tablespoons sunflower
  seed oil
1 cup mashed soft tofu

1. Sift dry ingredients twice into a medium-sized bowl.
2. Add water, oil, and tofu, and whisk together till smooth or whiz in a blender. (Amount of water will vary slightly because flours differ–the batter should be thin enough to spread easily around pan, but thick enough that the crêpe doesn't crumble when cooked and flipped.) Allow batter to rest from fifteen to thirty minutes.
3. Lightly grease a lightweight, ten-inch crêpe pan (with edges that curve up gently). Pour a bit over a quarter cup of batter into medium-hot pan. Tilt carefully all around so batter forms a thin, even layer. Cook over medium-high heat till edges lift away from sides of pan and center starts to bubble (one to two minutes).
4. Loosen with spatula and flip crêpe over. Cook till other side is freckled (about one minute). You may need to grease the pan lightly between crêpes–use a brush.

Crêpes

While experimenting with tofu, I produced a new crêpe. It can be used as a substitute for manicotti tubes, enchilada rolls, or in any way that you'd enjoy the usual crêpe.

Stack crêpes as you cook them and cover with a towel to keep them moist and warm till ready to eat. (These crêpes may also be frozen, stacked in a plastic bag or wrap.)

Serve immediately, spread with yogurt, nuts, cinnamon, raisins, or with savories such as mashed beans, grated cheese, and left-over salad greens. Or fill and bake for **Enchiladas**, layered crêpes, or manicotti.

Spinach-Cottage Cheese Stuffed Crêpes

(about 14 crêpes or 2 each for 7 people)

1 recipe crêpe batter, such as Tofu Crêpes
1 1/2 pounds fresh spinach
2 tablespoons extra-virgin olive oil
3 tablespoons diced onion
1 garlic clove, minced
1 cup chopped button mushrooms
3 tablespoons whole-wheat pastry flour
3 cups hot milk, either soy or dairy
1 tablespoon dry white wine
1 cup grated gruyère or other cheese
1/2 teaspoon sea salt (optional)
freshly ground black pepper
dash nutmeg
1 cup cottage cheese
1 tablespoon nutritional yeast
1 large beaten egg

1. Make crêpes and keep warm.
2. Blanch spinach and drain well. Place in a towel, and squeeze out as much moisture as possible. Chop and set aside.
3. In a heavy-bottomed saucepan, heat oil and sauté onion, garlic, and mushrooms until limp. Add flour and stir about two minutes. Stir in milk. Bring to a simmer, stirring constantly, and cook until moderately thick.
4. Add wine, grated cheese, salt, pepper, and nutmeg, and stir until well blended.
5. Place chopped spinach into a medium-sized bowl and add cottage cheese, yeast, egg, and enough of the sauce, if necessary, to bind nicely. (You're aiming for a ham-burgerlike consistency.)
6. Preheat oven to 350°F. Butter a nine- by thirteen-inch lasagna pan. Place two heaping tablespoons of filling on each crêpe, off-center. Roll up and place side by side in pan.

»

Pour enough sauce over to cover nicely. Bake ten to twenty to thirty minutes or until bubbly. Heat remaining sauce, pour it over the crêpes, and serve with a fresh salad.

Enchilada Sauce

(3 cups)

2 tablespoons sunflower
    seed oil
1 medium-sized onion,
    minced
3 1/2 cups tomato purée
2 garlic cloves, minced
1/2 teaspoon cayenne
1 teaspoon cumin
1/4 teaspoon dried
    oregano, crumbled
1/2-1 teaspoon sea salt

1. In a skillet sauté onion in oil until limp.
2. Add tomato purée, garlic, spices, and salt, and simmer twenty minutes or until thick and flavorful. For those who enjoy a really hot sauce, add more cayenne. Children usually prefer it on the mild side.

Enchiladas

(6 servings)

To make enchiladas, corn or wheat tortillas are wrapped around a savory filling and baked in a savory sauce–a Mexican dish I first tasted in southern California. It makes an easy dinner, popular with adults and children alike.

The first step is to purchase traditional corn tortillas, or make whatever flatbread one fancies.

Nutty Enchilada Filling

(for 12 enchiladas, or 6 servings)

1/2 cup walnuts or
    cashew nuts,
    chopped fine
1 cup cooked red kidney
    beans, chopped
1 cup any fresh vegetable,
    such as zucchini (in
    summertime), diced
1 medium-sized onion,
    diced
2 tablespoons green bell
    pepper, diced

1 stalk celery, diced
1/2 teaspoon sea salt
freshly ground black
    pepper
1/2 teaspoon powdered
    fennel (whiz seeds in
    blender)
1/8 teaspoon cayenne
    (optional)
1/4 cup chopped fresh
    parsley
enough Enchilada Sauce
    to moisten, but only
    if necessary

In a large bowl, mix all ingredients together.

Assembling Enchiladas

(6 servings)

**12 corn or wheat
  tortillas
Nutty Enchilada Filling
3 cups Enchilada Sauce
2/3 cup sharp, grated
  cheddar cheese
  (optional)
5 black olives, sliced
  (optional)
1/4 cup finely chopped
  fresh parsley**

1. Tortillas need to be moist and flexible. The easiest method, if they've been stored, is to moisten hands with water and rub each tortilla. Pop it for a moment into a hot, ungreased frying pan, then wrap it in a towel immediately and keep warm till ready for use. Or moisten, stack, wrap, and place in a 350°F oven till steamy (about fifteen minutes).

2. Butter an eight- by twelve-inch baking pan and pour in about a quarter inch of sauce to thoroughly moisten the bottom.
3. Pile two tablespoons filling on one side of tortilla, near an edge, and roll it up. Place seam-side down in pan. Arrange rolls close together and side by side.
4. Top with sauce. Coat every tortilla edge so it will not harden during cooking. Top with cheese, and olives if desired.
5. Bake for about thirty minutes at 350°F, or until enchiladas are just heated through.

Serve, garnished with chopped parsley, with a tossed salad.

Mexican Soufflé

(4 servings)

6 (6-inch) corn tortillas
   or crêpes
1 cup canned green chili
   salsa
4 large eggs
1 tablespoon masa
   harina (tortilla flour)
   or whole-wheat
   pastry flour
1 cup grated monterey
   jack or sharp cheddar
   cheese
3-4 finely chopped,
   canned California
   green chilies (rinsed,
   seeded, and pith
   removed)
Hungarian paprika
pimentos or pickled
   mild red pepper,
   finely chopped for
   garnish

1. Purchase tortillas or make them out of masa harina, or make six-inch corn or wheat crêpes.

2. In the bottom of a greased two-quart (eight-inch) casserole dish, place one tortilla or crêpe, dipped in green chili salsa. Arrange remaining tortillas or crêpes, also dipped in salsa on both sides, around the sides, overlapping each other and the central tortilla and up the sides. (They won't fit snugly into the bottom but it doesn't matter.) They should extend about two inches above the rim of the casserole.

3. Separate eggs. In a medium-sized bowl beat whites until stiff. With the same beater whip yolks in another bowl till slightly thickened.

4. Beat flour into the egg yolks and stir in one-half cup cheese and the chilies.

5. Add a little egg white; then fold yolk mixture into whites. Pour into the lined casserole and fold tortillas or crêpes down over filling. Spoon remaining green chili salsa on top, and sprinkle with remaining cheese. Dust with paprika.

6. Bake thirty minutes at 375°F.

Serve, garnished with pimentos or pickled mild red pepper, with a tossed salad, and additional tortillas or crêpes.

Soufflé

Along with the quiche, France is home to the soufflé supreme. The soufflé frightens many a new cook, but it's really very simple. A soufflé with a Mexican flavor suits the Maine climate wonderfully. And try Maine Shrimp Rice Soufflé.

Shrimp

*Late January, February, and sometimes March are the best times for shrimp in Maine—succulent little crustacea which turn light pink when **barely** cooked.*

Cleaning Shrimp

Maine shrimp are small and tender and usually purchased in bulk. When that heavy packet arrives in your kitchen, run a sinkful of cold water and dump them into it. Get out one pot for shells, another for pure shrimp meat. Swirl each shrimp in the water (using cool running tap water if you like) to wash it thoroughly. Twist and squeeze off head section, snip off tail fins with fingers, and pull the limp body from the tail without losing the last tidbits from the end. This can take time, so get a friend to join you! Then, either pop shrimp into freezer bags or make something succulent on the spot.

Maine Shrimp Rice Soufflé

(4–6 servings)

3 large eggs
1/4 teaspoon cream of tartar
1 cup cold, cooked short-grain brown rice
1/2 cup milk
1/4 pound grated cheddar cheese
1/2 cup raw, shelled, tiny Maine shrimp, minced
sea salt to taste

1. Separate eggs. Beat whites with cream of tartar till stiff.

Shrimp Stew

(4–6 servings)

1 cup water, slightly salted
1 bay leaf
2 heaping cups tiny, cleaned Maine shrimp
2 cups diced potato
1 cup diced onion
1/4 cup diced celery stalk
3 cups milk (to be scalded)
1/4 well-washed lemon rind
1/4 cup cold milk
2 tablespoons cornstarch or arrowroot
sea salt to taste
several grindings of black pepper
Hungarian paprika

2. In a medium-sized bowl beat yolks till fluffy. Add rice. Then add remaining ingredients, except whites, and stir well.
3. Fold three tablespoons of egg white into the yolk sauce, then fold the sauce into the rest of the egg whites.
4. Pour gently into a well-buttered, six-cup, straight-sided casserole or soufflé dish. Bake at 300°F for thirty-five to forty minutes, or till browned on top and nicely set.

Serve with a tossed salad and fresh bread.

3 tablespoons dry sherry (optional)
1/4 teaspoon angostura bitters for garnish
2 tablespoons chopped fresh parsley for garnish

1. Combine water and bay leaf in a small saucepan and bring to a boil. Add shrimp, and simmer about two minutes at the most. (A bit longer if shrimp are frozen, but *do not overcook*.) Drain shrimp and set aside.
2. Put potato, onion, and celery into the cooking water and bring to a boil. Simmer, uncovered, till *just* tender. By this time some of the water will have cooked down. »

3. Scald milk in a large, flameproof serving pot with lemon rind. Remove rind, and add shrimp and drained vegetables (removing bay leaf). Save the cooking liquor.

4. Dissolve cornstarch or arrowroot in one-quarter cup cold milk and add it to the hot cooking liquor. Whisk till very thick. Season with salt and pepper. Then add slowly to the milk/shrimp/vegetable mixture, stirring constantly.

5. Serve very hot, but *do not boil.* Add dry sherry if desired. Sprinkle with parsley.

Serve in hot bowls with a few drops angostura bitters, with fresh rolls and a tossed salad.

Note: The best flavor is obtained by allowing the bisque to rest overnight. In this case follow steps one through three, and set aside. Save the cooking water. On serving day, bring it to a boil and proceed with steps four through five. Serve as above.

Simple Shrimp Fry

(2 ample servings)

2 tablespoons clarified butter, extra-virgin olive oil, or sunflower seed oil
2 medium-sized Spanish onions, sliced into rounds
1/4 cup chopped green bell pepper (optional)
1 small clove garlic, minced
2 cups tiny, shelled fresh or frozen Maine shrimp
1/2 cup sweet white wine
1/2 teaspoon sea salt
freshly ground black pepper

1. Heat a large cast-iron skillet for about one minute. Add butter or oil and immediately pop in the onions, pepper, and garlic. Lower heat and sauté gently till onions are limp and nearly translucent.

2. Just before they are done, add shrimp and sauté one minute only, stirring gently.

3. Add wine, salt, and pepper and simmer till just hot and blended.

Serve immediately over heaps of steaming brown rice, accompanied by a tossed salad of mixed greens with a straightforward oil and lemon dressing.

Note: **Dandelion Wine** would complement this dish beautifully.

Simply fried, Maine shrimp is unsurpassed. Cooking must be hot and quick to keep the delicate flesh tender.

From clipper ship days, Maine has been attuned to the Far East. This shrimp dish is savory with shoyu.

Shrimp with Peppers and Tofu

(6 servings or about 24 bits)

1 cup minced Maine
    shrimp
8 ounces soft tofu,
    mashed
1/2-1 teaspoon sea salt
2 finely chopped
    scallions or 1 small
    keeper onion, diced
4 teaspoons cornstarch
1 tablespoon water
3 medium-sized red or
    green bell peppers
1 teaspoon cornstarch
1 small clove garlic,
    minced
1 tablespoon shoyu
1 tablespoon dry sherry
    or saké (see Glossary)
1 tablespoon maple
    syrup
6 tablespoons water
3 cups peanut oil
1 cup white unbleached
    flour

1. Drain tofu well, and knead it with your fingers until it's very smooth. You should have one cupful. Mince shrimp fine and, using hands, combine in a medium-sized bowl with tofu, salt, scallions, and four teaspoons cornstarch. What you are aiming for is a stiff consistency–soft but not runny. Set aside.
2. Cut each pepper into quarters. Remove seeds and membranes, and rinse well. Then cut each quarter in two to make eight bite-sized pieces.
3. Mound tofu/shrimp mixture on top of each pepper bit. Smooth it down neatly.
4. To make sauce, in a small bowl combine a teaspoon cornstarch with a tablespoon water and stir to dissolve. Then add garlic, shoyu, sherry or saké, maple syrup, and six tablespoons water. Set aside.
5. Heat wok and add oil. When 350°F is reached, dip the tofu-side of each tidbit in flour and slide a few into the hot oil, shrimp-side down. Fry until golden. Drain on a rack. Repeat until all have been cooked.
6. When done, pour oil out of wok (and save, drained, for the next fry) and wipe out the wok. Replace it on its ring, heat it, and pour in the sauce. Bring to a boil and boil one minute to thicken, stirring constantly. Add the pepper bits and heat through.

Serve with a whole grain or noodles, a crisp salad, and fresh rolls.

With a good tempura, the batter seems more a seasoning than batter. Tempura must be eaten immediately—it's best if the cook does the frying after all diners are seated, and they must eat when served, without waiting for their neighbors.

Japanese Tempura Batter

(enough to coat 15-25 bite-sized items)

1 egg yolk
1 cup ice water
1 cup sifted unbleached
    white flour
3 cups peanut or other stable
    saturated vegetable oil
1 cup flour in a soup bowl or
    pan

1. Beat egg yolk very slightly in a small bowl. Add ice water. Mix with only one or two strokes!
2. Add flour, and mix again with only one or two strokes. Batter should be lumpy with some undissolved flour showing.
3. Pour oil into heated wok, and heat to 350°F. Maintain this temperature carefully.

4. Dip each tempura item in the plain flour so that all sides are coated. Then dip into batter. Chopsticks are best for this work. Shake to remove excess.
5. Slide the item into the oil. Oil is ready when a bit of batter sinks slightly, then comes right back up surrounded by little bubbles. Fry about three minutes or till lightly golden.

Serve and eat immediately as a first course.
Each diner dips individual bites in **Dipping Sauce** or lemon juice. Traditional condiments include prepared horse-radish, mustard, and grated daikon.

Dipping Sauce

(1 1/3 cups sauce)

1 cup water
1-2 tablespoons komé miso
    (see Glossary)
4 tablespoons saké (see
    Glossary) or dry sherry or
    light beer

1/2 teaspoon honey
    (optional)
1 tablespoon freshly grated
    ginger root

1. Combine all ingredients except ginger until dissolved.
2. Add ginger.

Batters

*Batters, of course, are light coverings which protect and season food as it is fried. (See **Beer Batter** for cooking brook trout, and **Baking Powder Batter** for dandelion blossoms, as well as the section on Fats for a discussion of deep-frying oils.) Maine has a long tradition of batter-fried seafood, but in the past the batters too often have been rather rich and heavy. The trend now is to lightness. The Japanese have developed a thin, airy batter which is unsurpassed— tempura batter.*

Almost anything cut into bite-sized bits can be used for tempura: shrimp, oysters, clams, barely cooked bits of squash, turnip, sweet potato, white potato, eggplant, raw pieces of celery, small onions or onion rings, mushrooms, peppers, sunchokes, sliced carrots, broccoli or cauliflower florets (blanched), leeks, pea pods, string beans, tofu cubes (marinated in shoyu), tempeh, fiddleheads, milkweed or day lily buds, bean balls...

*Another batter
which blankets bits
of seafood
beautifully is this
one from the
Cheechako
Restaurant in
Damariscotta, now
closed but quite
famed among
Mainers and summer
people, given to me
by Lawson Aldrich.
Lawson and his son,
Tom, give the
following advice
about deep-fat
frying: maintain an
even temperature of
about 375°F for deep-
fat frying at all
times, and fry
quickly so that oil is
not absorbed or flesh
overcooked. To keep
oil absolutely clean,
filter through old
dish towels after
every use. (And
see the discussion of
oils under Fats in the
Glossary.)*

Cheechako Breading Batter for Seafood

(enough to coat seafood for 6 servings)

**1-2 cups unbleached
   white flour in a
   soup bowl or pan
2 eggs
1 quart water
2 tablespoons vinegar
1 teaspoon white sugar
2 cups finely crumbled
   white cracker crumbs**

1. Dredge items to be deep-fried in the unbleached flour, being careful to coat all surfaces. Shake off excess.

2. Whisk together remaining ingredients, except cracker crumbs. (Vinegar retards fat absorption and sugar promotes browning.)
3. Dip each item to be fried quickly into the wash, squeezing gently to remove excess.
4. Dredge in cracker crumbs and fry in deep hot fat–375°F– till golden brown, about three minutes.

Serve with lemon wedges and tossed green salad or fresh broccoli spears on the side, with pasta, whole grain, polenta (see Glossary), or potato.

*Beer batter has been
a down-Maine
favorite for
generations.
Seasoned with
celery seeds, it's
excellent for
blanketing bland
seafood or
vegetables. The
Cheechako also
offered beer battered
specialties. This
batter is especially
good for frying
shrimp (two
minutes) and
mushrooms (three
minutes).*

Cheechako Beer Batter (adapted)

(enough to coat about 2 cups ingredients, such as 2 large sliced onions or 1 pound cubed tofu)

**1 cup light beer
1 cup unbleached white
   flour
1/2 teaspoon sea salt
1/4 teaspoon celery
   seeds
1/8 teaspoon freshly
   ground black
   pepper
1/2 teaspoon white
   sugar**

Whisk all ingredients together until creamy. Use immediately. Leftover batter may be dropped into hot fat and fried till golden. Cooled, the tidbits are good scattered on soups or salads in place of croutons.

Whole-Wheat Batter

(enough to coat 1 pound cubed tofu, or about 2 cups of bite-sized ingredients)

2 eggs
1/4 cup whole-wheat
    pastry flour
2 tablespoons cornstarch
2 tablespoons dry sherry,
    saké, or light beer
1/2 teaspoon sea salt

1. Whisk eggs in a medium-sized bowl until light and fluffy.
2. Add remaining ingredients and whisk well.
3. Dip in items to be fried and refrigerate them for thirty minutes.
4. Deep-fry at 350-375°F until golden.

Fats

Of course what you deep-fry your battered tidbits in is vastly important—not only for taste but for the sake of your health. Currently, nutritionists, the producers of vegetable oils, and cooks appear confused.

Traditionally, Maine was a lard and butter cuisine. In the old days, pork greased the frying pans, flavored many dishes, and provided crisp brown cubes to top many a helping. But now, influenced by the saturated fat/cholesterol controversy, Maine favors margarine and vegetable oils along with the rest of the country.

This may be a change for the better, and yet it often seems that there is a lot of misinformation about the different qualities of poly-unsaturated, monounsaturated, and saturated fats. Chemists have isolated thirty-four different saturated fats, twenty-six monounsaturated fats, and eighteen polyunsaturated fats—

of which only a handful predominate in food–and all fats fall into these three categories, based on the amount of hydrogen that can be added to them chemically. A saturated fat already possesses all the hydrogen atoms it can hold. Monounsaturated fats can hold two additional hydrogen atoms. Polyunsaturated fats can accommodate at least four additional hydrogen atoms. And all foods contain a mixture of the three types of fat.

For the sake of simplicity, nutritionists often refer to the fat in a particular food as "saturated" even though some monounsaturated and polyunsaturated fat is present–they have developed a "shorthand" way to refer to the relative amounts of the three kinds of fat. Saturated refers to a fat in which saturated fats supply one third or more of the fat. Polyunsaturated describes vegetable oils and fish fats whose fat is less than fifteen

percent saturated, and at least one third poly-unsaturated. And monounsaturated applies to fats which are also less than fifteen percent saturated, but less than one third polyunsaturated fat.

This classification of common fats is illustrated in the chart on the opposite page.

Saturated	Monounsaturated	Polyunsaturated
		(starting with the most polyunsaturated)
Beef, pork, and lamb fats	Olive oil	Safflower oil
Milk fat	Peanut oil	Sunflower seed oil
Coconut oil		Corn oil
Palm oil		Soybean oil
		Sesame seed oil
		many fish oils

Note:

Coconut oil and **Palm oil** *raise* blood serum cholesterol.
Olive oil and **Peanut oil** are *neutral*, but peanut oil is considered saturated.
Sunflower seed, **Corn**, **Soybean**, and **Sesame seed** oils *lower* cholesterol content.

Cholesterol information is currently being revised. Recent research suggests that a high cholesterol intake may not be the only or even the major culprit in arterial disease. The American diet is generally low in all the B vitamins, and a B-6 deficiency may well play a vital role. It's interesting to note that as bread became increasingly "refined," losing most of its B vitamins, vitamin E and trace minerals, figures for heart disease began climbing.

Researchers now feel that low-cholesterol polyunsaturated vegetable oils, touted for a few decades as the solution to the nation's epidemic of heart disease, may in fact be dangerous to cook with. Fresh vegetable oils confer the three essential fatty acids (linoleic, linolenic, and arachidonic), but when heated, chemical changes occur which may increase atherosclerosis, the likelihood of cancer, and premature aging.

Where does all of this complex and confusing information leave the cook,

standing alone in the kitchen with a bottle of oil in one hand, a pound of butter in the other, and two children waiting for dinner? I'd recommend: (1) Use as little fat as possible. (All the fat one needs can probably be obtained from basic foods without the addition of any free fat.) (2) Use only a highly saturated, highly stable vegetable oil for deep-fat frying, such as peanut oil. (3) Use a stable highly saturated fat, such as clarified butter, for prolonged pan-frying. (4) Use a highly polyunsaturated cold-pressed vegetable oil for the quick stir-fry, especially one that lowers cholesterol levels, such as sunflower seed oil, or the neutral monounsaturate, extra-virgin olive oil. (5) Use only cold-pressed oils from the first pressing (rich in essential fatty acids) for salad dressings, such as light sunflower seed oil. (Though equally beneficial, sesame seed oil has a stronger flavor more suited to stir-fries.)

(6) Once opened, any oil should be capped and refrigerated to prevent oxidation. (7) Never use margarines. For more detail about individual oils and fats, please refer to the Glossary.

Midwinter Beet Stew (Borscht)

(6 servings)

5 medium-sized beets, cooked, skinned, and diced OR 1 quart home-canned beets, drained and diced
2 large onions, chopped
1 well-washed, unpeeled potato, cut into small cubes
1/2 head red cabbage, finely shredded
2 cups stewed tomatoes or tomato purée
1 sprig dill or 1 teaspoon dill seed
1 tablespoon soy flour
2 tablespoons brewer's or nutritional yeast
1 teaspoon sea salt
freshly ground black pepper
1 clove garlic, minced

1. Into a heavy-bottomed saucepan combine onions, potato, cabbage, and tomatoes. Simmer till vegetables are tender and blended–at least an hour. Add water as necessary, adjusting consistency to your taste.
2. Add remaining ingredients and heat thoroughly.

Top each bowl with a dollop of thick yogurt and serve hot, accompanied by a tossed green salad and whole-grain bread.

No classic Maine childhood would be complete without the staple "simple red flannel hash." Here is an updated version.

Red Flannel Hash

(6 servings)

2 cups cooked white potato cubes (1/4-inch)
3 cups cooked beet cubes (1/4-inch)
1/4 cup minced onion
1 tablespoon minced parsley
1/2 teaspoon sea salt
1/4 teaspoon Hungarian paprika
1 teaspoon komé miso (see Glossary)
2 tablespoons milk
2 tablespoons sunflower oil
sea salt to taste
freshly ground black pepper to taste
dash freshly ground nutmeg
minced parsley for garnish
yogurt for garnish

1. Dissolve miso in milk. Mix all ingredients, except oil, together.
2. In a skillet, heat sunflower oil. Pat hash into

Root Cellar, Attic, and Winter Garden Cooking
While carrots, parsnips, and sunchokes can remain under heavy garden mulch all winter, some vegetables are more likely to stay firm packed in moist sand or fall leaves and stored in the cellar. Turnips, rutabagas, beets, celeriac, and daikon radish prefer this treatment. Other vegetables hibernate well on cold cellar floors in bushel baskets–potatoes and apples for example. Onions and garlic can hang in braids on the cellar staircase. Winter squash can festoon the tops of closets, preferring a moderate temperature.

Beets
All over northern Europe winter root vegetables are highly prized when the weather is blustery. Our giant Lutz Green Leaf beets remain huge and firm; and in February we enjoy a thick beet soup introduced to Maine by Russian and Polish emigrés.

skillet, and sauté over moderate heat until heated through.

Serve garnished with more minced parsley, a lot of freshly ground black pepper, and a dollop of yogurt.

Carrots

Carrots are a midwinter necessity. Young carrots may be canned to make wonderful soup additions months later. If you have your own garden, it is a great pleasure to shovel off the snow and poke your pitchfork through layers of hay into the still-diggable soil, hoisting up a fresh orange gem.

Carrots are probably at their best eaten raw—with dips, grated in salads, added to aspics—but they are also indispensable as additions to loaves, breads, muffins, pancakes, cakes, burgers, and stews. And they are absolutely delicious puréed or steamed whole and garnished with a dash of dill weed or rosemary.

Midwinter Root Cellar Stir-Fry

(4-6 servings)

1 cup carrot matchsticks, 1-inch long
1 cup turnip matchsticks, 1-inch long
1 cup celeriac root matchsticks, 1-inch long
juice of 1 lemon plus enough water to measure 1 cup total volume
2 tablespoons sunflower seed oil
1 large clove garlic, minced
2 teaspoons powdered ginger or freshly grated ginger root
1 small sliced onion
1/2 teaspoon sea salt or to taste
1/4 cup white wine or Dandelion Wine
1 tablespoon cornstarch
2 cups frozen broccoli florets and sliced stems
1 cup sliced mushrooms
1 teaspoon freshly ground black pepper
1 teaspoon dried thyme
1/4-1/2 cup Shoyu Sunnies

1. Prepare carrots and turnips. Wash a big celeriac root, peel about half of it, and cut into matchsticks. Place these in a bowl and pour on the lemon juice/water mixture to prevent browning.
2. Heat oil in wok (see **The Wok**), and sauté garlic and ginger for a moment. Drain celeriac, reserving soaking water, and add, along with carrots, turnips, and onion; toss about two minutes until coated with oil. Add salt and wine. Cover, and steam over medium heat until vegetables are *barely tender*, about five minutes.
3. In a small bowl, add cornstarch to the reserved soaking water and set aside. Add all remaining ingredients to wok except **Shoyu Sunnies**, and simmer until hot. Pour in the cornstarch sauce, turn heat to high, and cook until gravy is clear and thick.

Serve sprinkled with **Shoyu Sunnies**, with brown rice, a green salad, and fresh bread.

Carrot Nut Soup

(4-6 servings)

3 tablespoons sunflower
    seed oil
3/4 cup chopped onion
2 cups grated carrot,
    tightly packed
1/2 cup peeled, chopped
    apples
2 tablespoons tomato
    purée
2 1/2 cups water
1 teaspoon sea salt
    (optional)
1/4 cup brown rice, oat
    groats, or whole
    barley (rinsed
    quickly)
1/2 cup raisins
1/2 cup cashew pieces
1/2 cup milk
yogurt for garnish
2 tablespoons finely chopped
    fresh parsley for garnish

1. Heat oil in a large, heavy-bottomed saucepan, and sauté onion and carrot until the onions are transparent. Add apples, tomato purée, water, salt, and rice or other whole grain. Bring to a boil.
2. Lower heat and simmer forty-five minutes.
3. Add raisins and cashews. Simmer till raisins are plump, about five minutes.

Serve hot topped with a dollop of yogurt, sprinkled with finely chopped fresh parsley.

Note: This make a fine sauce for **Tofu Balls.** Thin it with milk or water to a gravy consistency.

Baked Kennebecs

1 large Kennebec potato
    per person
garnishes of choice

1. Scrub potatoes well.
2. Place in a preheated 425°F oven and bake one to one and a quarter hours. About halfway through baking, pierce each potato with a table fork to allow steam to escape. (And be wary–they might explode.)
3. When the flesh is soft,

they're done. (Don't wrap them in foil because that makes them steam rather than bake.) They should be dry and fluffy.

Cut open, and serve topped with a dollop of yogurt, a dash of sea salt, freshly ground black pepper, grated lemon rind, and a sprinkling of finely chopped fresh parsley; or try **Cottage Cheese-Yogurt Dressing,** or a tahini-based dressing (see Index).

White Potato

The potato, that Maine institution, has kept many populations healthy through impoverished winters. It's considered a complete food, though the entire potato must be eaten because major nutrients are hidden just beneath the skin. To boost usable protein a little higher, it should be combined with milk or cheese. Baking and steaming are the best cooking methods for preserving vitamin content.

Related to the tomato, pepper, tobacco, petunia, and poisonous night-shade plants, potato contains good-quality complex carbohydrates. And potatoes in themselves are not fattening. It's the gravy, sour cream, and butter traditionally added that are high in calories.

Maine cooks have always known that one must discard any green skin or flesh from potatoes. When exposed to light while growing, the tubers can develop a toxic substance called solanine which turns them green.

Maine winter appetites are still satisfied by potatoes–baked, mashed, and fried. Of the hundreds of varieties, I most recommend the early red Norland for new potatoes; the big Kennebec for baking, and the Caribe, with its somewhat waxy flesh, for salads and boiling.

Leftover potatoes are never a problem. Mashed potatoes make an especially good baked dish for company.

Piquant Potato Bake

(4-6 servings)

4 large potatoes (4 cups cooked and mashed)
3 large eggs
1 tablespoon Dijon mustard
1 cup grated cheddar cheese
1 cup thick yogurt
1 teaspoon sea salt (optional)
4 tablespoons parmesan cheese

1. Cook potatoes in their skins. Peel, then mash coarsely with a potato masher. (Or use leftover mashed potatoes.)
2. Beat eggs until fluffy with mustard and sea salt. Add cheddar cheese and yogurt, and mix well. Fold into mashed potato and mix thoroughly. Spoon into a well-buttered two-quart casserole.
3. Sprinkle with parmesan cheese. Bake at 350°F until hot all through, about forty-five minutes. Sides should be browned and crusty, and the top golden.

Serve with a tossed salad or cooked leafy greens and fresh rolls.

Baked Stuffed Potatoes

(6 servings)

6 large baking potatoes
1 recipe Cottage Cheese-Yogurt Dressing flavored with dill weed and 1 tablespoon lemon juice
1 teaspoon chopped fresh dill weed OR 1 tablespoon chopped fresh chives
parmesan cheese or Hungarian paprika for garnish

1. Scrub potatoes well.
2. Place in a preheated 425°F oven and bake for one to one and a quarter hours. Pierce with a fork after the first half hour to prevent explosions.
3. When the potatoes are done, cut a thin slice off the top of each one, lengthwise. Scoop the insides into a bowl and mash.
4. Then add **Cottage Cheese-Yogurt Dressing,** and beat with an electric mixer until well combined. Consistency should be stiff but creamy. Add dill weed or chives to taste.
5. Lightly spoon mixture back into shells until piled high and fluffy. Place potatoes on a cookie sheet. Sprinkle with grated　　　　　»

parmesan cheese or Hungarian paprika, and bake in a preheated 425°F oven about thirty minutes, or until very hot and slightly browned on top.

Serve, sprinkled with finely chopped fresh chives or fresh dill.

Note: Rather than **Cottage Cheese-Yogurt Dressing**, use either of the following:

(These alternatives are sufficient for four large baked potatoes.)

a) 1 cup yogurt
1 small onion, diced
1 teaspoon dried dillweed, crumbled

b) 1 cup yogurt
1 heaping tablespoon finely chopped fresh parsley
2 scallions, chopped fine
sea salt to taste
few drops hot pepper sauce

Shepherd's Pie
(for folks who keep potatoes, not sheep)
(4-6 servings)

6 medium-sized white boiling potatoes
2 large eggs
1 cup grated sharp cheese (optional)
1/4-1/2 cup yogurt, if necessary (optional)
1/2 teaspoon sea salt
freshly ground black pepper
4 cups any leftover cooked, cubed vegetables OR 3 cups vegetables plus 1 cup tofu, poultry, or whatever protein food you fancy
1 cup water
1/4 cup shoyu
1/2 cup finely chopped fresh parsley
freshly ground black pepper

1 tablespoon white wine or Dandelion Wine
1 tablespoon cornstarch or arrowroot
Hungarian paprika

1. Scrub potato skins well. Cook potatoes until tender. When barely done, drain and cool until you can handle them. Then peel and mash coarsely.
2. Beat eggs till fluffy. Add cheese and mashed potatoes. Beat until smooth. If potatoes are too dry, add enough yogurt to moisten and lend a rather piquant flavor. Add salt and pepper. Set aside.
3. In a large bowl, toss together leftovers, such as cubed tofu, tempeh (see Glossary), tofu balls, quartered vegetarian burgers or **Falafel**, cooked carrot slices, string beans, peas or

Mother made a dish called Shepherd's Pie—savory meat and vegetables sauced with gravy and topped with browned pastry. A wonderful dish for leftovers, it can also be made with a potato topping.

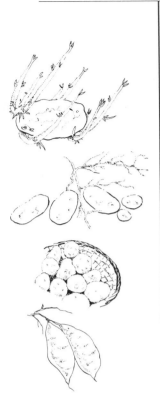

pea pods, blanched cauliflower or broccoli florets, cubed zucchini or cooked eggplant, chopped green or red bell pepper, onions or celery stalk, cooked red kidney or other dried beans.

4. In a small saucepan, bring remaining ingredients to a boil. Cook for one minute to thicken, stirring constantly. Then combine with vegetables, using just enough to make mixture resemble a stew, not a soup.

5. Pour into a well-buttered seven-and-a-half- by eleven-inch lasagna pan. Smooth potatoes over the top, making thick swirls. Dust with paprika. Bake in a 350°F oven until vegetables are hot and potatoes are browned.

Serve with salad and fresh whole-grain rolls.

Mint Custard

(4-6 servings)

**4 medium-sized
    potatoes (about 4
    cups, cubed)**
1 1/2 cups boiling water
1 1/2 cups milk
1 teaspoon sea salt
1 small onion, minced
3 large eggs
**1/2 cup chopped fresh
    mint or 1 tablespoon
    dried, crumbled**

1. Preheat oven to 350°F. Peel potatoes, wash, and cut into small cubes.

2. Drop into boiling water and cook until tender, five to eight minutes. Drain, saving water for stock or bread-making.

3. Scald milk. Add salt and onion.

4. In a small bowl, beat eggs till fluffy. Stir into milk *very slowly* to prevent curdling.

5. Mix mint into the cooked potatoes, and combine with milk.

6. Pour into a lightly buttered, two-quart casserole dish, and place in a pan of warm water. Bake at 350°F for forty-five minutes.

Serve for brunch with croissants, fruit salad, and champagne! Or as a dinner entrée, accompanied by a tossed green salad and fresh rolls.

Grated Potato Quiche

(6 servings)

3 medium-sized white
    potatoes
1 medium-sized onion
1 beaten egg
1/2 cup mung bean
    sprouts or other
    vegetable, diced
4 tablespoons minced
    shrimp (optional)
1 cup grated sharp
    cheddar cheese
3 large eggs
1 cup milk
1/4 teaspoon freshly
    ground black pepper
1/2 teaspoon sea salt
    (optional)
1/4 teaspoon dry
    mustard
1/4 teaspoon Hungarian
    paprika
1/8 teaspoon cayenne
    (optional)
3 tablespoons chopped
    parsley

1. Scrub potatoes, but don't peel. Shred them into a large bowl.
2. Dice onion, add to potato, and drain off any liquid.
3. Add egg and combine thoroughly.
4. Press onto sides and bottom of a well-buttered, ten-inch pie plate. Be sure potato "crust" doesn't rise higher than sides of plate.
5. Inside potato crust, layer bean sprouts and cheese.
6. Beat remaining ingredients together in a small bowl. Pour over the cheese and sprouts.
7. Bake forty-five minutes at 375°F, or till a knife comes out clean and top and crust are golden.

Serve with a tossed salad and fresh rolls.

Scalloped Potatoes

(4 servings)

3 large peeled raw
    potatoes, thinly sliced
1 thinly sliced large
    white onion
sea salt
freshly ground black
    pepper
6 teaspoons butter
2 tablespoons water
chopped fresh parsley
    for garnish

1. Place a thick layer of potatoes into a heavy, buttered skillet, and add onion.
2. Sprinkle with salt and pepper.
3. Add another layer of peeled raw potatoes and onion, and sprinkle with salt and pepper. Repeat until all ingredients are used up. Dot with butter and add water.
4. Turn heat on to medium-low, cover tightly, and allow to simmer about fifteen

Scalloped potatoes have always been a favorite with Mainers. This version is cooked with butter. Because of the high fat content I do not recommend serving it often, but its flavor is delicious! You could substitute olive oil–for a southern Mediterranean flavor.

minutes. Check now and again to see that potatoes are not burning. If necessary, add more water. Remove cover, and allow to cook until done, perhaps another fifteen minutes. A nice browned layer should form on the bottom but the potatoes will be tender. Using a metal spatula, turn the potatoes out onto a platter. Sprinkle with chopped fresh parsley.

Potato dumplings are always welcome in Maine. These New Maine dumplings filled with tempeh are particularly tasty–a centerpiece for any meal.

Potato Dumplings

(10 dumplings about the size of tennis balls)

**2 pounds peeled
    potatoes
2 tablespoons extra-
    virgin olive oil
1/4 cup diced onions
1 cup crumbled tempeh
    (see Glossary)
1/2 teaspoon allspice
1 tablespoon finely
    chopped fresh
    parsley
1 1/8 cups whole-wheat
    pastry flour
unbleached white flour,
    if necessary, to stiffen
    dough
1 lightly beaten large
    egg
1/2 teaspoon sea salt
1 teaspoon finely grated
    lemon rind
16 cups water
1 teaspoon sea salt
more olive oil
    (optional)
3 tablespoons parmesan
    cheese for garnish
2 tablespoons finely
    chopped fresh parsley**

1. In a large saucepan cook potatoes until about three-quarters done.
2. Pop into a colander over boiling water, and steam until tender and dry.
3. Rice potatoes into a big bowl and allow to cool.
4. Heat oil in a skillet and sauté onions until limp. Set aside in a bowl. Sauté tempeh until browned, and combine with onions. Add allspice, and allow to cool.
5. Add whole-wheat flour, egg, salt, and lemon rind to the cooled potatoes. With hands, knead into a dough. (Knead in some unbleached white flour if necessary.) Turn out onto a surface well dusted with unbleached flour and make a roll two inches thick. Cut the roll into ten pieces, and form them into large balls.
6. Make a hollow in the center of each ball, and place a tablespoon of tempeh filling in it. Pull dough up around filling, smooth, and form spherical dumplings.
7. Bring a large pot of salted water to a boil. Slide five dumplings in gently with a

»

slotted spoon. Cook, turning once, about ten minutes. They'll float. Using a slotted or wire spoon, drain, and transfer to a heated platter.
8. Preheat oven to 325°F. Place dumplings in a shallow, well-oiled ceramic baking dish. Drizzle dumplings with a little olive oil, sprinkle with parmesan cheese, and bake till very hot, about fifteen minutes.

Serve, sprinkled with parsley, with a crisp winter salad, and vegetables of choice. They're also excellent sauced with a hot tomato sauce, such as **Enchilada Sauce**, or with **Mushroom Gravy**.

Note: Substitute minced, cooked poultry or fish for the tempeh, and omit sautéing.

Turnip Delight

(6 servings)

2 medium-sized, well-washed, unpeeled white potatoes, cut into large chunks
1 medium-sized well-washed, unpeeled sweet potato (optional), cut into large chunks
1 medium-sized peeled turnip, cut into large chunks
1 medium onion, peeled and quartered
3/4 cup milk
1 egg, plus 1 egg per person
1/2 teaspoon sea salt, plus more to sprinkle
2 tablespoons fresh ginger root, peeled and sliced thinly
freshly ground black pepper
a little grated nutmeg
chopped fresh parsley for garnish

1. Steam turnips and potatoes until tender. Peel the sweet and white potatoes. (If you lack sweet potatoes use more turnip and white potato.) Mash all three together in a large bowl.
2. In blender, purée onion, milk, one egg, salt, and ginger until smooth. Beat into the turnip/potato mixture, and pour into a well-buttered two- to three-quart casserole.
3. On top, make little nests–one for each person–and drop an egg into each nest. Sprinkle with pepper, salt, and nutmeg.
4. Cover, and bake at 325°F about forty-five minutes, or till turnip is steaming and eggs are nicely set.

Serve, sprinkled with chopped parsley, with fresh bread, and a green salad.

Rutabagas and Turnips

Turnips, or, better yet, the purple-shouldered rutabaga, are good winter keepers and excellent fare. Peeled, cut into chunks, and simmered till tender in a little water, the smooth, tasty flesh seems very Nordic. Add a dash of cinnamon along with some sea salt and white pepper and it's truly succulent. In my childhood turnips were the last item left in our cellar come spring, still firm and fresh. If your children don't like turnips, try this dish to surprise them.

Gingered Turnips with Maple Syrup
(4-6 servings)

1 **(3-inch diameter) medium-sized turnip (4 cups cut up into matchsticks)**
3 **tablespoons maple syrup**
juice of 1 lemon
1 **tablespoon cornstarch or arrowroot**
1 **teaspoon powdered ginger**
2 **whole cloves or 1/8 teaspoon powdered cloves**
1 **cup hot turnip-cooking liquor**
1/4 teaspoon cinnamon

1. Peel turnip, halve, quarter, and cut it into matchsticks. Steam in a colander over boiling water until tender but not overdone (ten to twenty minutes). Place matchsticks into a large enameled skillet.
2. Whisk together remaining ingredients. Pour over turnip, bring to a boil; cover, and boil one minute or until sauce is thick and clear. Sprinkle with cinnamon.

Serve hot as a side dish to any winter meal.

Rutabaga, Apple, and Port
(4-6 servings)

1 **large rutabaga, or equiv-alent (4 cups prepared)**
3 **large tart winter keeper apples (4 cups prepared)**
juice of 1 lemon
1/4 well-washed lemon rind
1/2 cup port
1 **teaspoon caraway seeds**
1/4 teaspoon sea salt
a few grindings of fresh nutmeg

Rutabaga, sometimes called swede, is eaten regularly in Sweden. And in Maine! Scandinavian Americans traditionally serve it instead of squash at Thanksgiving and Christmas. Mother often cooked swedes and apples together with molasses. Port is a companion to apples of long-standing (almost a necessity in England). So combining rutabaga, apples, and port is a happy marriage.

1. Peel and cut rutabaga into half-inch cubes. Steam in a colander over boiling water until barely tender but still crisp (about eight minutes).
2. Peel apples, core, and cut into small slices. Dip into freshly squeezed lemon juice to prevent browning and increase tartness.
3. Place turnip and apples in a large enameled skillet, and add remaining ingredients.
4. Cover and steam until apples are sauced and port is reduced–it won't take long. Stir gently once or twice. What results are tender but firm cubes of rutabaga in a port-flavored apple sauce.

Serve as an elegant side dish to any meal.

Note: You may substitute potato for half the rutabaga.

Winter Squash Soup Supreme

(6-8 servings)

1 large winter buttercup
squash (about 4 cups,
cooked and peeled)
2-3 cups hot water,
divided
1 cup non-instant,
low-fat powdered
milk, divided in half
1 tablespoon powdered
cumin
1 teaspoon powdered
cinnamon
1 teaspoon powdered
marjoram
freshly chopped chives
or parsley for garnish

1. Wash squash, cut into
wedges, and remove seeds,
but don't peel. (Save seeds.
Wash them, place on a
cookie sheet, sprinkle with
salt, and toast lightly in a
325°F oven till browned.
These make good snacks.
See also **Toasted Pumpkin
and Squash Seeds**.)

2. Steam squash in a
colander set over boiling
water until pleasantly soft.
Scrape out the flesh when
tender and cool, discarding
peel. The resulting flesh
should be quite dry.
3. Purée half the squash
with a cup of hot water in
blender till smooth. Add
half the milk powder,
cumin, cinnamon, and
marjoram, and blend again.
(You may need to add more
water.) Empty into soup
kettle.
4. Place the rest of the
squash in blender with
remaining milk powder and
one cup hot water. Blend
again, adding more water if
necessary. By now you
should have a light-orange
mixture, thick and creamy.
Check to see if cumin is
strong enough for your taste.

Serve hot, sprinkled with
freshly chopped chives or
parsley, with a tossed salad,
and fresh bread.

Winter Squash and Pumpkins

*Tucked in the attic,
or underneath the
bed, handsome
squash wait
faithfully for mid-
winter cooking. The
solid, green-skinned
buttercup is my
favorite. With
sweet flesh which
cooks up as dry as
that of baked
potatoes, its nutty
flavor is unmatched.
But each variety has
its own special
virtues.*

*Winter squash has
always played an
important part in
Maine cuisine.
Usually served at
Thanksgiving and
Christmas as a side
dish for turkey or
other fowl, it's good
year-round if stored
in a dry, moderately
warm area of the
house. Besides
making a lovely side
dish–with no
seasoning needed–it
also thickens soups
admirably.*

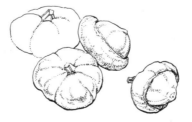

Stuffed Buttercups

1/2 buttercup squash per
    person
sunflower seeds
chopped apple dipped in
    lemon juice to
    prevent browning
raisins
grated lemon rind
lemon juice
cinnamon
maple syrup

1. Wash squash, cut in half, and scoop out seeds. (Save them to roast or toast.)

2. Into each squash bowl, place a dollop each of seeds, apples, and raisins, a quarter teaspoon lemon rind, a dash each lemon juice and cinnamon, and one to two tablespoons maple syrup.
3. Place cut-side up in a baking pan, and pour in water about an inch deep. Cover. Bake until tender, forty-five to sixty minutes.

Serve on a heated ceramic platter–to the particular enjoyment of children–and complement with a cooked whole-grain and a crisp salad.

Another favorite of children is the stuffed pumpkin–perhaps their very own which they've initialed during the summer.

Stuffed Pumpkin
(or Squash)
(6 servings)

1 **medium-sized pumpkin**
    (or 2 buttercup squashes)
1 **cup short-grain brown**
    rice, whole barley, or
    oat groats
1 **tablespoon extra-virgin**
    olive or sunflower seed
    oil
1 **medium-sized onion,**
    diced
1 **cup frozen broccoli florets**
    and sliced stems,
    chopped
freshly ground black pepper
1/2 **teaspoon dried basil**
1 **cup toasted Shoyu**
    Sunnies

1. Choose a medium-sized pumpkin (or two large buttercup squashes), and wash well. Slice off pumpkin or squash top (to make a lid), cutting it on a slant so lid won't fall through later.
2. Remove all seeds and stringy material (and save seeds for roasting). Score inside several times, and sprinkle with salt and black pepper. Place, cut-side down, in a shallow pan filled with a quarter inch water. Place the lid beside the pumpkin. Bake at 350°F for one hour, or until tender when pierced with a fork. (Be sure not to let it get mushy.) Drain.
3. While pumpkin is baking, cook rice in water. When

»

done, heat oil in a skillet and sauté onion till limp.

4. Add broccoli, and sauté until just separated and tender.

5. Pour pepper, basil, and **Shoyu Sunnies** into a bowl with one and a half cups rice and fluff together. (Depending on pumpkin or squash size, you may use all the rice.) Add sautéed vegetables.

6. Spoon rice mixture lightly into pumpkin shell. Replace lid, and put the whole thing into the oven again at 325°F. Heat thoroughly, perhaps a half hour or more.

7. Bring the steaming pumpkin to table–a feast for the eye!

Serve by spooning the rice out of the pumpkin along with pumpkin meat itself.

Onion Soup

(6-8 servings)

2 tablespoons sunflower
    seed oil
2 tablespoons butter
6 large onions, sliced
    very thin
1 heaping tablespoon
    whole-wheat pastry
    flour
1 tablespoon nutritional
    yeast
6 cups vegetable stock or
    water
about 4 tablespoons
    komé miso (see
    Glossary)
1/2 cup cold water
6 tablespoons brandy or
    dry sherry
1 tablespoon maple
    syrup
2 tablespoons finely
    chopped fresh
    parsley
6 slices of toasted
    French bread
6 tablespoons parmesan
    cheese

1. Heat a heavy cast-iron wok or kettle. Add butter and oil, and heat. Toss onions in the fat, then sauté until limp and translucent and some, at least, are beginning to turn brown. Sprinkle with flour and yeast. Mix well, and cook, while you stir, for about two minutes.

2. Add stock, and simmer slowly until onion is very tender–about a half hour. Dissolve miso in a half cup of cold water. Add slowly to soup, to taste.

3. Add brandy or dry sherry, and parsley. Lay a slice of dry toast in each individual bowl (I cut mine into disks with a biscuit cutter.) Pour the soup over it, and sprinkle with parmesan cheese. (Or pour soup into a large casserole, place the toasted bread on top, and sprinkle the toast

Onions

Is there any vegetable more wonderful, when you come to think of it, than the onion? Strong in flavor when raw, transformed by cooking into a light-tasting globe of mellowness, packed with vitamins. And, if peeling onions bothers you, try blanching them for one minute in boiling water, and then drowning them in cold water before peeling. This is an especially good method to use when preparing creamed onions at Thanksgiving.

with parmesan cheese.) Heat
in the oven for ten minutes
or until the cheese is slightly
browned.

Serve very hot with a salad,
fresh rolls, and fruit.

Baked Whole Onions with Dried Plums

(6 servings)

6 medium-sized onions
12 pitted prunes
3 lemon slices
1/2 stick cinnamon
1-1 1/2 cups water,
    divided
1/4 cup maple syrup
1 teaspoon Dijon
    mustard
1 tablespoon red wine
    vinegar
a tiny bit of ground
    cloves
1/2 teaspoon sea salt
freshly ground black
    pepper
1 garlic clove, minced
1 teaspoon komé miso
    (see Glossary)
1 teaspoon sesame seed oil

1. Preheat oven to 400°F.
2. Peel onions.
3. Cut a cross in the top of
each one a quarter-inch deep.
Place in a heavy, lightly
buttered shallow seven-and-
a-half- by eleven-inch pan
with prunes, lemon slices,
and cinnamon stick.
Add one cup water and
cover tightly.
4. Bake in a 400°F oven one
half hour. Add more water
if prunes are not plump.
5. Make a basting sauce of
remaining ingredients.
Baste onions often, and
continue baking another
half hour or until onions are
soft and prunes are plump.

Serve as the side dish to any
tasty winter meal.

Tapping a Maple Tree

1. At the beginning of the season, hang buckets on the south side of the tree where the flow will be heavier. At the end of the season, hang on the north side.

2. Drill a hole in the maple about three feet from the ground, using a hand drill with a seven-sixteenth-inch bit, and bore the hole about two inches straight in.

3. Tap in a metal spile. Never tap above or below an old scar–leave a space at least three inches between scars and where you tap.

4. Hang a galvanized bucket from the spile hook. Attach a removable lid to keep out bark and rain.

5. Set up a large container somewhere near the tree(s) into which the contents of galvanized buckets can be poured as they're emptied once or twice a day (we use a big plastic garbage container). If ice forms inside buckets, simply pry loose and throw out: this way you'll have less water to boil down.

6. Bacteria live in sap (as they do in milk), so the quicker sap can be boiled into syrup after leaving the tree the better. No more than twenty-four hours should elapse, according to commercial syrup-makers. Strain sap through several layers of cheesecloth as you pour it into large, flat evaporating pans on your stove. Boiling down out-of-doors is preferable: some *forty gallons of sap produce approximately one gallon of syrup*. If done inside the house, furnishings, ceilings, and walls become saturated with water.

7. Simmer over moderate to high heat until sap darkens and reaches a thick consistency (at 219°F on a candy thermometer–the boiling point of sap at sea level). The longer and hotter the boiling, the darker the color and heavier the taste.

8. As it reaches the last stages, sap will cook down quickly and foam up, so watch closely, remove quickly, and pour into clean storage containers. At 180°F syrup contains no bacteria and will sterilize containers. Fill almost to the top, cap, then lay containers on their sides. (Hot syrup will sterilize the seal as well.)

9. To make candy, cook foaming syrup even further until it reaches 234°F on a candy thermometer (or until a few drops will form a very soft ball in cold water). Remove from heat, and beat quickly with a rotary beater. Then pour into slightly oiled molds such as muffin tins. (You can also buy special rubberized molds, in the shapes of leaves, for instance.) Heat bottom of tins slightly to remove.

10. Maple syrup will keep in

Maple Syrup

It always seems like spring when the sap starts running in the dead of winter! In Maine this happens during late February and the first weeks of March when nighttime temperatures fall below freezing but days are relatively warm.

*The sugar maple (**Acer saccharum**) produces the best syrup, although other maples and even birches can be tapped as well. Try tapping your own trees as a small family project and for a great deal of fun. Choose only maple trees that have reached a diameter of at least ten to twelve inches. A tree this size can bear one bucket. Hang two buckets on trees twenty to twenty-four inches in diameter, and three buckets on trees twenty-four to thirty inches. Larger trees with a good crown may take from four to five buckets without injury.*

your cellar for a long time if you sterilized container caps (see above). Once uncapped, it will also keep well in the refrigerator.

I propose a maple-sugary but low-fat topping for any apple, squash, pumpkin, blueberry, or rhubarb dessert.

Maple Sugar Topping

1 cup low-fat cottage cheese
1 teaspoon pure vanilla
1 teaspoon grated lemon rind
1/4 cup maple syrup
chopped nuts

Combine cottage cheese, vanilla, lemon rind, and maple syrup in blender, and whiz until thick.
Top frappé with nuts.

*Maple sugar candy is the finest treat a Maine child can dream up. And if it comes once a year in a holiday atmosphere, who's to complain? It's the **constant** eating of candy that ruins so many beautiful teeth, personalities, figures, and constitutions!*

Maple Sugar Babies

2 cups maple syrup
1 cup heavy cream
sea salt
2 cups chopped walnuts, lightly toasted

1. In a heavy two-quart saucepan combine maple syrup with cream and salt to taste. Bring to 238°F on a candy thermometer, or until a sample forms a soft ball in cold water.
2. Remove from heat. Cool, and then beat about two minutes until creamy.

3. Stir in walnuts, and drop by tablespoons onto a well-greased cookie sheet. Cool.
4. Wrap each "baby" in waxed paper, and store for two weeks before eating (if you can).

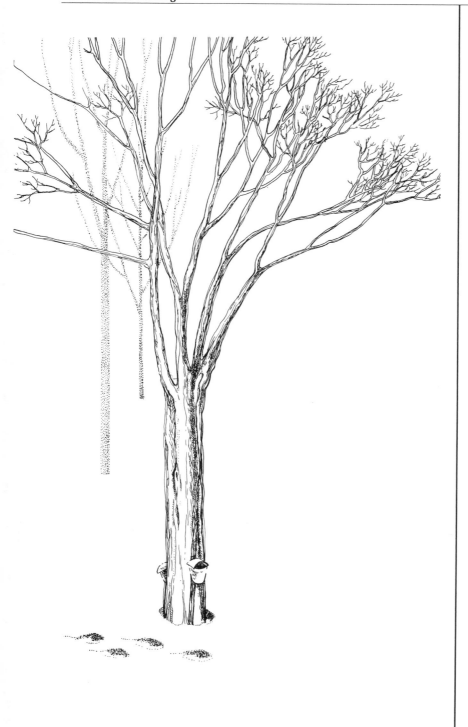

Index

Acknowledgments

Unless you have the patience of Job, and the lightheartedness of a kitten, never let a member of your family write a book! Especially a cookbook! To my children, Jessica and Julian, therefore, go many a hug for the times when they cried, "Mama, Mama!" and Mama wasn't listening; to my patient, loving husband a prolonged squeeze for ensuring that his wife had the perserverance of Samson (often a complete lack of a sense of humor along with it) and for hanging in there himself; tears and smiles to my dear Aunt Mae and her delicious biscuits which I shall miss always; to my grandmother and her own perserverance through the thicks and thins; to my beloved mother whose hands while kneading bread on Saturdays remain forever in my memory; to Harriet Rogers, publisher's assistant, who patted my head when it needed patting; to my publisher himself who believed in my ability to complete this work; and hugs especially to my dear editor, Julia Ackerman, without whom this book would be a lot less readable and, at times, a lot less tasty. I give you all my heartfelt thanks.